TOLKIEN
and
THE LORD
OF THE RINGS

TOLKIEN
and
THE LORD
OF THE RINGS

A Guide to Middle-earth

COLIN DURIEZ

HiddenSpring

Published in Great Britain in 2001 by
Azure
1 Marylebone Road
London NW1 4DU

Cover picture: 'Rivendell' by Rodney Matthews
Cover design: Andrea Rossi

ISBN 1-58768-017-3

Published in North America in 2001 by

HiddenSpring

An imprint of Paulist Press
997 Macarthur Boulevard
Mahwah, New Jersey 07430

www.hiddenspringbooks.com

Typeset by Pioneer Associates, Perthshire
Printed in Great Britain by
Omnia Books, Glasgow

CONTENTS

103778

Colin Duriez has written and lectured extensively on Tolkien and *The Lord of the Rings*. He is also the author of *The C.S. Lewis Encyclopedia*, and, with David Porter, *The Inklings Handbook*. He is General Books Editor for Intervarsity Press in Leicester.

To my mother,
Madge
Anar kaluva tielyanna

PREFACE

J.R.R. Tolkien is such a widely read author that it is difficult to believe that, once upon a time, his publishers were convinced that *The Lord of the Rings* might well make a financial loss for them. In those unenlightened days, the learned Professor could mutter the word 'orc' at uncouth behaviour, or exclaim 'Mordor in our midst' at an ugly example of modern life, without his meaning being known to the general public. Now the very word 'hobbit' has entered the English language, with its own place in dictionaries. The readership of his books is over 150 million (the print run of the first US paperback edition of *The Silmarillion* alone was reportedly well over 2 million). He is read throughout the world in many languages.

Several polls of readers have made *The Lord of the Rings* their first choice. In 1996 the British bookshop chain, Waterstones, and a network TV programme, *Book Choice*, commissioned a poll of readers to determine the five books 'you consider the greatest of the century'. The response was impressive. Around 26,000 readers responded, with 5,000 giving the first place to *The Lord of the Rings*, placing it in the number one position as the book of the century. Other polls repeated this preference. In 2000 Tom Shippey published *J.R.R. Tolkien: Author of the Century*. He is a literary scholar who like Tolkien has held the Chair of English Language and Medieval Literature at Leeds University. His book opens with the increasingly plausible claim, 'The dominant literary mode of the twentieth century has been the fantastic', a claim he defends rigorously in the book. He speculates:

When the time comes to look back at the century, it seems very likely that future literary historians ... will see as its most representative and distinctive works books like J.R.R. Tolkien's *The Lord of the Rings*, and also George Orwell's *Nineteen Eighty-Four* and *Animal Farm*, William Golding's *Lord of the Flies* and *The Inheritors*, Kurt Vonnegut's *Slaughterhouse-Five* and *Cat's Cradle*, Ursula Le Guin's *The Left Hand of Darkness* and *The Dispossessed*, Thomas Pynchon's *The Crying of Lot-49* and *Gravity's Rainbow*.

Not only is Tolkien read on a vast scale, but his work is present in many media – on audiotape and CD, in computer and board games, in illustration (by such as Rodney Matthews, John Howe, Ted Naismith, and Alan Lee), in drama adaptations, and on film. Tolkien's status as a global phenomenon is reinforced by the appearance of a three-part film by Peter Jackson (2001–3), each part representing a volume of *The Lord of the Rings*. Using the latest computer techniques, and filmed in the unspoiled landscapes of New Zealand, it employs actors of the calibre of Cate Blanchett as Galadriel, Christopher Lee as Saruman, Ian Holm as Bilbo Baggins, Liv Tyler as Arwen, Ian McKellan as Gandalf, and Bernard Hill as Théoden. Peter Jackson described the work as

the holy grail of cinema ... I really think it would have been impossible to do *The Lord of the Rings* before the advent of computers ... With computers, we've arrived at a time when anything you can imagine can be put on to film, and ... anything Tolkien could imagine can be put on film.

Explorations of virtual reality, particularly in film, have opened up the big philosophical and theological questions about the scope of reality. Does it extend beyond what can be measured, and beyond what can be seen, touched and heard? The denials of modernism, which tried to put reality into a closed box, seem increasingly hollow.

The Lord of the Rings is a fantasy about *actual* reality. Underpinning it is Tolkien's carefully worked out idea of sub-creation† (see Chapter 9), in which the human maker imagines God's world after him, just as the early scientists – and today's cosmologists like Stephen Hawking – think God's thoughts after him. For Tolkien, the moral and spiritual world is as real as the physical world – indeed, each is part of one creation, and a successful sub-creation like the linguistic world of Middle-earth captures them all in an organic whole. The result is an image of reality that is making a claim to reliable knowledge.

Even readers who have ventured into Middle-earth through reading *The Hobbit* or *The Lord of the Rings* may not realize the full treasures to be found in Tolkien's other writings, and in his thinking. This book tries to explain the relationship between the two familiar works and Tolkien's less well-known life work *The Silmarillion*. This is a work Tolkien never finished, and which was reconstructed and published by his son, Christopher Tolkien, after his death. I argue that it provides a necessary backdrop to the adventures of the Ring. Furthermore I try to show that the relationship between Tolkien's life, his work as an Oxford scholar, his close friends (especially C.S. Lewis) and his fiction is itself fascinating.

There are, of course, many readers of Tolkien who may have travelled in *The Silmarillion*. Many find this book strangely different from the other, more popular works. Some are overwhelmed by the proliferation of new names and places, yet attracted by a sense of depth and richness – and of even more of a world to explore.

My book hopes to introduce, or remind readers of, the abundance that exists in Tolkien's thought and imagination. It makes no claim to be exhaustive, but to provide helpful pointers. Selection was the most difficult of my tasks. The book is made up of interweaving sections, relating to his life, thought and writings, with the main focus upon *The Lord of the Rings* and its background – Middle-earth itself. To allow readers to follow through themes and subjects, fictional and actual, which capture their interest I have used asterisks, and other symbols, within articles and entries to show other references. If this omits a significant cross-reference I give it at the article's end. Where appropriate, I have added further reading. At the end of the book is a list of J.R.R. Tolkien's works (most of which are described within Chapter 9). For descriptions of *The Hobbit*, *The Lord of the Rings*, and *The Silmarillion*, the reader is referred to Part Two.

The key to symbols of reference is:

* Entry in Part Three: An A–Z of Tolkien's Middle-earth, Chapter 6: Beings, Places, Things and Events

† Entry in Part Four: A Look Behind Tolkien's Life and Work, Chapter 7: Key Themes, Concepts and Images in Tolkien

‡ Entry in Part Four: A Look Behind Tolkien's Life and Work, Chapter 8: People and Places in His Life
Chapter 9: Tolkien's Writings

Significant works of art and literature – like Tolkien's *The Lord of the Rings*, and the background of its invented mythology,† set in his world of Middle-earth* – challenge the human understanding and imagination.† The challenge is just as real, I believe, as when a new philosophy or scientific theory is thought out. Human beings are always in the process of being shaped. Without challenge, we specialize and stagnate. Tolkien, significantly, was particularly antagonistic to mechanization, represented in Sauron,* Mordor,* Saruman,* and the despoiling of the Shire.*

We are all on a journey† – for which the quest† to destroy the Ring in *The Lord of the Rings* is an image, with applicability to us. Tolkien, by challenging us, helps us to go in a right direction, and arrive at a certain destination. One of the songs of Middle-earth characteristically speaks of the road† going ever on and on, a seminal image in the stories. As Bilbo said to Frodo,* 'It's a dangerous business . . . going out of your door.'

Tolkien's portrayal of new possibilities helps us to have the refreshment and moral strength to persevere over what is true, noble, right, pure, lovely and admirable. Tolkien challenges the spirit of our age, which says that there is no meaningful journey – either because there is no road, or because all roads lead to the same destination. The fact that Tolkien is so popular with readers in numerous countries shows that many people are attracted by the hope that shines through his work.

This book is enlarged and substantially reworked from my *The Tolkien and Middle-earth Handbook* (1992). My thanks are due, in writing this new book, to many people, far too many to acknowledge. The ideas started out as a paper given at L'Abri in Switzerland in 1969, and slowly grew, with the encouragement of Francis Schaeffer and Hans Rookmaaker (whose pioneering ideas on symbolism and reality opened up many vistas). My many friends in the Tolkien Society have helped to keep me exploring Tolkien's writings and context, and given me the opportunity to try out on them my attempts to understand Middle-earth. I am most thankful for the friendships gained through Tolkien's legacy. It has also been my privilege to meet notable and inspiring literary scholars who were big enough to take Tolkien's writings seriously, such as Professor Tom Shippey, Verlyn Flieger, Colin Manlove, Professor Jakub Lichański of Warsaw University, and Chris Garbowski at various conferences held to explore the work of Tolkien or his friend C.S. Lewis or the literary mode of the fantastic. Their labours have helped to make my little book possible. My thanks as well to Alison Barr of SPCK for all her encouragement, to Claire Sauer for her much-appreciated and cheerful editorial work on my typescript and to Joanne Hill for checking the proofs. The Marion E. Wade Collection also provided invaluable resources, although my visit there was, alas, all too brief.

COLIN DURIEZ

Part One

THE MIND BEHIND MIDDLE-EARTH

— ONE —

THE LIFE AND WORK
OF J.R.R. TOLKIEN

I was born in 1892 and lived for my early years in 'the Shire' in a pre-mechanical age. Or more important, I am a Christian (which can be deduced from my stories), and in fact a Roman Catholic. The latter 'fact' perhaps cannot be deduced . . . I am in fact a Hobbit (in all but size). I like gardens, trees and unmechanized farmlands; I smoke a pipe and like good plain food . . . I like, and even dare to wear in these dull days, ornamental waistcoats. I am fond of mushrooms (out of a field); have a very simple sense of humour (which even my appreciative critics find tiresome); I go to bed late and get up late (when possible). I do not travel much.

(Letter, 25 October 1958)

J.R.R. Tolkien's most familiar creation, the hobbits* of Middle-earth,* belonged only to his private world until September 1937. Before then they were known only to his children, to his great friend C.S. Lewis,‡ and to a few other people. The print run of what is now a children's classic – *The Hobbit, or There and Back Again*‡ (1937) – in its first edition was 1,500 copies. Forty years later, in 1977, the initial print run for the first US edition of Tolkien's *The Silmarillion*‡ was over 300,000 copies, and two years later the run for the first US paperback edition was reportedly over two and a half million copies.

John Ronald Reuel Tolkien was born on 3 January 1892 in Bloemfontein, South Africa, the first son of English citizens Arthur Reuel‡ and Mabel Tolkien.‡ At the time of his father's death in

1896, Ronald Tolkien and his brother Hilary‡ were in England with his mother because of his health. They remained in England after his father's death and occupied a rented house in Sarehole,‡ Warwickshire, outside Birmingham.‡ In Sarehole there was an old brick mill with a tall chimney. Though it was powered by a steam engine, a stream ran under its great wheel. The mill, with its frightening miller's son, made a deep impression on Tolkien's imagination. In *The Lord of the Rings*‡ (1954–55) he wrote of a mill in Hobbiton,* located on the Water, which was torn down and replaced by a brick building which polluted both the air and water.

In his letters Tolkien remembered his mother as 'a gifted lady of great beauty and wit, greatly stricken by God with grief and suffering, who died in youth (at 34) of a disease hastened by persecution of her faith'. Her non-conformist family was opposed to her move to Roman Catholicism, which took place in 1900. 'It is to my mother,' wrote Tolkien, 'who taught me (until I obtained a scholarship) that I owe my tastes for philology, especially of Germanic languages, and for romance.' The boys' education required that the family move into Birmingham.

Father Francis Morgan‡ was a Roman Catholic parish priest attached to the Birmingham Oratory, founded by John Henry Newman. He provided friendship and counsel for the fatherless family. Half-Spanish, Father Morgan was an extrovert whose enthusiasm helped the Tolkien family. With the boys often ill and the mother developing diabetes, Father Morgan helped to move them to Rednal, in the countryside, for the summer of 1904. The feeling there was like that of Sarehole. Mabel Tolkien died here later that year, and Father Morgan was left with the responsibility of the boys. He helped them financially, found them lodgings in Birmingham, and took them on holidays.

In 1908 Father Morgan found better lodgings for the orphaned brothers on Duchess Road in Birmingham. Here Tolkien fell in love with another lodger, Edith Bratt,‡ who was slightly older than him. She was attractive, small and slender, with grey eyes. Father

Morgan (like King Thingol in Tolkien's tale of Beren* and Lúthien*) disapproved of their love. He was fearful that Tolkien would be distracted from his studies, and ordered Tolkien not to see Edith until he was 21. It meant a long separation, but Tolkien was loyal to his benefactor, the only father he had really known. When Tolkien wrote of their eventual engagement, Father Morgan accepted it without a fuss. The two were formally engaged when Tolkien was 22, after Edith was received into the Roman Catholic Church. Edith was ever associated in Tolkien's mind with a fictional character he created early on in the development of *The Silmarillion* – Lúthien. The story had such a personal meaning for Tolkien, that Lúthien and her lover Beren were pet names for Edith and himself. The conception of the story was tied up with an incident where the two of them had wandered in a small wood in Roos, north of the Humber estuary. There, among hemlock, she danced and sang to him. Beren, in the story, encounters Lúthien dancing among hemlock in the woods of Neldoreth.* For both Beren and Tolkien it was a time of memories of danger: Tolkien was on leave from the battles of the First World War. When Edith died in 1971, he included 'Lúthien' on her gravestone.

While Tolkien was a schoolboy in King Edward VI Grammar School, he formed a club with several friends, the key members aside from Tolkien being G.B. Smith,‡ R.Q. 'Rob' Gilson,‡ and Christopher Wiseman.‡ Only Wiseman and Tolkien survived World War I. The group was called the Tea Club (TC) at first, and then later the Barrovian Society (BS), the last because the tearoom in Barrow's Stores on Corporation Street in Birmingham became a favourite place to meet. Gilson was the son of the head teacher at King Edward's School. G.B. Smith was also a close friend who commented on some of Tolkien's early poems, including his original verses about Eärendil* (then written 'Earendel'). Smith was killed on active service in the winter of 1916. He wrote to Tolkien shortly before his death, speaking of how the TCBS‡ – the 'immortal four' – would live on, even if he died that night. Smith concluded: 'May

God bless you, my dear John Ronald, and may you say the things I have tried to say long after I am not there to say them, if such be my lot.'

Though he was from a Methodist family, Wiseman found a great affinity with the Roman Catholic Tolkien. According to Tolkien's biographer, Humphrey Carpenter, Wiseman and Tolkien shared an interest in Latin and Greek, Rugby football, and a zest for discussing anything under the sun. Wiseman was also sympathetic with Tolkien's experiments in invented language, as he was studying the hieroglyphics and language of ancient Egypt. Tolkien and Wiseman continued to meet after Wiseman entered Cambridge University. Wiseman served in the Royal Navy during World War I and later became head of Queen's College, a private school in Taunton. Although the two men did not meet frequently, the friendship with Wiseman was never entirely forgotten.

Tolkien's friends enjoyed his interest in Norse sagas and medieval English literature. After leaving school the four continued to meet occasionally, and to write to each other, until the war destroyed their association. The TCBS left a permanent mark on Tolkien's character, which he captured in the idea of 'fellowship', as in the Fellowship of the Ring. Friendship, later, with C.S. Lewis helped to satisfy this important side of his nature.

After graduating from Exeter College, Oxford,‡ in 1915 and marrying Edith in 1916, Tolkien had his share of bitter action at the front lines. It was during the years of World War I that Tolkien began working on *The Silmarillion* (1977), writing 'The Fall of Gondolin' in 1917 while convalescing. In fact most of the legendary cycle of *The Silmarillion* was already constructed before 1930 – before the writing and publication of *The Hobbit*, the forerunner of *The Lord of the Rings*. In the latter books there are numerous references to matters covered by *The Silmarillion*: ruins of once-great places, sites of battles long ago, strange and beautiful names from the deep past, and elven swords made in Gondolin,* before its fall,† for the Goblin Wars.

In a letter written many years later, Tolkien outlined to an interested publisher the relationship between his life and his imaginary world. He emphasized that the origin of his fiction was in language. 'I do not remember a time', he recalled, 'when I was not building it. Many children make up, or begin to make up, imaginary languages. I have been at it since I could write. But I have never stopped, and of course, as a professional philologist (especially interested in linguistic aesthetics), I have changed in taste, improved in theory, and probably in craft. Behind my stories is now a nexus of languages (mostly only structurally sketched) . . . Out of these languages are made nearly all the names that appear in my legends. This gives them a certain character (a cohesion, a consistency of linguistic style, and an illusion of historicity) to the nomenclature.'

Tolkien's lifelong study and teaching of languages was the source of his imaginative creations. Just as science-fiction writers generally make use of plausible technological inventions and possibilities, Tolkien used his deep and expert knowledge of language in his fiction. He created in his youth two forms of the Elvish* tongue, inspired by his discovery of Welsh and Finnish, starting a process which led to the creation of a history and a geography to surround these languages, and peoples to speak them (and other tongues). He explains: 'I had to posit a basic and phonetic structure of Primitive Elvish, and then modify this by a series of changes (such as actually do occur in known languages) so that the two end results would have a consistent structure and character, but be quite different.' In a letter to W.H. Auden‡ Tolkien confessed that he always had had a 'sensibility to linguistic pattern which affects me emotionally like colour or music'.

Equally important to language in Tolkien's complicated make-up was a passion for myth† and for fairy story,† particularly, he says in his letters, for 'heroic legend on the brink of fairy-tale and history'. Tolkien revealed that he was an undergraduate before 'thought and experience' made it clear to him that story and language were 'integrally related'. His imaginative and scientific interests were not on opposite poles. Myth and fairy story, he saw, must contain moral and religious truth, but implicitly, not explicitly (as allegory†). Both in his linguistic and his imaginative interests he was constantly seeking 'material, things of a certain tone and air'. Myths, fairy stories, and ancient words constantly inspired and sustained the unfolding creations of his mind and imagination† – his elven languages and the early seeds of *The Silmarillion*. The tone and quality he sought, he identified with northern and western Europe, particularly England. He sought to embody this quality in his fiction and invented languages.

The stories he invented in his youth – such as 'The Fall of Gondolin' – came to him as something given, rather than as conscious creation. This sense of givenness and discovery remained with him throughout his life. Paradoxically, *The Silmarillion* belongs to this period even though a full and developed version was not published until after Tolkien's death. The mythology, history, and tales of Middle-earth* are found in unfinished drafts dating over half a century, with considerable developments and changes in narrative structure.

The seeds of *The Silmarillion* lay in his childhood, his schooldays, and his undergraduate fascination with language. As a schoolboy Tolkien was delighted to acquire a second-hand copy of Joseph Wright's‡ *Primer of the Gothic Language* (1892). As a student at Oxford, Tolkien chose comparative philology as his special subject, so he had Wright as a lecturer and tutor. One of Wright's achievements was his six-volume English dialect dictionary. Wright communicated to Tolkien his love for philology and was a demanding teacher and a formative influence on his life. After the interruptions of war, Tolkien returned to Oxford, working on a new edition of the *Oxford English Dictionary*. Over the years Tolkien was associated with three Oxford colleges: Exeter, Pembroke and Merton. Between 1911 and 1915 he was an undergraduate at Exeter College, studying at first classics and then English language and literature. In 1925 he returned from Leeds University to become

Professor of Anglo-Saxon at Pembroke College. After he changed chairs to become Professor of English Language and Literature in 1945, he became a fellow of Merton College.

It was at Leeds, not Oxford, however, that Tolkien began his distinguished career as a university teacher. E.V. Gordon,‡ a Canadian who had been a Rhodes scholar at Oxford, was appointed soon after Tolkien to teach in the English department at Leeds University. The two men became firm friends and were soon collaborating on a major piece of scholarship, a new edition of *Sir Gawain and the Green Knight*‡ (1925). This presentation of the text of the finest of all the English medieval romances helped to stimulate study of this work, much loved by Tolkien. The edition also contains a major glossary.

In 1975, two years after Tolkien's death, *Sir Gawain and the Green Knight, Pearl, and Sir Orfeo*, including Tolkien's own translations of three major medieval English poems, was published. Both *Sir Gawain and the Green Knight* and *Pearl* are thought to be by the same unknown author from the West Midlands, an area of England with which Tolkien identified and upon which he based the Shire.* Tolkien's area of teaching at Leeds University, and later Oxford, was essentially philology. According to T.A. Shippey, in his book *The Road to Middle-earth* (1982), Tolkien's fiction results from the interaction between his imagination and his professional work as a philologist. In his science-fiction novel *Out of the Silent Planet* (1938), C.S. Lewis put something of his friend into the fictional character of the philologist Elwin Ransom. In 1944 Tolkien wrote to his son Christopher‡: 'As a philologist I may have some part in him, and recognize some of my opinions Lewisified in him.'

The name Elwin means 'elf friend' and is a version of the name of the central character in Tolkien's unfinished story, *The Lost Road*. In that story he is named Alboin. From a child he has invented, or rather discovered, strange and beautiful words, leading him to the theory that they are fragments from an ancient world. This slightly autobiographical story tells us much about the love which motivated Tolkien's work in philology, and how it was intimately tied up with his invented mythology of Middle-earth. Owen Barfield said of Lewis that he was in love with the imagination. It could be said of Tolkien that he was in love with language.

When he moved south from Leeds to Oxford in 1925, Tolkien taught mostly Old English, Middle English, and the history of the English language. This work was intimately related to his construction of the languages, peoples and history of the three Ages of Middle-earth.* He commented in a letter that he sought to create a mythology for England, but it might be argued that he also tried to create a mythology for the English language. The earliest expression of the mythology embodied in *The Silmarillion*, a poem written in 1914 about the voyage of Eärendil, was inspired by a line from Cynewulf's Old English poem 'Christ', *Eala Earendel engla beorhtost* ('Behold Earendel brightest of angels').

In the year Tolkien took up the chair of Anglo-Saxon, the distinguished poet W.H. Auden came to Oxford as an undergraduate. There Auden developed a particular liking for Old English literature. Like Tolkien, Auden had a deep interest in northern mythology and was influenced by Tolkien while at Oxford. In later years Tolkien was greatly encouraged by Auden's enthusiasm for *The Lord of the Rings*. He wrote on the quest† hero† in Tolkien's work, corresponded about and discussed with him the meaning of his work, and counteracted through reviews some of the negative criticism of the trilogy. *The Lord of the Rings*, he believed, does 'justice to our experience of social-historical realities'.

It was in 1926 that Tolkien met C.S. Lewis, who had been teaching at Magdalen College for one year. They met at the English faculty meeting on 11 May, and Lewis was not amused, recording in his diary his first impression of Tolkien:

He is a smooth, pale, fluent little chap. Can't read Spenser because of the forms – thinks language is the real thing in the

English School – thinks all literature is written for the amuse-
ment of men between thirty and forty – we ought to vote
ourselves out of existence if we are honest . . . No harm in him:
only needs a smack or two.

Any initial antipathy, however, was soon forgotten. Within a year
or so they were meeting in each other's rooms and talking far into
the night. Tolkien eventually moved from being among Lewis'
second order of friends to his first.

These conversations proved crucial both for the two men's writings and for Lewis' conversion to Christianity. As Lewis remarked
in *Surprised by Joy* (1955):

> Friendship with Tolkien . . . marked the breakdown of two old
> prejudices. At my first coming into the world I had been (implic-
> itly) warned never to trust a Papist, and at my first coming into
> the English Faculty (explicitly) never to trust a philologist. Tolkien
> was both.

A typical note of the time occurs in a letter from Lewis to his Ulster
friend Arthur Greeves in December 1929: 'Tolkien came back with
me to college and sat discoursing of the gods and giants of Asgard
for three hours.'

It is to this period that the origins of the Inklings‡ belongs. This
literary group of male friends centred around the friendship of the
two men, and other friends of Lewis'. In a letter to Donald Swann
on 14 October 1966, Tolkien explains that the title originally
belonged to an undergraduate group (of a type common in Oxford
in those days). He speaks of reading an early version of his poem,
'Errantry', to them (later set to music by Swann):

> I read it to an undergraduate club that used to hear its members
> read unpublished poems or short tales, and voted some of them
> into the minute book. They invented the name *Inklings*, and not

I or Lewis, though we were among the few 'senior' members. (The club lasted the usual year or two of undergraduate societies; and the name became transferred to the circle of C.S. Lewis when only he and I were left of it.)

This poem was linked into Tolkien's developing stories of Middle-earth in a complex way. Similarly, he recalled sharing with Lewis other elements of his work on *The Silmarillion*. The pattern of their future lives, including their later club, the Inklings, was being formed. Tolkien remembered that 'In the early days of our association Jack used to come to my house and I read aloud to him The Silmarillion so far as it had then gone, including a long poem: "Beren and Lúthien"'. Lewis was given the unfinished poem to take home to read and was delighted by it, offering Tolkien suggestions for improvement.

Also important in Tolkien's life at this time was the Kolbitar,‡ an informal reading club he initiated soon after beginning to lecture at Oxford. Its purpose was to explore Icelandic literature such as the Poetic Edda. The name referred to those who crowd so close to the fire in winter that they seem to 'bite the coal'. Lewis attended meetings, as did Nevill Coghill.‡ In some ways it was a forerunner of the Inklings, though more focused than the Inklings' meetings ever were.

The gist of one of the long conversations between Lewis and Tolkien was recorded in October 1931 by Lewis in another letter to Arthur Greeves, and in Tolkien's poem to Lewis, 'Mythopoeia'.‡ It was a crucial factor in Lewis' conversion to Christianity. Tolkien argued that human stories tend to fall into certain patterns and can embody myth. In the Christian Gospels there are all the best elements of good stories, including fairy stories, with the astounding additional factor that everything is also true in the actual, primary world. They combine mythic and historical, factual truth, with no divorce between the two. Lewis' conversion deepened the friendship, a friendship only later eclipsed by Lewis' acquaintance with

Charles Williams‡ and what Tolkien called his 'strange marriage' to Joy Davidman.

In 1936 Tolkien published his seminal essay, 'Beowulf: The Monsters and the Critics'.‡ On 8 March 1939 Tolkien gave his equally significant Andrew Lang lecture at St Andrews University. 'On Fairy Stories'‡ was later published in *Essays Presented to Charles Williams* (1947) – the Inklings' tribute to the writer who had a great deal in common with Tolkien and Lewis. It set out Tolkien's basic ideas concerning imagination, fantasy, fairy story, and sub-creation.† By being tales of elves,* Tolkien's stories of Middle-earth fall into the category of fairy story.

Also belonging to this period of Tolkien's life – it was not in fact published until 1982 – was the writing of *Mr Bliss*.‡ This is a children's story, illustrated throughout by Tolkien in colour. He was an accomplished illustrator (*see Pictures by J.R.R. Tolkien‡*).

Of more abiding significance from this period is his creation of the strange figure of Tom Bombadil,* 'Master of wood, water and hill'. He was a nature† spirit, a name-giver, mastered by none and refusing possession† himself. Tom Bombadil was well-known to Tolkien's children. He was a Dutch doll belonging to Michael Tolkien as a young child. He became the hero of a poem, 'The Adventures of Tom Bombadil', published in 1934 in the *Oxford Magazine*. Tom Bombadil eventually re-emerged in *The Lord of the Rings*.

Tolkien's *The Hobbit* was eventually published on 21 September 1937. It had long been familiar to Lewis and to Tolkien's children. The writing of the book probably began in 1930 or 1931. Lewis was shown a draft before the end of 1932. Tolkien's eldest sons remember the story being told to them before the 1930s. At first the story was independent of his burgeoning mythological cycle, *The Silmarillion*, and only later became drawn into the single invented world and history. The tale introduced hobbits into this mythological world and its history, dramatically affecting the course of the greater structure. *The Hobbit* belongs to the Third

Age* of Middle-earth and chronologically precedes *The Lord of the Rings*.

Bilbo's* discovery of the Ring† provided Tolkien with the link between *The Hobbit* and its large sequel, *The Lord of the Rings*. However, it proved necessary for Tolkien substantially to rewrite chapter 5 of the former book to provide proper continuity between the two works over the great significance of the ruling Ring. This involved Bilbo deceiving his friends over crucial details about how he acquired the Ring. He drafted this in 1947, in the midst of composing *The Lord of the Rings*. The new edition, incorporating the revised chapter, first appeared in 1951.

What is striking about *The Hobbit* is Tolkien's skill in adjusting the scale of his great mythology of the earlier ages of Middle-earth to the level of children. Names are simple, in complete contrast to the complexities of *The Silmarillion*. Erebor* is simply the Lonely Mountain.* Esgaroth* is usually called Lake-town. Elrond's* home in Rivendell* is described as the Last Homely House, west of the Mountains.

Tolkien continued with the adult sequel to *The Hobbit*, *The Lord of the Rings*, more and more leaving aside his first love, *The Silmarillion*. The writing of the sequel was a long, painstaking task. In the midst of it he wrote *Leaf by Niggle*‡ and *Farmer Giles of Ham*‡ (1949). *Leaf by Niggle*, a short allegory, was first published in January 1945 in the *Dublin Review* and was republished in *Tree and Leaf*‡ (1964). The allegory, an unusual form for Tolkien, is also atypical in that it has autobiographical elements, concerning the nature and dilemmas of imaginative creation.

Tolkien's little story suggests the link between art and reality. Even in heaven there will be a place for the artist to add his or her own touch to the created world. The allegorical element could be interpreted with Niggle the painter signifying Tolkien the writer, and Niggle's leaf the tales of Middle-earth (or perhaps just *The Hobbit*).

Farmer Giles of Ham is a lighthearted short story more obviously of interest to children, but full of a philologist's playfulness.

It is set before the days of King Arthur, in the valley of the Thames. The Little Kingdom has similarities with the Shire, particularly the sheltered and homely life of Ham. Farmer Giles is like a complacent Hobbit, with unexpected qualities.

Meanwhile, work continued slowly on *The Lord of the Rings*. Some of it was written and sent in instalments to one of his four children, Christopher, on service in World War II with the Royal Air Force. At one point Tolkien did not touch the manuscript for a whole year. He wrote it in the evenings, for he was fully engaged in his university work and other matters. During the World War II years, and afterwards, he read portions to the Inklings, or simply to Lewis alone, or to Lewis and Charles Williams.

From the early to mid-1930s the Inklings had played an increasingly important part in Tolkien's life. They were particularly important during the writing of *The Lord of the Rings*. The group did not have any consistent documentation such as the careful minuting of the fictional Notion Club, Tolkien's unfinished portrait of an Inklings-type group of friends, set in the future.

Tolkien was undoubtedly a central figure in the literary group of friends held together by the zest and enthusiasm of Lewis. Tolkien described it in a letter as an 'undetermined and unelected circle of friends who gathered around C.S.L[ewis]., and met in his rooms in Magdalen . . . Our habit was to read aloud compositions of various kinds (and lengths!).'

Lewis gives a rare insight into the Inklings, in his preface to *Essays Presented to Charles Williams*, to which Tolkien contributed. Lewis points out that three of the essays in the collection are on literature and, specifically, one aspect of literature, the 'narrative art'. That, Lewis says, is natural enough. Williams'

All Hallows Eve and my own Perelandra (as well as Professor Tolkien's unfinished sequel to The Hobbit) had all been read aloud, each chapter as it was written. They owe a good deal to the hard-hitting criticism of the circle. The problems of narrative as such – seldom heard of in modern critical writings – were constantly before our minds.

Later, near the end of its life as a reading group, the Inklings swelled to include Colin Hardie, Lord David Cecil, John Wain and others. Christopher Tolkien attended as soon as he returned from war service with the RAF in South Africa, and he became a significant member. It was upon this larger group that Tolkien drew inspiration for his unfinished 'The Notion Club Papers',‡ and it is likely that he read it all to them. Warren ('Warnie') Lewis, the brother of C.S. Lewis, records in his diary of 22 August 1946 about 'Tollers' reading 'a magnificent myth which is to knit up and concludes his Papers of the Notions Club'. This would have been 'The Drowning of Anadune' (published with the Notion Club Papers in *Sauron Defeated*).

There were two patterns of Inklings meetings: Tuesday mornings in 'The Bird and Baby' pub (The Eagle and Child, St Giles) – except when Lewis took the chair in Cambridge, when Monday mornings were more suitable – and Thursday evenings, usually in Lewis' rooms in Magdalen but sometimes in Tolkien's rooms in Merton College. The Thursday evenings were of more literary interest, as here members would read to each other work in progress, receiving criticism and encouragement. Much of the 'new Hobbit', *The Lord of the Rings*, was read in this way, sometimes by Christopher instead of his father. After 1951 the term 'the Inklings' no longer appears in the diaries of Warren Lewis, and it is probable that some time around 1949 the Thursday meetings ended, though the Tuesday meetings (or Monday ones) continued until 1963. The key years of the Inklings, in terms of their literary significance, were probably from the early 1930s until near the end of 1949.

The death of Williams in 1945 was a great blow to the group, particularly Lewis. There was a gradual cooling of the friendship between Lewis and Tolkien, which was the heart around which the Inklings formed and grew. The situation was not helped by Hugo

Dyson‡ exercising a veto against Tolkien reading from the unfinished *Lord of the Rings* at Inklings meetings. A later complexity was introduced by Lewis' at first only intellectual friendship with Joy Davidman. Not all of Lewis' friends appealed to Tolkien, or at least not to the same extent, as in the case of Charles Williams. Tolkien however influenced Lewis deeply, and Lewis was of great importance to Tolkien.

The central influence on Lewis was Tolkien's Christianity. Lewis was originally an atheist, and Tolkien helped him come to faith. The pattern of his persuasion is vividly captured in the poem 'Mythopoeia', published in *Tree and Leaf*. The second, related element of Tolkien's influence was his view of the relation of myth and fact. The view can be seen as a theology of story (*see* Story, Tolkien's theology of†). Tolkien had worked out a complex view of the relation of story and myth to reality. Tolkien saw the Gospel narratives – a story created by God himself in the real events of history – as having broken into the 'seamless web of story'. Story – whether preceding or subsequent to the Gospel events – is joyfully alive with God's presence. The importance of story became central to Lewis, expressed for example in his *An Experiment in Criticism* (1961).

The third element, also related, is Tolkien's distinctive doctrine of sub-creation, the view that the highest function of art is the creation of convincing secondary or other worlds. Without the impact of Tolkien's view of sub-creation on Lewis we might not have had Malacandra, Perelandra, or Glome, particularly Perelandra, one of his most successful creations, or even Narnia.

Turning the other way, what was Lewis' importance to Tolkien? Lewis clearly did not influence Tolkien's writing in the way Tolkien influenced his. In Lewis, rather, Tolkien found a ready listener and appreciator. This listening was institutionalized in the Inklings' Thursday night gatherings, where much of *The Lord of the Rings* was read. In fact, Tolkien confesses that without Lewis' encouragement it is unlikely that he would have finished *The Lord of the*

Rings. We might speculate that if the Thursday meetings had continued, with the associated dynamic of Tolkien and Lewis' friendship, there would exist today tellings of the tales of Beren and Lúthien, and perhaps also of Túrin Turambar,* and other key stories of the First Age,* nearer the scale of *The Lord of the Rings.*

The two friends had a great number of shared beliefs. These convictions derived from shared tastes, and particularly from their common faith which, though orthodox, had an original cast. They saw the imagination as the organ of meaning rather than of truth (which made their romanticism distinctive). Imaginative invention was justifiable in its own right – it did not have to serve in a didactic medium and did not have the burden of carrying conceptual truths. Though Lewis was more allegorical and explicit than Tolkien, both writers valued a symbolic perception of reality. A further central preoccupation of Lewis and Tolkien was imaginative invention (most obviously expressed in Tolkien's concept of sub-creation). This was related to their view of the function of imagination as the organ of meaning rather than of truth. Products of the imagination were a form of knowledge, but knowledge discovered by making, essentially not accessible in any other way.

They also shared a sense of the value of otherness – or other-worldliness. Great stories take us outside the prison of our own selves and our presuppositions about reality. Insofar as stories reflect the divine maker, they help us face the ultimate Other – God himself, distinct as creator from all else, including ourselves. The well of fantasy and imaginative invention is every person's direct knowledge of the Other. In *Of This and Other Worlds* (1982) Lewis writes that 'To construct plausible and moving "other worlds" you must draw on the only real "other world" we know, that of the spirit.' For both men this all-pervasive sense of the other was focused in a quality of the numinous.† Each successfully embodied this quality in their fiction.

Both Tolkien and Lewis were preoccupied with pre-Christian paganism, particularly what might be called enlightened paganism.

Most of Tolkien's fiction is set in a pre-Christian world, as was his great model, *Beowulf*, according to his own interpretation of that poem. Even while an atheist, Lewis was attracted by pagan myths of the North and the idea of a dying god. In one of his Latin Letters, Lewis speculates that some modern people may need to be brought to pre-Christian pagan insights in preparation for more adequately receiving the Christian gospel. Tolkien undoubtedly shared this view of pre-evangelism. To point out these shared concerns is not to downplay important differences, often of emphasis, between Tolkien and Lewis. Their differences gave a dynamic to their friendship.

Tolkien was also influenced by Owen Barfield,‡ who is considered one of the core Inklings, such was his impact on the group, even though he rarely was able to attend meetings. Barfield's distinction between allegory and myth rings true of Tolkien's perception, leading to his dislike of allegory and his concern, for example, about Lewis' fondness for allegory. We can also find Tolkien-like concepts in Barfield's view of prehistoric human consciousness, which he saw as unitary, not fragmented into subject and object. It was, as Barfield notes in *Poetic Diction* (1952),

a kind of thinking which is at the same time perceiving – a picture-thinking, a figurative, or imaginative, consciousness, which we can only grasp today by true analogy with the imagery of our poets, and, to some extent, with our own dreams.

Such an attention to dreams, and to shifts in consciousness with developments in language, is typical also of Tolkien, highlighted in his unfinished 'Notion Club Papers'.

In 1945 Tolkien was appointed to a new chair at Oxford, Merton Professor of English Language and Literature, reflecting his wider interests. He was not now so cool to the idea of teaching literature at the university as he had been previously. Tolkien retained the chair until his retirement in 1959. In 1954 he played a key role in securing a Cambridge literary Professorship for C.S. Lewis, who had been passed over by his own university. The scholarly storyteller's retirement years were spent revising *The Lord of the Rings*, brushing up and publishing some shorter pieces of story and poetry, and intermittently working on various drafts of *The Silmarillion*. Tolkien also spent much time dodging reporters and youthful Americans, as the 1960s marked the exploding popularity of his fantasies, when his readership went in numbers from thousands to millions, all over the world.

An interviewer at the time of this new popularity, Daphne Castell, tried to capture his personal manner:

> He talks very quickly, striding up and down the converted garage which serves as his study, waving his pipe, making little jabs with it to mark important points; and now and then jamming it back in, and talking round it . . . He has the habits of speech of the true story-teller . . . Every sentence is important, and lively, and striking . . .

His voice is captured on several recordings of poems and other extracts from his fiction.

Out of this period of consolidation, however, came *Smith of Wootton Major*‡ (1967), a profound story which is written simply enough for a child to enjoy. This short story was Tolkien's last finished work and complements his essay 'On Fairy Stories' in tracing the relationship between the world of faerie and the primary world. The story seems deceptively simple at first, and though children can enjoy it, it is not a children's story. Tolkien described it as 'an old man's book, already weighted with the presage of "bereavement"'. It was as if, like Smith in the story with his elfen star, Tolkien expected his imagination to come to an end. He was also preoccupied in this story with a theme associated with George MacDonald,‡ but which permeates all his work – 'good' death.†

Tolkien's great achievement and life work is the invention, or sub-creation, of Middle-earth. Strictly speaking, Middle-earth is only part of the world. It is an old name for the world, taken from northern mythology and occurring in Old English literature. Much of Tolkien's invention concerns the history, annals, languages and chronology, and geography of Middle-earth. He was concerned to make an inwardly consistent sub-creation. *The History of Middle-earth*‡ (1983–96) is the title of a series of 12 volumes of unfinished or preliminary material edited and published after Tolkien's death by his son, Christopher, who also provided a valuable, detailed commentary (*see* Chapter 5: How *The Lord of the Rings* Relates to *The Silmarillion*).

TWO

A BRIEF CHRONOLOGY

1857   Arthur Reuel Tolkien (father) born in Birmingham, England.

1870   Mabel Suffield (mother) is born in Birmingham, her family originally from Evesham, Worcestershire, England.

1889   Birth of Edith Bratt.

1892   John Ronald Reuel Tolkien born in Bloemfontein, in South Africa, 3 January, where his father worked for Lloyds Bank.

1894   Birth of Hilary Arthur Reuel Tolkien.

1896   Death of Arthur Tolkien, aged 40. The family moves near to Sarehole Mill, then outside the city of Birmingham.

1900   He enters King Edward VI School, Birmingham.

1904   Death of Mabel (Suffield) Tolkien from diabetes, aged 34.

1908   He meets Edith Bratt in his lodgings.

1909   Their romance is discovered by Father Morgan.

1911   Enters Exeter College, Oxford to read classics.

1915   First Class in English Language and Literature. He is commissioned in the Lancashire Fusiliers.

1916   Marries Edith Bratt. He serves from July to November in the Battle of the Somme. Returns to England suffering from 'trench fever'.

1917   His son, John, born. Begins writing the tales which will become *The Silmarillion*.

1918   The war finished, he takes up work with the new *Oxford English Dictionary*.

1920 Appointed Reader in English Literature at Leeds University. His second son, Michael, born.

1924 Appointed to the Chair of English Language at Leeds. His third son, Christopher, born.

1925 Elected to the Chair of Anglo-Saxon at Oxford University (as Rawlinson and Bosworth Professor).

1926 Friendship with C.S. Lewis begins.

1929 His daughter, Priscilla, born.

1930 Begins to write *The Hobbit*.

1936 His lecture, 'Beowulf: The Monsters and the Critics'.

1937 *The Hobbit* is published. He begins a sequel, which will become *The Lord of the Rings*.

1939 His lecture, 'On Fairy Stories'.

1945 Takes up Chair of English Language and Literature at Oxford University (as Merton Professor). Sudden death of his friend and fellow Inkling, Charles Williams.

1954 Publication of first two volumes of *The Lord of the Rings*.

1955 Publication of final volume of *The Lord of the Rings*.

1959 Retires from his work at Oxford.

1965 Increasing popularity on American college campuses after an unauthorized paperback edition of *The Lord of the Rings* is issued.

1968 He and his wife move to Bournemouth.

1963 Death of his friend and fellow Inkling, C.S. Lewis.

1971 Death of Edith Tolkien. He returns to Oxford.

1973 Dies on 2 September.

1977 Publication of *The Silmarillion*, edited by Christopher Tolkien.

1980 Publication of *Unfinished Tales*, edited by Christopher Tolkien, the first of a number of publications of early versions of *The Silmarillion*, and other stories and annals from the first three Ages of Middle-earth. Most notable is *The Lays of Beleriand* (1986) from *The History of Middle-earth* (1983–96).

Further reading

Humphrey Carpenter, *J.R.R. Tolkien: A Biography* (1977).

Humphrey Carpenter, *The Inklings: C.S. Lewis, J.R.R. Tolkien, Charles Williams and Their Friends* (1978).

Daphne Castell, 'The Realms of Tolkien', *New Worlds SF*, vol. 50, no. 168 (1966).

Daniel Grotta, *The Biography of J.R.R. Tolkien: Architect of Middle-earth* (1976, 1978).

The Letters of J.R.R. Tolkien, edited by Humphrey Carpenter with the assistance of Christopher Tolkien (1981).

Tom Shippey, *J.R.R. Tolkien: Author of the Century* (2000).

Part Two

'THE BOOK OF THE CENTURY'

THREE

INTRODUCING
THE LORD OF THE RINGS

THE HOBBIT: THE PRELUDE TO
THE LORD OF THE RINGS

The Hobbit, a children's story, belongs to the Third Age* of Middle-earth,* and chronologically precedes *The Lord of the Rings*. The tale was published in 1937, 17 years before its successor. Its events, particularly the discovery of a Ring of power,† provide the conditions for the quest† that is at the centre of the later book. Seen in the light of *The Lord of the Rings*, the discovery of the Ring, and Bilbo's* encounter with Gollum,* turns out to be more significant than the successful raid on Smaug* the dragon's† hoard of treasure. The finding of the Ring is reiterated in the later book as an essential component of its plot. It is a vital piece of 'back-story'.

Mr Bilbo Baggins, then a peace-loving, middle-aged hobbit,* is hero† of the tale, the bare bones of which are as follows:

A party of dwarves,* 13 in number, are on a quest for their long-lost treasure, which is jealously guarded by a dragon.† Their leader is the great Thorin Oakenshield.* They employ Bilbo Baggins as their burglar to steal it, at the recommendation of the wizard,† Gandalf* the Grey. The reluctant Mr Baggins would rather spend a quiet day with his pipe and pot of tea in his comfortable hobbit-hole than partake in any unrespectable adventure.

The dwarves become increasingly thankful for the fact that they employed him, despite initial misgivings, as he gets them out of many scrapes. He seems to have extraordinary luck, but there is an underlying sense of providence† at work in events.

After near disaster with three trolls,* the party find refreshment at the Last Homely House at Rivendell,* kept by elves* under the leadership of Elrond* Half-elven. They continue further up the slopes of the orc*-infested Misty Mountains.* Sheltering from a thunder battle between giants in a seemingly deserted cave, they are suddenly overwhelmed by the goblin hordes, with the exception of the quick-witted Gandalf. The wizard rescues them as they are brought before the fat goblin chief. As they make their escape, Bilbo is knocked unconscious and left behind in the darkness.

Reviving, Bilbo discovers a Ring lying beside him in the tunnel. It is the ruling Ring that forms the subject of *The Lord of the Rings*, but Bilbo is to discover only its magical property of invisibility at this stage. After putting the Ring in his pocket, Bilbo stumbles along the black tunnel. Eventually, he comes across a subterranean lake, where Gollum dwells, a luminous-eyed corruption of a stoor* hobbit, his life preserved over centuries by the Ring he has now lost for the first time. After a battle of riddles, Bilbo escapes, seemingly by luck, by slipping on the Ring. Following the vengeful Gollum, who cannot see him, he finds his way out of the mountains, on the other side.

Bilbo later gives a false account of the finding of the Ring, preserved in the first edition of *The Hobbit*. He does this because the pernicious influence of the Ring is beginning to work. Gandalf and the others realize this and the true story eventually emerges, incorporated into the second edition. Tolkien developed the plot in this way as the story of *The Lord of the Rings* developed.

Reunited with Gandalf and the dwarves, Bilbo sets off with them on the next stage of their journey: across the forbidding forest of Mirkwood.* They are almost burnt alive by orcs, only to be rescued by eagles,† who whisk them aloft to safety high in the mountains. After rest and food, they are lifted on their way, and soon encounter Beorn,* who can assume animal or human shape. His house is near the fringe of Mirkwood.

Beorn gives them provisions for their journey through the

dangerous forest, and warns them not to leave the elven path that runs through it. At this point Gandalf leaves them for pressing 'business in the south' of Mirkwood. The power of the Necromancer – revealed in *The Lord of the Rings* as Sauron* – is growing. He tells them that they have no cause to worry while they have the resourceful Mr Baggins with them. As so often, Gandalf interprets the underlying pattern of providence in the world of Middle-earth.

After a long, dark and cheerless journey† through the evil-ridden undergrowth of Mirkwood, the party is enchanted off the path by the sight of mysterious lights. They desperately hope for food for their shrunken stomachs. Thorin is taken by the wood-elves. The remainder, except Bilbo, are captured and cocooned by hideous and bloated spiders.* The plucky hobbit rescues them, and rises in the esteem of the dwarves, who had regarded him as an unlikely hero.

By slipping on the Ring, Bilbo narrowly escapes capture by the wood-elves, who are suspicious of the trespassers in their part of the forest. The elves are ruled by Thranduil,* father of Legolas* (who doesn't appear in this story). Bilbo trails the elves and their prisoners to their stronghold built into a rocky hill. This stronghold is a relic of the once great elven kingdoms in Middle-earth. The hobbit's resourcefulness is tested to the full in rescuing them.

After a cramped and foodless journey (for the dwarves) in empty barrels down a river, and (for Bilbo) a cold, wet, virtually foodless journey on a barrel, the party arrive at Lake-town, or Esgaroth, on the Long Lake, south of the Lonely Mountain* where Smaug* the dragon dwells, jealously guarding his hoard of lost treasure.

Reaching the Lonely Mountain Bilbo and the dwarves search fruitlessly for the secret back-door into the dragon's lair. With the help of their map, and apparent luck, the door is discovered (another instance of providence at work). The reluctant hobbit is dispatched down the dark tunnel. A little afterwards, a white-faced Bilbo reappears, clutching a stolen trophy. He urges the dwarves to enter the comparative safety of the tunnel before the vengeful dragon can blast fire and destruction on that part of the mountain.

Bilbo, invisible now he is wearing the Ring, ventures once more to the dragon's hoard. The dragon awakes and there ensues a conversation between the two which, like the earlier riddles with Gollum, require all Bilbo's quick wits. He escapes with singed ankles and head to tell the dwarves that the dragon is out to destroy them. After blasting the mountainside, Smaug wings off to devastate Lake-town. Here, a well-aimed arrow from Bard,* the Bowman pierces the dragon in his only vulnerable spot – a weakness discovered by Bilbo and passed on to Bard by a messenger bird.

In Smaug's absence, Bilbo and the dwarves are able to cross his lair and emerge from the mountain by the main entrance. To the dismay of the dwarves both the Woodland Elves and the men of Lake-town make a claim to a share in the treasure. Bilbo desperately tries to mediate as battle threatens.

Just as all looks at its worst, the sky darkens with evil birds, foreshadowing the arrival of a great army of goblins and wolves. Against this common enemy the dwarves are reunited with men and elves. Thus begins the Battle of Five Armies, in which the forces of evil† are dominant. At the moment when all seems lost, the noble eagles – symbols of providence – intervene and save the day.

Bilbo and Gandalf – who returned before the battle – journey back to the peaceful Shire.* Bilbo has refused most of his share of the treasure, having seen the results of greed. The events have changed him for ever, but even more, the Ring he secretly possesses will shape the events recorded in *The Lord of the Rings*.

Significant information about the background to 'The quest of Erebor' (the events of *The Hobbit*) is found in *Unfinished Tales*.‡ There we learn of the reluctance of the dwarves to take along a hobbit, the great persuasion Gandalf had to muster for Thorin, and the place that providence played in the unfolding of events.

The Lord of the Rings, its sequel, appeared in 1954–55. This great tale of the Third Age* of Middle-earth is written in six parts. Each of the three volumes published contains two of the parts. The volumes are: *The Fellowship of the Ring*, *The Two Towers*, and *The Return of the King*. The evolution of the work is traced in the four parts of *The History of the Lord of the Rings*, edited by Christopher Tolkien.‡

The Lord of the Rings is a heroic romance, telling of the quest to destroy the one, ruling Ring of power, before it can fall into the hands of its maker, Sauron, the dark lord of the title (who appeared as the Necromancer of Mirkwood in *The Hobbit*). As a consistent, unified story, it stands independently of the invented mythology† and historical chronicles of Middle-earth. Events of the past provide a backdrop and haunting dimension to the story. (See Chapter 5: How *The Lord of the Rings* Relates to *The Silmarillion*.)

THE LORD OF THE RINGS

In *The Lord of the Rings* the wizard, Gandalf, discovers that the Ring found by Bilbo is in fact the One Ring, controlling the Rings of Power forged in the Second Age* in Eregion.* Frodo,* inheritor of the Ring, flees from the comfort of the Shire with his companions. On his trail are the Black Riders* sent from Mordor* by Sauron. With the help of the Ranger,* Aragorn,* they succeed in reaching the security of Rivendell. There Elrond holds a great Council where it is decided that the Ring must be destroyed, and that Frodo should be the Ring-bearer. The Company of the Ring* is also chosen to help him on the desperate quest. The Ring can only be destroyed in the Mountain of Fire, Mount Doom,* in Mordor, where it was forged.

Frustrated in their attempt to cross the Misty Mountains in the snow, the Company are led by Gandalf into the underground‡ ways of Moria.* Here dwells a dreadful Balrog.* Gandalf, in great sacrifice,† gives his life fighting the spirit of the underworld to allow the others to escape. The Company is led on by Aragorn, revealed as the secret heir of the ancient Kings of the West. They pass through the blessed realm of Lórien* and then down the great River Anduin.* The creature Gollum is by now on their trail, seeking back his lost Ring.

Boromir* tries to seize the Ring by force to use against the enemy. A party of orcs attack, killing him as he defends Merry* and Pippin,* the hobbits. Frodo and Sam* have, by now, parted from the rest of the Company, heading eastwards, their destination, Mordor. The remainder of the Company follow the track of the orcs who have captured Merry and Pippin, going westwards.

The story now follows the progress of Frodo and Sam, and the others remaining in the Company, in parallel.

Frodo and Sam move slowly towards Mordor, now led by the treacherous Gollum, intent on betrayal, yet held back from this treachery by the rags of his lost nature. Finding the main entrance to Mordor impassable, Frodo accepts Gollum's offer to lead them to a secret entrance. There he leads them into Shelob's* lair. After many perils (including the near death of Frodo) the two make their way to Mount Doom, with no hope of return. At the final moment Frodo cannot throw the Ring into the Cracks of Doom. Gollum bites off the ring-finger, but falls to his death with the Ring. The quest is over. As Mordor disintegrates, and the wraith of Sauron fades, the two are rescued by eagles and reunited with their friends, where they are hailed as heroes.

In the parallel story, after the capture of Merry and Pippin, they are tracked by Aragorn, Legolas and Gimli* to the Forest of Fangorn,* into which they have disappeared after escaping the orcs. In the Forest, the hobbits meet the Ent* Treebeard,* guardian of the woodland. The Ents assault and capture Isengard,* the stronghold of the traitor, Saruman.* Here the hobbits are reunited with the others of the Company, as well as Gandalf, returned from the dead.

Gandalf and the others had healed the aged king of Rohan,* Théoden,* and revealed the poisonous deception of Wormtongue,* secret servant of Saruman. With Théoden's forces, most of the Company move towards Minas Tirith,* now under threat from Sauron's forces. Aragorn, Legolas and Gimli, however, pass through the Paths of the Dead to gather the spirits of long-dead warriors bound by a dreadful oath. These they lead southwards to attack the enemy there.

Without the destruction of the Ring, the alliance against Mordor would have failed. Though there was no certainty of the success of the quest of Frodo and Sam, the people of Gondor* and Rohan, and the other allies, are prepared to fight to the death against the dreadful enemy.

The story ends with the gradual healing† of the land, preparing the way for the domination of humankind. The fading of the elves is complete as the last ships pass over the sea to the Undying Lands of the West. On them are the Ring-bearers Bilbo and Frodo. Sam follows later, after a happy life in the Shire, with his beloved Rosie.*

FOUR

A Guide to
The Lord of the Rings and
Its History

This is a guide to the plot and history which includes references to relevant chapters in *The Lord of the Rings*,‡ which are not always in chronological sequence. The calendar only partly resembles the modern calendar. Each month, for instance, has 30 days.

The Fellowship of the Ring

The first volume of *The Lord of the Rings*, comprising Books One and Two, tells of Gandalf's* discovery that the magical Ring* possessed by Frodo,* the hobbit* is in fact the One Ring,* controlling all the other Rings of Power.† It records the formation of the Company of the Ring* to support the Ring-bearer, and their perilous journey on the way to destroy the Ring. It is set in the Third Age* of Middle-earth* (*see* Chapter 5: How *The Lord of the Rings* Relates to *The Silmarillion*).

Book One

Book One tells of Bilbo's* farewell party, as he leaves for retirement in Rivendell;* Gandalf's account of the history of the Ring to Frodo long after; Frodo's sad departure from Hobbiton* with Sam* and Pippin;* encounters with Sauron's* Black Riders;* their arrival at Buckland;* the journey through the Old Forest,* and visit to the House of Tom Bombadil;* the capture of Frodo by a barrow-wight;

their stay at Bree,* where Aragorn* joins them; and the attacks by Black Riders, where Frodo is badly wounded.

3001

22 September Bilbo Baggins, long after the adventures recounted in *The Hobbit*, throws a farewell eleventy-first birthday party. His possession of the dark ruling Ring has stretched out his life far beyond the normal expectation of a hobbit. Using the Ring, Bilbo conveniently disappears from the party and leaves Bag End for Rivendell, never to return. Gandalf, suspicious of the Ring, warns Frodo never to use the Ring, which Bilbo reluctantly left for him (I, 1: A Long-Expected Party).

3018

12 April Gandalf returns to Hobbiton to tell Frodo the full history of the Ring that he has discovered, and Gollum's* part in it. Frodo starts his preparations to leave to destroy the Ring in the Cracks of Doom (I, 2: The Shadow of the Past).

20 June Sauron* attacks Osgiliath in Gondor.* Around this time Thranduil* is also attacked, allowing Gollum to escape. (Legolas* brings news of the escape to the Great Council* at Rivendell on 25 October – II, 2: The Council of Elrond.)

4 July Boromir* leaves Minas Tirith* bound for Rivendell.
10 July Gandalf is imprisoned by the treacherous Saruman* in Orthanc.* (This is not recounted until 25 October – II, 2: The Council of Elrond.)

August All trace of Gollum is lost. It is probable that he hid from his pursuers in Moria.*

18 September Gandalf escapes Orthanc.

23, 24 September A Black Rider reaches Hobbiton at dusk. Frodo departs Bag End. After two close encounters with a Black Rider, Gildor and his elves* invite Frodo, Sam and Pippin to their camp in Woody End (I, 3: Three is Company). Borne by Shadowfax* Gandalf leaves Rohan.*

25 September The companions meet Farmer Maggot, and cross the ferry over the River Baraduin (Brandywine) to Bucklebury. In Crickhollow Frodo discovers that his cousins and Sam have known about his plans and the Ring all along (I, 4: A Short Cut to Mushrooms; I, 5: A Conspiracy Unmasked).

26 September They face the perils of the Old Forest, and are rescued by Tom Bombadil (I, 7: In the House of Tom Bombadil).

27 September They spend a second night with Bombadil and Goldberry.*

28 September The hobbits captured on the Downs by a barrow-wight (I, 8: Fog on the Barrow Downs).

29 September The party reach the East Road and arrive at Bree after nightfall. Frodo creates a sensation at the inn when the Ring makes him invisible (I, 9: At the Sign of the Prancing Pony). The hobbits become acquainted with Strider* (Aragorn), a Ranger,* and king in disguise (I, 10: Strider). Gandalf, by now in the Shire,* speaks to the Gaffer.

30 September Crickhollow and the inn at Bree are both raided by the Black Riders of Sauron in the early hours. Frodo and his companions leave Bree with Strider in their company, heading for Weathertop over the unpleasant Midgewater Marshes (I, 11: A Knife in the Dark). Gandalf visits Crickhollow, and gets to Bree that night.

1 October Gandalf sets off from Bree.

3 October He battles the dark forces at night on Weathertop.*

6 October Frodo and company reach Weathertop, where their camp comes under attack at night. Before this they see the ruins of Amon Sûl* and Aragorn recounts the tale of Beren* and Lúthien.*

Frodo suffers a severe wound (I, 11: A Knife in the Dark. *See also* II, 2: The Council of Elrond; III, Appendix A: The Northern Kingdom and the Dúnedain).

9 October Glorfindel* sets out from Rivendell to look for Frodo and friends.

7–13 October The travellers move slowly due to Frodo's wound, eventually reaching the Last Bridge.

13–20 October They come across the trolls* turned to stone during Bilbo's adventures recounted in *The Hobbit*. Glorfindel meets them and guides the party to the Ford of Bruinen. Frodo escapes the Black Riders, but collapses. Gandalf reaches Rivendell on 18 October (I, 12: Flight to the Ford).

Book Two

Book Two narrates Frodo's healing† in Rivendell. It tells of the Great Council of Elrond,* in which it is decided to form the Company of the Ring, and to take what seems a foolish course of bearing the Ring to Mordor.* It recounts the dangerous journey south, and through Moria, where Gandalf is lost fighting the Balrog.* It describes the passage of the Company through Lórien,* and their meeting Galadriel.* Leaving Lórien, the Company travels south once again, on the River Anduin,* until they reach the Falls of Rauros. Here Boromir* tries to seize the Ring from Frodo, the Company is divided, as Sam and Frodo set out alone for Mordor, and the remainder are scattered by a sudden orc* attack.

3018

24 October Frodo comes round in Rivendell, and feels restored. He is reunited with Bilbo at a feast that evening. Boromir arrives (II, 1: Many Meetings).

25 October The Council of Elrond. Here the full story of the Ring and its danger to elves, dwarves,* hobbits and men is revealed. Despite Boromir's misgivings the Council decides that the Ring must be consigned to the fires of Mordor, where it was forged. Frodo offers to bear the Ring (II, 2: The Council of Elrond).

25 December The Company of the Ring leaves Rivendell at nightfall. The Fellowship is nine in number, to match the number of Nazgûl* (II, 3: The Ring Goes South).

3019

13 January Wolves attack in the night, after the Company is forced to change path because of snowstorms. They reach the West-gate of Moria at nightfall. It is here that Gollum begins to shadow the Ring-bearer (II, 3: The Ring Goes South).

14–15 January They are forced into the underworld† of the dwarf mines of Moria, as the only way left to cross the Misty Mountains.* After spending the night in Hall Twenty-one they reach the Bridge of Khazad-dûm,* where Gandalf is lost fighting the fiery Balrog and the Company are thrown into confusion. They reach Nimrodel late at night (II, 4: A Journey in the Dark; II, 5: The Bridge of Khazad-Dûm).

16–17 February The Company reaches Caras Galadon* in Lórien at evening, and meets Galadriel, holder of one of the three elf-rings. As Frodo looks into the waters at her invitation in order to see what may be in the future he realizes that the enchanting elven beauty of Lórien is destined to pass away whether or not the Ring is destroyed. They stay long in the elf-kingdom, a vestige of the kingdoms of earlier Ages (II, 6: Lothlórien; II, 7: The Mirror of Galadriel).

23 February Gandalf pursues his enemy right to the height of Zirak-zigil.

25 February After defeating the Balrog, he dies, and his body lies on the peak.

14 March Gandalf returns to life, but remains in a trance.

16 March The Fellowship of the Ring bid farewell to Lórien, a departure observed by the skulking Gollum (II, 8: Farewell to Lórien).

17 March Gandalf is carried to Lórien by Gwaihir.

23 March The company follow the River Anduin as far as they can, surviving an orc attack near Sarn Gebir (II, 9: The Great River). They face the choice of going with the Ring towards Minas Tirith (Boromir's wish), or continuing to Mordor.

25 March They pass the Argonath and make camp at Parth Galen on the shores of the Lake of Nen Hithoel (II, 9: The Great River; II, 10: The Breaking of the Fellowship). Théodred, son of Théoden,* slain upon the West Marches (III, 6: The King of the Golden Hall).

THE TWO TOWERS

This, the second volume of *The Lord of the Rings*, comprises Books Three and Four. It tells the adventures of the members of the Company of the Ring after the break up of their fellowship, up to the beginning of a great darkness from Mordor and the start of the War of the Ring.*

Book Three

Book Three marks a division of the narrative, following the fortunes of the company other than Frodo and Sam, who had set off for Mordor. The Book tells of the confession and death of Boromir; the pursuit of the orcs who had taken Merry* and Pippin; the meeting with Eomer and the Riders of Rohan;* the escape of the hobbits from the orcs; the reappearance of Gandalf; Merry and Pippin's meeting with the Ent* Treebeard;* the meeting with King Théoden and Gandalf's removal of the deception upon him; the battle of Helm's Deep; the destruction of Isengard* by the Ents; the reunion of Aragorn, Gimli, Legolas and Gandalf with Merry and Pippin; Pippin's look into the Palantir.*

Book Four

Book Four is chronologically parallel to Book Three, telling how Frodo and Sam fared as they made their dangerous way to Mordor. It recounts how Gollum joins the two as their reluctant guide; their passage across the Dead Marshes;* their arrival at the Black Gate; their journey beyond through Ithilien* and meeting with Faramir* of Gondor;* their parting from Faramir at the Cross Roads as they move towards Cirith Ungol;* their arrival at Shelob's* lair and the treachery of Gollum; Shelob's attack on Frodo and his capture by orcs of Mordor; and Sam's pursuit into their headquarters, now bearing the Ring.

3019

26 February The Fellowship is scattered with the death of Boromir; killed by orcs serving Saruman. Merry and Pippin taken. Frodo and Sam enter alone into the eastern Emyn Muil. Aragorn, Gimli and Legolas start tracking the orcs (II, 10: The Breaking of the Fellowship; III, 1: The Departure of Boromir).

27–28 February Eomer, ignoring Théoden's orders, sets out from Eastfold at night to pursue the orcs. He overtakes them just outside Fangorn Forest.* Aragorn learns from Eomer that Rohan is at war with Saruman (III, 2: The Riders of Rohan).

29 February Merry and Pippin escape their orc captors and meet Treebeard, the Ent. The Rohirrim attack at dawn and destroy the orcs (III, 3: The Uruk-Hai). Frodo and Sam descend the cliffs of Emyn Muil and discover Gollum (IV, 1: The Taming of Sméagol). Faramir sees the funeral boat of Boromir.

30 February The Entmoot begins (III, 4: Treebeard). Eomer, heading for Edoras, encounters Aragorn.

1 March Frodo and Sam, led by Gollum, start to cross the Dead Marshes at dawn. They see faces of corpses from an ancient battle in the waters (IV, 2: The Passage of the Marshes). Meanwhile, the

Entmoot continues. Aragorn and his companions meet Gandalf the White, then set out for Edoras (III, 4: Treebeard; III, 5: The White Rider). Faramir leaves Minas Tirith for Ithilien.

2 March Frodo and the others reach the end of the Marshes (IV, 2: The Passage of the Marshes). Gandalf enters Edoras and brings healing to Théoden. The Rohirrim set out west against Saruman (III, 5: The White Rider; III, 6: The King of the Golden Hall). There is another battle at the Fords of Isen, where Erkenbrand is defeated. The Entmoot ends that afternoon. The Ents decide to march on Isengard.

3 March Théoden retreats to Helm's Deep, where the desperate Battle of the Homburg begins (III, 7: Helm's Deep). Ents complete the destruction of Isengard.

4 March The battle over, Théoden and Gandalf set out for Isengard (III, 8: The Road to Isengard). Frodo, Sam and Gollum arrive at the slag-mounds near Mordor (IV, 2: The Passage of the Marshes).

5 March Theoden and his party reach Isengard at noon. Negotiations with Saruman in Orthanc. Gandalf sets out with Pippin for Minas Tirith (III, 9: Flotsam and Jetsam; III, 10: The Voice of Saruman; III, 11: The Palantir). Frodo and the others hide in sight of the Morannon, and leave at nightfall, following a new route, at Gollum's suggestion (IV, 3: The Black Gate is Closed).

7 March After encountering men of Gondor in Ithilien, Frodo and Sam are taken by Faramir to Henneth Annûn (IV, 4: Of Herbs and Stewed Rabbits; IV, 5: The Window on the West). Aragorn comes to Dunharrow at nightfall (V, 2: The Passing of the Grey Company).

THE RETURN OF THE KING

Published in 1955, this is the third volume of *The Lord of the Rings*, comprising Books Five and Six, and extensive appendices. It tells of the conflicting strategies of Gandalf and Sauron, up to the end of the darkness gripping Middle-earth. The appendices provided the main source of information about the earlier Ages of Middle-earth until the publication of *The Silmarillion*‡ in 1977.

Book Five

Book Five tells of the arrival of Pippin and Gandalf at Minas Tirith; the passing of the Grey Company (those led by Aragorn on the Paths of the Dead); the muster of Rohan; the siege of Gondor; the ride of the Rohirrim; the Battle of the Pelennor Fields (*see* War of the Ring); the suicide of Denethor;* the restoration of Éowyn* and Faramir at the Houses of Healing; the last debate of the western allies; and the opening of the Black Gate of Mordor, when all seems lost.

Book Six

Book Six is parallel, for much of its narration, to Book Five. It tells of Sam searching for Frodo at the Tower of Cirith Ungol; their perilous journey into Mordor's land of shadow; their arrival at Mount Doom* and the end of the quest to destroy the Ring; the reunion at the Field of Cormallen; the crowning of Aragorn; the various partings; the hobbits' journey back to the Shire; the scouring of the Shire and the death of Saruman; and the passing of the Ring-bearers from Grey Havens.*

Some of the events below (concerning Sam and Frodo) are actually recounted in *The Two Towers*, Book Four.

3019

8 March Aragorn takes the 'Paths of the Dead' at dawn, and reaches Erech at midnight (V, 2: The Passing of the Grey Company).
9 March Gandalf arrives at Minas Tirith. Aragorn sets out from Erech and reaches Calembel. Faramir leaves Henneth Annûn. By evening Frodo reaches the Morgul Road. Théoden enters

Dunharrow. Darkness begins to pour out of Mordor (V, 3: The Muster of Rohan; IV, 7: Journey to the Cross Roads; IV, 8: The Stairs of Cirith Ungol).

10 March Rohan is mustered, and the Rohirrim ride from Harrowdale. Faramir is rescued by Gandalf outside the city gates. Sauron's army takes Cair Andros and moves into Anórien. Frodo passes east from the Cross Roads towards Mordor (V, 3: The Muster of Rohan; V, 4: The Siege of Gondor; IV, 8: The Stairs of Cirith Ungol).

11 March Gollum plots with Shelob, but seeing Frodo asleep nearly changes his mind. Aragorn gets to Linhir and crosses into Lebennin. The east of Rohan is invaded.

12 March Gollum leads Frodo into Shelob's lair (IV, 9: Shelob's Lair).

13 March Frodo is captured by the orcs of Cirith Ungol (IV, 10: The Choices of Master Samwise). In Gondor the Pelennor* is overrun, and Faramir is wounded. Aragorn reaches Pelargir and captures the fleet.

14 March Sam finds Frodo in the Tower (VI, 1: The Tower of Cirith Ungol). Minas Tirith is besieged.

15 March The Witch-king breaks the gates of the city, and in despair Denethor burns himself on a pyre. The Rohirrim arrive. In the Battle of the Pelennor, Théoden perishes. Frodo and Sam escape the orc stronghold and begin their journey north. Battles elsewhere in Middle-earth (V, 6: The Battle of the Pelennor Fields; VI, 1: The Tower of Cirith Ungol; VI, 2: The Land of Shadow).

16 March Frodo and Sam from the height of the Morgai can see Mount Doom in the distance (VI, 2: The Land of Shadow).

17 March Battle of Dale* in the north. Many, both dwarves and men, find refuge in Erebor,* under the Lonely Mountain. The orc Shagrat brings Frodo's cloak, mail-shirt, and sword to Sauron's stronghold.

18 March The Host of the West sets out from Minas Tirith (V, 10: The Black Gate Opens).

19 March The Western Army reaches Morgul-vale (V, 10: The Black Gate Opens). Frodo and Sam continue towards the Barad-dûr (VI, 3: Mount Doom).

23 March The Host pass Ithilien. Frodo and Sam cast away their arms and gear.

24 March Frodo and Sam complete their journey to the feet of Mount Doom (VI, 3: Mount Doom). The Host of the West encamps before the Black Gate of Mordor (V, 10: The Black Gate Opens).

25 March The Host is surrounded on the slag-hills (V, 10: The Black Gate Opens). Gollum seizes the Ring from Frodo and falls into the Cracks of Doom. Downfall of Barad-dûr and the passing of Sauron (VI, 3: Mount Doom). The quest† has ended.

3019

1 May The crowning of Aragorn as King Elessar. Arwen* sets out from Rivendell (VI, 5: The Steward and the King).

Mid-Year's Day Wedding of Elessar and Arwen (VI, 5: The Steward and the King).

22 September The hundred and twenty-ninth birthday of Bilbo. Saruman comes to the Shire.

5 October Gandalf and the four hobbits leave Rivendell (VI, 7: Homeward Bound).

28 October They reach Bree by evening.

30 October The four hobbits come to the Brandywine Bridge late in the day, and find it locked and bolted (VI, 8: The Scouring of the Shire).

1 November They are arrested at Frogmorton (VI, 8: The Scouring of the Shire).

2 November They come to Bywater and rally the folk of the Shire.

3 *November* The Battle of Bywater, and the passing of Saruman ('Sharky'). The end of the War of the Ring.

3021

29 *September* Frodo and Bilbo sail from the Grey Havens. The end of the Third Age (VI, 9: The Grey Havens).

FIVE

HOW *THE LORD OF THE RINGS* RELATES TO *THE SILMARILLION*

Behind the story of *The Lord of the Rings*‡ lies a complex history of earlier Ages of Middle-earth,* in which the very shape of the world changed. Its events span a vast range of time. This history, with many of its central figures, is constantly alluded to in the story. Tom Bombadil,* for instance, speaks of great changes in the world to Frodo* and his companions.

> When they caught his words again they found he had now wandered into strange regions beyond their memory and beyond their waking thought, into times when the world was wider, and the seas flowed straight into the western shore; and still on and back Tom went singing out into the ancient starlight, when only the Elf-sires were awake.

Later they find that Rivendell,* a haven of the dwindling elves,* is a place of storytelling. Here Bilbo* is translating the elven tales of past Ages. This is the house of Elrond,* who is son of Eärendil,* a figure who links the former and present Ages. Elrond is also father of Arwen,* who renounces her immortality to marry Aragorn* in the happier days after the destruction of the Ring.† The story of the love of Aragorn and Arwen echoes an ancient tale of Beren* and Lúthien,* which Aragorn had retold to Frodo, Sam* and the others beside Weathertop.*

The most striking presence of the older world in the times of

Bilbo, Frodo and the hobbits* of the Shire* is of course the one, ruling Ring,* forged by Sauron* in Eregion.* The rule of this Ring over the lesser ones of elves, dwarves,* and mortals is a central motif of *The Lord of the Rings*. It is an objective token of the power of evil,† and the spell it casts, which tests Bilbo, Frodo, Sam, Gandalf,* Saruman,* Gollum,* the tragic Boromir* and many others. There are numerous other relics of the older world, including many ruins and overgrown roads encountered by Frodo and his companions.

This ancient background, which continues throughout the events of *The Lord of the Rings* to have important consequences, is set out in *The Silmarillion*‡ (1977). This work Tolkien never completed. The tales of *The Silmarillion* are also collected in other posthumous publications, including the 12-volume *History of Middle-earth*,‡ edited by Christopher Tolkien,‡ his son.

Christopher Tolkien, one-time member of the Inklings‡ and an Early English scholar, is the person closest to his father's thinking. *The Silmarillion* is based on Tolkien's unfinished work, and is not intended to suggest a finished work, though his son's editorial work is highly skilled, and faithful to his father's intentions. The unfinished nature of the book is most apparent in several independent tales that are contained therein, such as Beren and Lúthien, the elf-maiden, Túrin Turambar,* Tuor* and the Fall of Gondolin,* and Eärendil the mariner.* These are in fact summaries of tales intended to be on a larger, more detailed, scale, and never completed. The condensed, summary nature of much of the published *Silmarillion* presents difficulties for many readers. This difficulty is compounded by the plethora of unfamiliar names. When J.E.A. Tyler updated his *Tolkien Companion* to include *The Silmarillion* he had to add about 1,800 new entries!

Later in this section I give an outline of one of the more important independent tales for which most detailed storytelling exists – that of Beren and Lúthien. The mythology† and earlier history of Middle-earth exists as background to this story, as it does for *The*

Lord of the Rings (though of course much more has happened by the time of the events surrounding the hobbits). Speaking of the tale of Beren and Lúthien, Tolkien commented: 'There are other stories almost equally full in treatment, and equally independent and yet linked to the general history.'

The tales of *The Silmarillion* evolved through all the years of Tolkien's adulthood, and strictly are only a part of the published book. The work chronicles the ancient days of the First Age* of Middle-earth. It begins with the creation of the Two Lamps* (*see* Light†) and concludes with the great battle in which Morgoth* is overthrown (*see* Battles of Beleriand*). The unifying thread of the annals and tales of *The Silmarillion* is, as its title suggests, the fate of the Silmarils,* the gems crafted by Fëanor.*

The published *Silmarillion* is divided into several sections. The first is the 'Ainulindalë'‡ – the account of the creation of the world. This is one of Tolkien's finest pieces of writing, perfectly taking philosophical and theological matter into artistic form. The second section is the 'Valaquenta' – the history of the Valar.* Then follows the main and largest section, the 'Quenta Silmarillion'‡ – *The Silmarillion* proper (the 'history of the Silmarils'). The next section is the 'Akallabêth',* the account of the Downfall of Númenor.* The final section concerns the history of the Rings of Power† and the Third Age.* Tolkien intended all these sections to appear in one book, giving a comprehensive history of Middle-earth. He comments at length on the development of the history of Middle-earth through the Three Ages in the important and lengthy Letter 131 in his *Letters*.‡

The mythology, history and tales of Middle-earth are, in fact, found in unfinished drafts spanning over half a century, with considerable developments and changes in narrative structure. Not least, some of the great tales have poetic and prose versions. The published *Silmarillion* provides a stable point of reference by which to read the unfinished publications (collected by Christopher Tolkien in *Unfinished Tales*‡ and *The History of Middle-earth*).

Further stability is provided by Tolkien's own often lengthy commentaries on *The Silmarillion* in his *Letters* (as in Letter 131, mentioned above).

To illustrate the spread of material in different publications, there are several versions of the creation of the world (Arda*): 'The music of the Ainur' (*The Book of Lost Tales* I, chapter 2); 'The Ambarkanta' ('The Shape of the World' – *The Shaping of Middle-earth*,* chapter 5); and the 'Ainulindalë' (*The Lost Road*, part 2, chapter 4). Earlier versions of *The Silmarillion* can be found as follows: *The Book of Lost Tales 1 and 2*‡ (the beginning of the tales that eventually became *The Silmarillion*); the earliest 'Silmarillion' (*The Shaping of Middle-earth*, chapter 2); 'The Quenta' (*The Shaping of Middle-earth*, chapter 3); and the 'Quenta Silmarillion' (*The Lost Road*, part 2, chapter 6).

Much of *The Silmarillion* was cast by Tolkien into the form of annals, in his concern for astonishing consistency and detail in dates and history. (Such consistency was part of his theory of sub-creation.†) There are therefore a number of summaries of the key events of the First Age, as follows: 'The Earliest Annals of Valinor' (*The Shaping of Middle-earth*, chapter 6); 'The Earliest Annals of Beleriand' (*The Shaping of Middle-earth*, chapter 7); 'The Later Annals of Valinor' (*The Lost Road*, part 2, chapter 2); and 'The Later Annals of Beleriand' (*The Lost Road*, part 2, chapter 3).

The Ages of Middle-earth

There were several Ages of Middle-earth. Prior to the Ages, Ilúvatar* (the creator-deity) created the world, first in conception in music† and then in giving it actual being. This is told in the 'Ainulindalë'. *The Silmarillion* then goes on to chronicle the history of the elves. Tolkien's mythology is distinctive in being centred upon elves rather than human beings, even though humans eventually get caught up in events and matters of interest to elves. In contrast, events of a very much later Third Age, are told and perceived from the perspective of halflings (hobbits) and humans. From this period they look back to the earlier Ages, and some stories are more relevant to them than others, such as the story of Beren and Lúthien, and others which concern the intermingling of humans and elves, or the doings of the people of Númenor. The high matters of elves and the Valar and attendant powers are translated into the common speech and thought-forms of hobbits and humans. One method Tolkien uses to convey this transposition and translation is by a frequent use of deliberate anachronism. Many features of the Shire of the hobbits resemble the West Midlands of Tolkien's childhood – potatoes, stewed rabbit, and even a reference to fish and chips by Sam Gamgee* appear in the story; and, most notably, Tolkien locates the northern lands of Middle-earth as early northern Europe, with Númenor (Atlantis) lying to the far west of the landmass, as in Celtic mythology. Tolkien explains: 'In presenting the matter of the Red Book, as a history for people of today to read, the whole of the linguistic setting has been translated as far as possible into terms of our own times' (see Red Book of Westmarch*).

Before the beginning of the First Age (taken as the rising of the sun) the Valar and later also many of the elves are established in the uttermost West, or Valinor.* Fëanor makes the great gems, the Silmarils, which provide the underlying motif for The Silmarillion. Morgoth darkens Middle-earth by destroying the Two Lamps and brings shadow to Valinor by extinguishing the Two Trees* (see below). He hides in the cold north of Middle-earth, north of Beleriand,* long drowned by the time of the events of The Lord of the Rings.

Beleriand in the First Age is the setting for the tales of Beren and Lúthien the elf-maiden, Túrin Turambar (or, The Children of Húrin*), and the Fall of Gondolin. In a momentous climax to the events, Eärendil the mariner sails to Valinor to intercede on behalf of the free peoples of Beleriand. In the Second Age* the star-shaped island of Númenor (Atlantis) is given to the Dúnedain,* the Men of the West, for their faithfulness in resisting Morgoth. Sauron, Morgoth's lieutenant, secretly forges the great Ring in Middle-earth. He succeeds in aiding the corruption of Númenor, resulting in its destruction. The very shape of the world is changed into a globe, and Valinor is no longer accessible, except by the Straight Road.* There is a great and successful western alliance against Mordor.*

In the Third Age, the Ring remains lost for many centuries. Gondor* is a great power. Hobbits migrate to the Shire. The events of *The Hobbit‡* and *The Lord of the Rings* take place (*see* Chapter 3: Introducing *The Lord of the Rings*). The Fourth Age* opened our present era of the domination of humankind, and the fading of the elves, where the Christian era gradually unfolds (*see* Christianity, Tolkien and†). The original geography* of Middle-earth changes into its present shape, though some parts, such as turn-of-the-century Warwickshire and Worcestershire, resemble that original world (in this case, the Shire). In unfinished stories of Tolkien, Aelfwine* voyages to Tol Eressëa;* and, in our own time, Alboin* finds the lost road,* travelling back in time to Númenor. According to his letters (Letter 211) we may now be in a Sixth or even Seventh Age.

The Lamps and the Two Trees

At the beginning of the history of Middle-earth two great globes are set on top of great pillars of stone in the north and south of Middle-earth by the Valar to light the world. The malicious destruction of the lamps by Morgoth (Melkor) marked the end of the Spring of the world. After the lamps, the world was lit by the two trees of Valinor, one white and one golden. The first was called Telperion* and the second Laurelin.* They illuminated Valinor, Eldamar and as far as Tol Eressëa. Their glory was such that the sun and moon were made out of their dying light. Before the destruction of the Two Trees by Morgoth and Ungoliant,* Fëanor captured their light in the Silmarils that he made.

The changing geography of the world

Two geocatastrophic events affected the geography of the world of Tolkien's sub-creation. The first was the ruin of Beleriand at the end of the First Age. The second was the even more dramatic drowning of Númenor in the Second Age, which resulted in a change in the world. It is only after the destruction of Númenor that the world is our familiar sphere. Aman* is removed from the physical world, and is only to be found by the Straight Road.*

At different times in the history of Tolkien's invented world there are significant landmasses: Aman, Númenor, Beleriand (to the north of Middle-earth), and Middle-earth (as it existed at the time of the events recorded in *The Hobbit* and *The Lord of the Rings*). These areas can be described geographically (as has been done in Fonstad's *The Atlas of Middle-earth*).

Aman was a great western continent. It lay between the great sea of Belegaer,* and the outer sea of Ekkaia, which was the boundary of the world. Parallel to the eastern coast of Aman ran the great mountain chain of the Pelori. Valinor was to be found west of the Pelori, and Eldamar between the mountains and the sea, near the pass of the Calacirya. North and south lay vast wastelands. The island of Tol Eressëa lay off the coast.

To the east of the great sea of Belegaer lay Middle-earth. In the First Age the northern region of Beleriand was significant, with settlements of elves, dwarves and humans. After its destruction, the more southerly regions became important. The star-shaped island of Númenor was raised in the middle of the great sea for a favoured habitation for the Dúnedain. These are the lands that are described in *The Silmarillion* and *Unfinished Tales*.

The relatively southern regions of Middle-earth are those that are familiar to the readers of *The Lord of the Rings*, and *The Hobbit*. Because of the growing importance of humans, and gradual decline of the elves, regions generally express the political boundaries of humans rather than elves. Physically, the north–south presence of the Misty Mountains* and the River Anduin* are significant. In the south the White Mountains of Gondor,* and the mountain chains of Mordor impose themselves. To the west, the Blue Mountains are a feature. The most important western feature is the long coast-line of the sea of Belegaer. Politically, the kingdoms of Gondor and Arnor* are important, as well as the southern lands of the Haradrim.*

The elven region of Eregion was important in the Second Age, with Grey Havens,* Rivendell* and Lórien* retaining their impor-tance into the Third Age. There were significant dwarf realms, including Khazad-dûm,* abandoned at the time the Company of the Ring* passed through the Misty Mountains.

The Shire was located in the ruined realm of Arnor, the north-ern kingdom founded by the Númenoreans. It was preserved from danger by its guardians, the Rangers of the North.* The southern kingdom, Gondor, remained a significant power in the days of the hobbits, and played an important part in the War of the Ring.*

FOUR GREAT STORIES OF *THE SILMARILLION*

Tolkien intended 'Tuor and the Fall of Gondolin' to be a major tale in *The Silmarillion*, standing independently of the history of the ancient days and the First Age. It was never completed on a grand scale. *The Silmarillion* contains a summary of the story, while in *Unfinished Tales* there is the first part of a detailed treatment showing, sadly, the promise of what was never achieved. 'The Fall of Gondolin' is the first of the tales of the First Age to be composed by Tolkien – during sick-leave from the army in 1917. The most complete form of 'The Fall of Gondolin' is to be found in *The Book of Lost Tales*,‡ but, unfortunately, this was written early in the development of *The Silmarillion*.

The tragedy of Túrin, 'The Tale of Túrin Turambar', is another of several stories from *The Silmarillion* that, according to Tolkien, stand independently of the history and mythology. The tale was conceived early, when Tolkien as a young man wished to make use of elements from the Finnish *Kalavala*. There is a hint of the story of Oedipus in it, as Tolkien was aware.

Húrin,* the father of Túrin, had been captured by Morgoth and bound upon the peak of Thangorodrim,* where he could better see the outworkings of Morgoth's curse or doom upon his family. The curse bedevils the life of Túrin, and other relations, including Túrin's sister, Nienor.* Yet the sorrow in Túrin's life comes not only from external causes, though compounded by them, but also because of a 'fatal flaw' that is the stuff of tragedy. Túrin's flaw was a mixture of pride and rashness of action. In the tension between internal motive and external malice in Túrin's life, Tolkien explores the problem of evil.† He says that, in the tale of Túrin 'are revealed most evil works of Morgoth', and that it was 'the worst of the works of Morgoth in the ancient world'.

There are several accounts of the tale of Túrin. That in *The Silmarillion* is in fact a summary of a story worked out in great detail by Tolkien. A longer, fuller and powerful version, sadly incomplete, appears in *Unfinished Tales* and an unfinished poetic version is recorded in *The Lays of Beleriand*.‡

Tolkien considered 'The Voyage of Eärendil the Mariner' another of the great stories of *The Silmarillion*, which stand independently of the history and annals of the First Age. For Tolkien Eärendil has a strategic role in bringing *The Silmarillion* to its conclusion. His descendants provide the main links to the persons in the tales of later Ages, particularly in the events recounted in *The Lord of the Rings*. It is a quest† story, in which Eärendil represents both elves and humans. He seeks a seaway back to Valinor, the Land of the Valar. He is an ambassador, interceding for the rescue of the exiles in Middle-earth. His wife Elwing* is of the line of Lúthien, still possessing the Silmaril.

Unfortunately, the tale, or tales, of Eärendil cannot be reconstructed from Tolkien's unfinished work in as great detail as the tales of Beren and Lúthien, and of Túrin Turambar.

Tolkien regarded the tale of Beren and Lúthien, set in an earlier period than the story of Eärendil, as the pivotal story of *The Silmarillion*, the key to its interlocking themes and events. The tale also determines the outcome of events for Ages to come, not least in its intermarriage of an elven princess and a mortal man, in which an elven quality† becomes incarnate in humanity. It is worth, therefore, outlining the story in greater length. The story had the potential to be told in a detail and length approaching that of *The Lord of the Rings*. As it was Tolkien never fully finished it. There are drafts in both prose and poetry. Tolkien began composing the first version, which was in poetry, in 1925. Late in 1929 he gave a large portion of the poem to his friend C.S. Lewis‡ to read, who commented on it in depth. While in the process of reading it, Lewis wrote to Tolkien:

I can quite honestly say that it is ages since I have had an evening of such delight: and the personal interest of reading a friend's work had very little to do with it. I should have enjoyed it just as well as if I'd picked it up in a bookshop, by an unknown author. The two things that come out clearly are the sense of reality in the background and the mythical value: the essence of a myth being that it should have no taint of allegory to the maker and yet should suggest incipient allegories to the reader. (7 December 1929)

What Lewis says of that early poetry from *The Silmarillion* is also strikingly true of Tolkien's later work, *The Lord of the Rings*, in its embodiment of myth† and background of place and history.

Barahir,* the father of Beren, resisted Morgoth and remained in the north of Beleriand, in Dorthonion.* Eventually, Barahir had only 12 companions remaining, and made his hide-out near a beautiful lake, Tarn Aeluin, to the east. By treachery, Sauron (familiar, Ages later, as the Dark Lord of Mordor) discovered his lair and ambushed the outlaws. Providentially, Beren had been sent away on a perilous spying mission, and was the sole survivor. Sauron's orcs* had hacked off the hand of Barahir upon which was the ring of Felagund, a gift for rescuing him in battle. Pursuing the orcs Beren, with great daring and 'defended by fate', retrieved the hand and thereafter wore the ring.

Aided by the birds and beasts Beren remained a solitary outlaw against Morgoth in Dorthonion for four more years. His fame spread throughout Beleriand, and even into the magically fenced realm of Doriath,* to the south of Dorthonion, beyond the mountain range of Gorgoroth, the Mountains of Terror. Finally forced to flee Dorthonion, Beren climbed the high regions of Gorgoroth. From here he saw, far off, the Hidden Kingdom of Doriath. It was 'put into his heart' to go there, where as yet no mortal man had gone.

The journey there alone was considered to be one of Beren's great deeds. He had to pass through the dangerous precipices and their preternaturally dark shadows. Beyond these, he crossed the wilderness of Dungortheb, where the good and evil powers of Queen Melian* and Sauron contested each other, and where spiders and nameless monsters prowled. Finally, he had to pass through the protective mazes that Melian had woven around Doriath.

Beren was grey and bowed by his journey. It was summertime when he wandered into the Forest of Neldoreth, through which flowed the river of Esgalduin. One evening, at moonrise, he came upon Lúthien. In the forest glades beside the river he saw her dancing upon the unfading grass. Seeing this most beautiful of all the children of Ilúvatar,* elves and mortals, healed† all memory of pain in Beren.

When she vanished from his sight he was as a person enchanted. Knowing no name for her, he called her Tinúviel,* which is Nightingale, daughter of twilight, in Elvish.* (Recalling this story deep into the future, Aragorn was to call Arwen Tinúviel when he first saw her in Rivendell.) Beren sought for her all winter, and then, on the eve of spring, Lúthien sang again, and danced, and her song awoke the spring. The spell of silence also broke from Beren, and he called aloud the name, Tinúviel. The trees† echoed the name, and Lúthien did not flee. As she looked on Beren, she fell in love with him. Tolkien writes: 'In his fate Lúthien was caught, and being immortal she shared in his mortality, and being free received his chain.'

Beyond Beren's hope she returned to him, and secretly they passed the spring and summer together through the forest. Daeron the renowned minstrel, whose compositions were inspired by the beauty of Lúthien, and who loved her, betrayed Beren and Lúthien to her father, King Thingol. The king sent his servants to drag Beren to the splendid Menegroth,* the Thousand Caves. Lúthien forestalled them by leading her lover to the throne of Thingol, treating him as she would a guest of honour.

In scorn and anger the king demanded to know why Beren had entered his forbidden realm. Beren, awed both by the splendour of Menegroth and the king, was silent, but Lúthien introduced him as a foe of Morgoth and a man whose deeds were sung even among the elves. As he looked at Lúthien, and glanced to Melian, her mother, it seemed to Beren as if words were given him. His quest, he said, was the greatest treasure of all, Lúthien, daughter of Thingol. Her worth was above all gold, silver, or jewels.

To secure, as he thought, the death of Beren, Thingol told him that he too desired a treasure that was withheld. If Beren could bring to him, in his hand, a Silmaril from the Iron Crown of Morgoth, then, if she wished, Lúthien could set her hand in his. With these words, he brought about the eventual end of the protected realm of Doriath, for he was caught within the curse or Doom of Mandos.* This doom had been brought on by the disobedience of the elves to the Valar, a disobedience especially associated with Fëanor.

Beren declared that, next time he came before the king, his hand would hold a silmaril from the Iron Crown.

Leaving Doriath unhindered, Beren passed westward and south to Nargothrond,* the realm of the elvish King Finrod Felagund.

It was Felagund who had given the ring to Beren's father, Barahir. When the king heard Beren's tale, and discovered who he was, and found out Thingol's desire for the silmaril, his heart was heavy. His oath to Barahir had to be fulfilled, but in so doing he would be drawn into the curse associated with the Silmarils.

Celegorm* and Curufin,* sons of Fëanor, dwelled in Felagund's halls. Their vow was to possess the jewels, which contained light from the Two Trees which had originally lit the uttermost West, or Valinor. They would not support Felegund in his wish to help Beren in his quest. Realizing his isolation, Felagund cast down his silver crown. Ten warriors however stood with him, and he left his brother, Orodreth,* to rule in his place.

On an autumn evening Beren, Felagund, and the band of men set off towards Angband,* stronghold of Morgoth in the utter north. As they neared the western pass in which Sauron's tower was located they surprised and killed a company of orcs, and disguised themselves as them. They fell nevertheless into Sauron's hands, and a contest of power ensued between Felagund and Sauron. Sauron's song† of power was of treachery and darkness; Felagund's of resistance and endurance. Felagund at last fell down, and the company were cast into a deep pit, the secret of their quest still unknown to Sauron. One by one, a werewolf started to devour the companions.

Far away in Doriath, Lúthien sensed the horror of these happenings, and discovered Beren's whereabouts from Melian, her mother. Her attempt to secretly leave the realm was betrayed by Daeron, and she was kept a prisoner in a great beech tree. By enchantment she escaped, only to fall into the hands of Celegorm and Curufin, who were hunting with their hounds away from Nargothrond. One hound, Huan,* had come long ago from Valinor, and could understand speech. He befriended Lúthien, and helped her escape the two sons of Fëanor, who schemed to have her marry Celegorm. For speed, Huan allowed her to ride on his back as they went together northwards towards Sauron's tower.

Only Beren and Felagund remained alive in the pits of Sauron. As the werewolf crept up to devour Beren, Felagund made a great effort. Bursting his bonds he struggled with the wolf, slaying it with his teeth and hands, yet was mortally wounded. Bidding farewell to Beren, the fair and beloved elf fulfilled his oath in death.†

As Beren mourned his friend in black despair, Lúthien stood on the bridge leading to Sauron's island tower. She sang a song that the mightiest of walls could not stop. Thinking he dreamed, Beren heard it, and himself sang a song challenging Sauron. It was a song he had composed in reverence to Elbereth,* praising the Seven Stars, the Sickle of the Valar placed in the heavens by her as a sign of the ultimate defeat of Morgoth.

Hearing Beren's song, Lúthien sang a greater song. Sauron recognized the singer and, smiling, thought to capture her for Morgoth. As he sent wolves, one by one, to capture her the hound Huan silently destroyed them. Even Sauron's greatest werewolf, the dreaded Draugluin, was no match for Huan. Then Sauron himself took on the form of a werewolf (for, as a Maia,* he could take on any earthly form) and challenged the hound of Valinor. Though in the battle Sauron shifted shape again and again, he failed to free himself from Huan's grip. At last, Sauron yielded and, taking the form of a vampire, fled eastwards to Taur-nu-Fuin,* and possessed the forest there.

Beren and Lúthien were now free to devote themselves to each other again. Huan, as well as many elves freed from Sauron's isle, returned to Nargothrond. Their return, with the story of Lúthien's bravery, stirred the people of the realm against Celegorm and Curufin. The unpopular brothers set off northwards, heading for Himring, where another brother, Maedhros,* dwelt. The faithful Huan was with them. The party encountered Beren and Lúthien on the borders of Doriath. They tried to kill Beren and capture Lúthien. Huan however protected the couple, but even so Beren was badly wounded. By her arts and her love she healed him.

Beren was torn between his oath to Thingol to gain the silmaril and his love for Lúthien. While she slept he left her in the care of Huan and slipped away.

Lúthien bade Huan follow Beren's northward trail towards Morgoth's stronghold at Thangorodrim. Passing the ruins of Sauron's isle, Huan took the skins of the werewolf Draugluin, and Sauron's messenger vampire. Wearing these fearful shapes, Huan and Lúthien sped northwards, overtaking Beren at last. Then, by the advice of Huan and the skill of Lúthien, Beren took on the shape of the werewolf, and Lúthien the bat-form, with its great fingered wings, barbed with iron claws. Howling, Beren rushed towards Morgoth's stronghold, with the bat that was Lúthien wheeling and flittering above him.

As they approached the gate of Angband, they were seen by Carcharoth,* the tormented and specially bred werewolf of Morgoth. Throwing off her disguise, Lúthien challenged the wolf, commanding him to sleep. The pair then passed through the gate, and down twisting stairs to the very throne of Morgoth. As Morgoth saw her beauty he lusted for her, leaving her free for a time as he gloated over his thought of possession.† This was his downfall, for she sang a song of enchantment that caused him and his court to fall into a deep sleep. As Morgoth slipped forward his crown fell off his head, allowing Beren to cut a silmaril from it. Its radiance shone through the flesh of Beren's hand as he held it.

Morgoth stirred in his sleep and, in sudden terror, Beren and Lúthien fled towards daylight. Carcharoth was waiting for them. Lúthien was exhausted by her efforts, but Beren held up the silmaril to dispel the wolf. Suddenly the wolf bit off Beren's hand holding the jewel. The fire from the silmaril tormented his innards, maddening him, and causing him to rush away howling. Beren lay dying from the poisoned wound while, with what strength she had, Lúthien tended to him. Just as the quest for the silmaril seemed doomed, three mighty eagles† came to their rescue. They were watchful in that region to help the victims of Morgoth. They were carried far south, over the hidden and beautiful city of Gondolin,* and eventually to the borders of Doriath.

After a long time, Beren revived to hear Lúthien singing soft and slow beside him. Her love had drawn him back from death. She and Beren came before the throne of Thingol, where the one-handed man claimed Lúthien for his wife. The silmaril, he said, was in his hand, holding up his empty arm.

News came that Carcharoth, still maddened by the silmaril burning inside him, had burst into Doriath. Beren, Thingol, Huan and others set off to chase him. As Huan attempted to dislodge the wolf, he sprang at Thingol. Beren leapt in front of the king and was mortally wounded. Huan fought Carcharoth to the death, and then himself died, in fulfilment of an ancient prophecy. The silmaril, cut from Carcharoth, was put in Beren's remaining hand, and he held it up and gave it to Thingol, saying the quest was achieved. Lúthien reached Beren before he died, and bade his spirit await her beyond the Western Sea.

Beren's spirit tarried until Lúthien came to the dim shores of the Outer Sea. Leaving her body, like a cut flower, Lúthien entered the halls of Mandos,* where Beren's spirit was. Kneeling before Mandos, the Vala, Lúthien sang. Her song mingled the themes of the sorrow of the elves and the grief of humankind, the two kindred races made by Ilúvatar to inhabit earth. Mandos was moved to pity, and he sought the advice of Manwë,* who governed the world under Ilúvatar's hand.

Lúthien was given the choice of going to Valinor or becoming mortal like Beren, taking him back to Middle-earth, to live there without certainty of either life or joy.

She chose mortality,† and Beren and she lived in mortal form in Ossiriand.* Lúthien herself was the product of a marriage between an elf and one of the Maiar, so she already had angelic blood in her veins. This angelic inheritance was thus added to the elvish inheritance she gave to Beren. For about 40 years the two lived in Tol Galen, and their only child, Dior,* was the father of Elwing, who married the great mariner Eärendil. After the deaths of Beren and Lúthien, Dior inherited the Nauglamir,* the necklace in which the silmaril was set.

Part Three

AN A–Z OF
TOLKIEN'S MIDDLE-EARTH

SIX

BEINGS, PLACES, THINGS AND EVENTS

Adûnaic

On the great island of Númenor,* Adûnaic was the common language of the Dúnedain,* the Men of the West. It was the ancestor of Westron,* or common speech, represented by English in Tolkien's writings about Middle-earth.* The name derives from adûn, 'west'.

Adûnakhôr, Tar-

In the Second Age* (born 2899), he was nineteenth king of Númenor.* Symbolically, he broke with tradition and took his name in Adûnaic* rather than in Elvish.* It blasphemously means 'Lord of the West'. He forbade the use of elven languages and persecuted those faithful to the true West† and the rule of Ilúvatar.*

A Elbereth Gilthoniel

An elven chant attributed to the elves* of Rivendell* in honour of Elbereth Gilthoniel, or Varda,* the greatest of the seven Queens of the Valar* (the angelic† guardians of Middle-earth), and most approachable by elves, humans and hobbits.* Only the first verse is recorded, written in Sindarin* Elvish.* The chant of praise and intercession was sung in the house of Elrond,* as recounted in *The Fellowship of the Ring*.‡ Sam Gamgee's* invocation of Elbereth in *The Two Towers*,‡ in Shelob's* lair on the fringes of Mordor,* echoes this chant. Tolkien translates both prayers in *The Road Goes Ever On*.‡

He translates the recorded stanza of the chant as:

O! Elbereth who lit the stars, from glittering crystal slanting falls with light like jewels from heaven on high the glory of the starry host. To lands remote I have looked afar, and now to thee, Fanuilos, bright spirit clothed in ever-white, I here will sing beyond the Sea, beyond the wide and sundering Sea.

Aelfwine

Originally called Eriol in the early form of Tolkien's mythology, *The Silmarillion*.‡ Aelfwine was a mariner to whom the tales of the First Age* were told. He provided a narrative framework for the tales. His name means 'elf-friend'. There are several versions of the Aelfwine story, but the basic idea is that a British mariner by chance finds the lost road that leads to the uttermost West and arrives at Tol Eressëa,* where he hears the tales of the elves.*
See also The Lost Road.‡

Afterlithe

The hobbit* name for July, from Old English *aefterlith*. Hobbit month-names reinforce the link between their language and that of the Rohirrim, who, like hobbits, originally dwelt in the north, east of the Misty Mountains.* Tolkien uses Old English sources for words and names of the Rohirrim.
See also Languages of Middle-earth.*

Afteryule

The hobbit* name corresponding to January, from Old English *aefter Geola* ('after Winter-Solstice').
See also Languages of Middle-earth.*

Ages of Middle-earth

See Chapter 5: How *The Lord of the Rings* Relates to *The Silmarillion*.

Aglarond

In *The Two Towers*,‡ the caverns of Helm's Deep (Sindarin*
Elvish,* 'glittering caves, place of glory'). Gimli the dwarf* was
astonished and enraptured at the beauty of these caves originally
worked by the men of Númenor,* and used by the Rohirrim as a
refuge and storage place. After the War of the Ring* Gimli settled
there with other dwarves and became Lord of the Glittering Caves.

Ainur

Angelic powers, 'The Holy Ones', created before the making of the
world by Ilúvatar.* Their order of being includes the Valar,* and
the lesser powers, the Maiar.* Some of their number, both of the
good and those turned to evil, entered the realm of the world and
participate in its events. The Ainur are male and female and,
though spiritual beings, can take on real physical bodies.
See also Angels;† Evil.†

Akallabêth

An Adûnaic* (or Númenorean) name given to Númenor* after its
destruction, meaning 'The Downfallen'. A section of *The Silmarillion*‡ is called this name. It concerns the history of Númenor from
its foundation to its destruction.

Aldarion, or Tar-Aldarion

The Mariner King of Númenor,* the sixth king of the island. His
story is told in 'Aldarion and Erendis', in *Unfinished Tales*.‡ His
only child was a daughter, Ancalime. The king altered the law of
succession so that a female could reign, and she became queen.

Almaren

An island in the middle of a great lake deep inland in Middle-
earth, the original dwelling place of the Valar.* It was ruined when
Morgoth* destroyed the Two Lamps* which illuminated the world.

Alqualondë

Harbour city of Telerin* elves* in Valinor,* the 'Haven of the swans'. As they entered the harbour ships passed through a large natural arch. The elven ships originally reached this haven from Middle-earth* with the aid of great swans.

Aman

The specific name of the vast western continent in which Valinor* lay.

See Chapter 5: How *The Lord of the Rings* Relates to *The Silmarillion*.

Amandil

The last lord of Andunie in Númenor,* leader of the faithful remnant and father of Elendil.*

Amon Obel

A prominent hill in the Forest of Brethil.* Túrin* dwelt here at the time when the woodmen made their stronghold at Amon Obel. He married Nienor* here, unaware that she was his sister.

Amon Rûdh

One of the oldest of the early settlements of dwarves* in Beleriand* in the First Age.* It was a hill rising steeply, with sheer rocky cliffs in places. Mim dwelt in its caverns, and Túrin's* outlaws made their hide-out here.

Amon Sûl

See Weathertop.

Amras

Elf,* and son of Fëanor,* twin brother of Amrod. The brothers were killed attacking the people of Eärendil* at the Mouths of Sirion,* in an attempt to recover one the silmarils* from Elwing.*

Amrod

Elf,* and son of Fëanor,* twin brother of Amras.*

Anárion

At the end of the Second Age* he escaped, with his father Elendil* and brother Isildur,* from the destruction of Númenor.* With them he founded the Númenorean realms in exile in Middle-earth.* He was lord of Minas Anor and died in the siege of Barad-dur, during the great alliance against Sauron.*

Anarríma

A constellation formed by Elbereth* before the creation of the elves* by Ilúvatar.*

Ancalagon

Greatest of the winged dragons† of Morgoth,* destroyed by Eärendil* at the end of the First Age.* His falling body broke Thangorodrim.*

Andram

In Sindarin* Elvish* this means 'The Long Wall'. It is a distinctive feature of the landscape of Beleriand,* an escarpment cutting right across the region.

See Chapter 5: How *The Lord of the Rings* Relates to *The Silmarillion.*

Anduin

The 'great river' of north-western Middle-earth, important during the Second and Third Ages.* It flowed from north to south around 1,500 miles, running between the Misty Mountains* and Mirkwood,* and further south between Gondor* and Mordor.* The hobbits* originated from the Anduin region, and the river plays an important part in the events of *The Lord of the Rings.*‡ The ruling Ring of Power† was lost in the river at the death of Isildur* and discovered there by Smeagol (Gollum*).

Anfauglith

An area north of Beleriand.* It was given this name (literally 'great-thirst-ash') after it was scorched in battle by Morgoth.* Before its desolation, the area was called Ard-galen.* By mistake, Túrin* killed his friend Beleg in this region.
See also Battles of Beleriand.*

Angband

The stronghold of Morgoth* in the icy north of Middle-earth,* north of Beleriand,* and originally destroyed by the Valar.* After Morgoth returned to Middle-earth with the stolen silmarils* he rebuilt Angband, along with Thangorodrim.* Here Morgoth used slaves and bred monsters and orcs.*

Anglachel

A sword forged by Eol from meteoritic iron.

Angmar

In the Third Age,* the Witch-kingdom ruled by the Lord of the Nazgûl,* the Witch-king.

Annúminas

The first capital of Arnor,* built by Elendil,* who kept a palantir* here. The name means 'tower of the west', or 'sunset-tower'. The city became deserted during Arnor's decline, but was re-established by Aragorn* as the northern capital of the Reunited Kingdom at the beginning of the Fourth Age.* It was located on the shore of Lake Evendim, not far from the Shire.*

Aragorn

In *The Lord of the Rings*‡ Aragorn was a member of the Company of the Ring,* the true heir of Isildur* in disguise. Frodo* and the other hobbits* encountered him in the inn at Bree* as a Ranger* known as Strider. In fact, Aragorn was the last Chieftain of the

Dúnedain.* After the War of the Ring* he was crowned, and restored the old northern and southern kingdoms. He was the Beren* of his day, like Beren marrying an elf-maiden, Arwen,* who resembled Lúthien* in beauty.

Aragorn had the characteristics of a Christian king, with his healing† hands, humility, the sacrifice of years as a Ranger, and power over evil.† In him, the wisdom of Númenor* was restored.

The Company of the Ring found him a wise companion, and a leader after the loss of Gandalf.* His strategy of passing through the Paths of the Dead helped to bring victory in the War of the Ring.

Arda

The world, or earth.
See Chapter 5: How *The Lord of the Rings* Relates to *The Silmarillion*.

Ard-galen

A large plain lying north of Dorthonion,* between it and Thango-rodrim.* It was wasted by Morgoth* during one war (*see* Battles of Beleriand*), an example of the effect of evil† on the natural world. The resulting desolation was named Anfauglith.*

Argonath

In *The Lord of the Rings*,* great carved rocks between which the River Anduin* flowed. They were statues of Isildur* and Anárion* built to mark the northern boundary of Gondor.*

Arkenstone

In *The Hobbit*,‡ a great white jewel found by Bilbo Baggins* in the hoard of Smaug,* the dragon.† It had been found originally beneath Erebor* by the dwarf,* Thráin I, and was the prized treasure of the kings of Erebor. It had a little of the glory of a silmaril.*

Army of the West

An alliance of men of Gondor* and Rohan* which marched to the

Gates of Mordor* to distract Sauron's* attention from the Ring-bearer, Frodo,* and Sam,* in *The Lord of the Rings*.‡

Arnor

The northern kingdom of the Númenoreans in Middle-earth.* Elendil* established it after escaping the destruction of Númenor.*

Athelas

In Middle-earth,* a healing† plant brought from Númenor.* It grew only in the places where Númenoreans had lived or camped. In the hands of Aragorn,* or other heirs of Elendil,* it had potent powers of restoration.

Arwen

The elven daughter of Elrond.* For most of the Third Age* of Middle-earth* she lived in Rivendell* and Lórien.* Aragorn* met her in Rivendell and they fell in love. Their love – the love of a mortal for an immortal elf* – echoed that of Beren* and Lúthien.* Like Lúthien, Arwen chose mortality (*see* Death†) by marrying Aragorn. Her dark beauty resembled that of Lúthien, and for it, and because she chose to leave the elves, she was called Evenstar. Her presence in *The Lord of the Rings*‡ helps to recall the great history of the First Age,* so represented in the story of Beren and Lúthien.

Aulë

One of the Valar,* or angelic† powers. He was master of crafts and husband of Yavanna.* Although Ilúvatar* made elves* and humans, Aulë made the dwarves, but could not make them live.*

Avallónë

Harbour and city of the elves* on the island of Tol Eressea.* Its quays were lit by lamps, and it had a distinctive white tower.

Baggins, Bilbo

The unlikely hero† of Tolkien's *The Hobbit*,‡ the title referring to him. He is a creature of paradox, summed up in his role as a bourgeois burglar in the story. Hobbits* aimed at respectability – not only by being comfortably off, but by not having any adventures or doing anything unexpected. Bilbo's reputation is tarnished for ever when he is suddenly caught up in the quest† for dragon's† treasure. He finds this more congenial than he thought. A new world is opened up to him as in later years he becomes something of a scholar, translating and retelling tales from the older days. The quest also develops his character, though he always retains the quality of homeliness‡ associated with hobbits and the Shire.*

Thorin Oakenshield's* remark concerning Bilbo is perhaps an apt summary of his many-sided character: 'a hobbit full of courage and resource far exceeding his size, and if I may say so possessed of good luck far exceeding the usual allowance'. The 'good luck' noticed by Thorin is in fact the unusual presence of providence† working out in events using him as a key agent. Thorin also notices his personal qualities. Free will is an important theme in Tolkien, particularly the voluntary commitment to the struggle against darkness and evil,† sometimes against all odds.

In Bilbo's make-up, Tolkien draws attention to unusual blood inherited from his mother. This unhobbitlike quality emerges and develops as Bilbo partakes in the adventure. Most important for him, however, is not the finding of the treasure (which leads to Smaug,* the dragon's, death), but his discovery of the One Ring.* In Tolkien's Middle-earth* tales there is not a novelistic delineation of character. Essentially, people or beings are in character as dwarves,* elves,* humans, ents,* Maiar,* orcs,* and so on. This is how we know them. Often, however, there is surprising individuality in this role. For example, Tom Bombadil,* Queen Melian,* and Gandalf* are all Maiar, yet dazzlingly distinct. Similarly, hobbits like Bilbo, Frodo,* Sam* or Merry* have their own marked traits.

We are told of Bilbo's love of maps; his liking for runes* and letters and cunning handwriting – although his own was 'a bit thin and spidery'; his passion for riddles – an asset which saves his life; his sudden burst of pity for Gollum,* and his kind-heartedness in returning the sleeping jailer's keys; his 'sharp inquisitive eyes'; his skill at stealth, shooting stones, blowing smoke-rings, and cooking; and his constant lament about not being back in his comfortable hobbit-hole. These traits reveal something of his character.

The effect of the Ring on his character is complex. In developing *The Lord of the Rings*‡ from seeds in *The Hobbit*, Tolkien was forced to change the account of Bilbo's finding of the Ring. The change, however, is convincing in terms of the Ring's power over an individual. Bilbo was never mastered by it, and voluntarily (with prompting from Gandalf) passed it on to Frodo, the new Ring-bearer.

Baggins, Frodo

Frodo is a hobbit* of the Shire,* and a hero† of *The Lord of the Rings*,‡ which is the source of information about him and his deeds. Frodo grew up in Buckland,* the only child of Drogo Baggins and Primula Brandybuck. After his parents' death, Frodo was adopted by his distant relation Bilbo Baggins,* hero of *The Hobbit*,‡ joining him in Bag End. Frodo was highly intelligent, with a gift for languages (he eventually learnt Sindarin* Elvish*). When Bilbo left the Shire, he passed on to him the One Ring,* not knowing its real nature. When Gandalf* discovered what the Ring was he advised Frodo to leave the Shire for Rivendell,* to escape the Nazgûl.* At Rivendell, the Company of the Ring* was formed. With the help of Sam Gamgee,* Frodo bore the Ring to Mount Doom, where it was destroyed, and the power of Sauron* broken. Never fully recovering from his suffering, Frodo passed over the Sea to the Undying Lands of Aman* for healing.† Frodo supplemented the writing of Bilbo in the Red Book of Westmarch* with his account of the War of the Ring* and the quest† that took him to Mount Doom.

Balar, Isle of

A large island in the Bay of Balar, to the south-west of Beleriand,*
into which the River Sirion* flowed. The elves* who chose to go to
Valinor* were transported there on a floating island, Tol Eressëa.*
Part of this broke off, forming the Isle of Balar.

Balrogs

Demons of fire that served Morgoth.* The name is Sindarin*
Elvish,* meaning 'Demon of Might'. In being, balrogs are Maiar,*
and carried whips of flame. The balrog killed by Gandalf* in *The
Lord of the Rings*‡ survived the destruction of Morgoth's strong-
hold in the First Age.*
See also Evil.†

Bard

In *The Hobbit*,‡ a notable archer who led the defence of Lake-town
against Smaug,* and who slew the dragon.†

Barrow Downs

In *The Lord of the Rings*,‡ the downs east of the Old Forest* get
their name from the Great Barrows, or stone-chambered burial
mounds. They dated back to ancient days, before humans had
crossed the Ered Luin* – the Blue Mountains – into Beleriand.*
Earlier in the Third Age* evil† spirits from Angmar* – the 'barrow-
wights' – had possessed the burial mounds, making the region an
area of dread.

Battles of Beleriand

In *The Silmarillion*‡ is recorded the troubled centuries during the
First Age* in which Morgoth* occupied Angmar.* The five major
battles and the final Great Battle provide a backdrop to the tales set
in Beleriand* and are not described in as much detail as the major
stories such as that of Beren and Lúthien.*

The First Battle was Morgoth's initial attempt to gain mastery of

Beleriand. The elves* then living there, led by King Thingol* of Doriath,* resisted a two-pronged attack in the East and West. As a result of the war, Melian* wove a girdle of magic protection around Doriath.

The Second Battle was called Dagor-nuin-Giliath, 'the Battle Under Stars'. Morgoth, hearing of the return of Fëanor* and his elves to Middle-earth,* attacked them in Mithrim before they were established. The battle took place before the first rising of the moon (hence the battle's name). In the conflict Fëanor was mortally wounded, and Maedhros* was captured by balrogs* and taken to Angband.*

The third battle was dubbed Dagor Aglareb, 'the Glorious Battle'. Fingolfin to the West and Maedhros to the East attacked Morgoth's assault forces of orcs.* As his army retreated across Ard-galen,* it was slaughtered. The battle was followed by a siege of Angband.

The fourth battle was graphically called Dagor Bragollach, or 'Battle of Sudden Flame'. In a long period of peace during the siege the elvish stronghold of Nargothrond* was completed, and Gondolin* established. Morgoth, however, was busy devising new weapons of horror associated with fire. Rivers of fire scorched Ard-galen, to the north of Beleriand. Armies of orcs were joined by balrogs and Glaurung the dragon.† Dorthonion* was taken. Finrod Felagund was rescued by Barahir, father of Beren.* Fingolfin was so angered by the great loss of elves and men that he challenged Morgoth to a duel. Though he was slain, he inflicted seven mighty wounds on Morgoth, bitter to his pride.

The fifth battle was a great defeat, called Niraeth Arnoediad, 'Battle of Unnumbered Tears'. A great alliance of elves, men, and dwarves* led by Maedhros failed in an offensive against Morgoth's stronghold. All of the northern highlands, with the exception of Gondolin, fell under the control of Morgoth. Glaurung the dragon and Gothmog the balrog helped to lead Morgoth's forces. Húrin,* father of Túrin Turambar,* was captured by Morgoth.

The final battle of Beleriand was called the Great Battle, or

War of Wrath. The Valar* responded to the intercession of Eärendil* and directly intervened against Morgoth's tyranny. During this battle Morgoth released his new evil, winged dragons. Their leader, Ancalagon,* the Black, was slain by Eärendil, and crashed down upon Thangorodrim.* Eagles,† led by Thorondor,* played an important part in defeating the dragons.

Belegaer

'The Great Sea' of the West that in the First Age* separated Middle-earth* from the Undying Lands of Tol Eressëa* and Valinor.* Also called the Western Sea. In the Second Age,* the great star-shaped island of Númenor* lay in it. After the reshaping of the earth following the downfall of Númenor, the Straight Road* (or Lost Road*) passed over it, leading beyond the planet to the Undying Lands. The Ring-bearers, Bilbo Baggins* and Frodo Baggins,* and later Sam Gamgee,* took this road, leaving Middle-earth from Grey Havens.*

Belegost

In *The Silmarillion*,‡ a city of the dwarves* in the Blue Mountains (Ered Luin*). They were friendly with King Thingol of Doriath.* After the Great Battle (*see* Battles of Beleriand*) at the end of the First Age,* many of its inhabitants moved east to Khazad-dûm,* under the Misty Mountains.*

Beleriand and its realms

In later Ages all the land that was swallowed up by sea in the north of Middle-earth* was described as Beleriand. All the area west of the Ered Luin,* the Blue Mountains, was engulfed. This vast range of mountains provided a distinctive boundary for Beleriand to the east. In fact Beleriand was only part of this area in the First Age,* with great areas to the north controlled by Morgoth,* the source of struggle and many wars (*see* Battles of Beleriand*). It was made up of four geographical regions. These were the northern territory of Morgoth, the central highlands, the main area of Beleriand, and the Ered Luin – the Blue Mountains.

(*See* Chapter 5: How *The Lord of the Rings* Relates to *The Silmarillion.*)

Further reading

Karen Wynn Fonstad, *The Atlas of Middle-earth* (1981).

J.R.R. Tolkien, 'Quenta Silmarillion' (sections 105–21), in *The Lost Road* (1987).

Beorn

In *The Hobbit*‡ he gives succour to Bilbo Baggins* and Thorin* and his company of dwarves.* He is chieftain of the Beornings (men of the Vales of Anduin), but is not typical, in being a skin-changer, able to shift shape (a quality shared by Lúthien* in the tale of Beren* and Lúthien). As well as a shape-changer Beorn is also a beserker, a wild warrior figure (hence our term 'going beserk') plucked by Tolkien from the northern imagination.† Beorn helped to win the Battle of the Five Armies, killing Bolg, leader of the orcs.*

Beren

In *The Silmarillion*,‡ the son of Barahir who cut a silmaril* from the Iron Crown of Morgoth* to gain the elf-maiden Lúthien* as his wife, as told in the tale of Beren* and Lúthien. After being killed by Carcharoth,* the wolf, he was allowed to return from the dead after Lúthien's intercession, and choice of mortality.† The two then lived in Tol Galen in Ossiriand,* to the east of Beleriand,* where their son Dior* was born. Beren avenged the murder of Thingol his father-in-law by dwarves,* and recovered the silmaril, now set in the Nauglamir.* The Númenorean kings descended from him. His granddaughter, Elwing,* married Eärendil,* the mariner.

Bilbo Baggins

See Baggins, Bilbo.*

Black Riders

See Nazgûl.*

Black Speech

Devised by Sauron* in the Second Age* and revived by him in the Third Age,* it may have been a perverted form of Quenya* Elvish.* The orcs* of Mordor* used a debased form of Black Speech. The only example of pure Black Speech given in Tolkien's writings is the inscription on the One Ring* in *The Lord of the Rings*.‡

See also Languages of Middle-earth.

Bombadil, Tom

Possibly one of the Maiar* (Tolkien was uncertain of his status), but certainly 'Master of wood, water and hill'. He was a nature† spirit, mastered by none and refusing possession† himself. Like the biblical Adam, he was a name-giver. In *The Lord of the Rings*,‡ he gave to the ponies of the hobbits* names that they 'answered to for the rest of their lives'. There is a comic, hobbitish* description of him in the collection of verse, *The Adventures of Tom Bombadil*.‡ Like the wizards,† he appeared like a man, though, unlike them, he had been in Middle-earth* from earliest days. As Bombadil told the hobbits:

> Eldest, that's what I am . . . Tom was here before the river and the trees; Tom remembers the first raindrop and the first acorn. He made paths before the Big People, and saw the Little People arriving . . . When the Elves passed westward, Tom was here already, before the seas were bent.

The bending of the seas refers to the sundering of Valinor* from Middle-earth after the destruction of Númenor.*

Tom Bombadil was the name given to him by hobbits (he was

known in Buckland*); he was known by other names to elves,* dwarves* and humans.

He was also well-known to Tolkien's children. Tom Bombadil was a Dutch doll belonging to Michael Tolkien. It had a splendid feather in its hat. He became the hero of the poem 'The Adventures of Tom Bombadil', published in 1934. Tom Bombadil eventually re-emerged in *The Lord of the Rings*.

Boromir

One of several tragic† figures in Middle-earth,* another being Túrin Turambar.* He appears in *The Lord of the Rings*,‡ and his 'fatal flaw' is pride. He disdains the idea of the hobbit,* Frodo Baggins,* bearing the One Ring* to Mordor.* Instead, he believed that its power should be used against the Dark Lord, Sauron.* Because of his pride, he was unable to overcome his lust for the Ring, and, in madness, tried to kill Frodo. This act proved providential† in driving Frodo to leave the Fellowship of the Ring just before an orc* attack. Repentant, Boromir bravely sacrificed† his life defending the hobbits, Merry Brandybuck* and Pippin Took.*

Boromir was the son of the proud Denethor,* Steward* of Gondor,* and brother of the wise Faramir.* Had he lived he himself would have become Steward. Boromir had gone to Rivendell* to seek the answer to a dream he and his brother had had, and thus was chosen to join the Company of the Ring.*

Brandybuck, Meriadoc

'Merry' and Pippin Took* were the closest friends of Frodo Baggins* in the Shire,* and were allowed to join the Fellowship of the Ring* in *The Lord of the Rings*.‡ After the death of Boromir,* Merry, with Pippin, was taken captive by orcs* of Saruman.* After escaping into Fangorn Forest,* they travelled with the Ent* attack on Isengard.* Merry pledged service to King Théoden* of Rohan.* He secretly rode with Éowyn,* Théoden's niece, to Gondor* where they killed the Lord of the Nazgûl.*

After the War of the Ring* Merry returned to the Shire where he helped to clean up the forces of Saruman. He eventually became Master of Buckland.* In later life he became something of a scholar, writing such works as *Herblore of the Shire, The Reckoning of Years,* and *Old Words and Names in the Shire.*

Bree

In *The Lord of the Rings,*‡ the main settlement of the Breeland; a town of both men and hobbits.* It was located at the crossing of the Great East Road and the North Road. Frodo* and his friends stayed here at the ancient Prancing Pony Inn.* In *The Return of the Shadow* (1988; *see History of Middle-earth*‡) is reproduced Tolkien's sketch, showing the plan of Bree.

Brethil, Forest of

In *The Silmarillion,*‡ this is a forested part of Beleriand* associated with the story of Túrin,* who lived with the people of Brethil before he slew the dragon,† Glaurung. Though originally the possession of the elven king, Thingol, Brethil was given to the Haladin* in return for guarding the strategic Crossings of Teiglin.

Buckland

A region of the Shire* in *The Lord of the Rings,*‡ located to the east, before the Old Forest.* It was the family territory of the Brandy-bucks, nominally ruled by the Master of Buckland. Frodo's* mother was a Brandybuck, and he grew up here, until adopted by Bilbo.*

Cair Andros

In *The Lord of the Rings,*‡ an island in the River Anduin.* It lies about 50 miles north of Minas Tirith.* The island is shaped like a ship, hence its name, Sindarin* Elvish* meaning 'ship long-foam'. Another significant river island in Middle-earth* is Tol Sirion.* There is a small river island on the Avon at Warwick,‡ beside the castle, which Tolkien would have known.

Calaquendi

In *The Silmarillion*,‡ these are 'Elves of the Light': elves* who lived, or at one time had lived, in Valinor.* They were the High Elves.*

Caras Galadon

In *The Lord of the Rings*,‡ the 'City of the Trees' in Lórien.*

Carcharoth

In *The Silmarillion*,‡ Morgoth's* great wolf of Angband,* especially bred for evil† deeds. He bit off the hand of Beren* which clutched a silmaril* stolen back from Morgoth. In agony he ran from Angband and eventually entered Doriath,* where he was killed by Huan,* the hound of Valinor,* after mortally wounding Beren. His name is translated as 'the red maw'.

Celeborn (1)

A white tree† which grew in Tol Eressëa,* a seedling of Galathilion. In a later Age, Nimloth* grew from its seed.

Celeborn (2)

An elf* of Doriath* in the First Age* and relation of King Thingol* who married Galadriel.* He remained with her in Middle-earth* after the destruction of Beleriand.* In *The Lord of the Rings*‡ he dwells in Lórien.* Galadriel tells the Company of the Ring:* 'Together through ages of the world we have fought the long defeat.' Part of their story is found in *Unfinished Tales*.‡

Celebrimbor

A Noldorin* elf* whose name means, 'Hand of Silver', son of Curufin* of the House of Fëanor.* After the death of Finrod Felagund he remained in Nargothrond,* though his father was expelled. In the Second Age* he was the most notable of the smiths of Eregion.* He made the Three Rings* of the Elves. When Sauron* made the One Ring* to rule the others Celebrimbor realized his evil† intent. He was slain by Sauron when Eregion was occupied.

Celegorm

The third son of Fëanor* in *The Silmarillion*.‡ He was a Noldorin* elf.* With his brother Curufin* he was Lord of the region of Himlad, north-east of Doriath.* They fled to Nargothrond* when Morgoth's* forces overwhelmed the region. He was master of Huan,* the hound of Valinor,* given him by the Vala,* Oromë,* who had taught him much about animals and hunting. In the tale of Beren and Lúthien, the elf-maiden‡ he falls in love with Lúthien* and plots to marry her. He and his brother try to murder Beren.* He was eventually killed by Dior* at Menegroth* when he and his brothers tried to regain the Silmaril* recovered by Beren.

Chieftains of the Dúnedain

The two kingdoms of the ancient Númenoreans in the north and south were Arnor* and Gondor.* Whereas Gondor was tended by Stewards* when the line of kings failed, the more devastated northern kingdom never lost its royal line. The heirs of Isildur* took on the disguise of Rangers* in the wild, though they retained the long life-span (*see* Death†). The Aragorn* of the Company of the Ring* in *The Lord of the Rings*‡ was the sixteenth and last Chieftain. The Chieftains were brought up in Rivendell,* educated in the rich history of Middle-earth.* Here, in Elrond's* house, were kept the heirlooms of the Line of Isildur, including the Ring of Barahir* and the broken sword which figured in prophecies of the returning king.

The Chieftains along with other Rangers acted as guardians, protecting Eriador* from orcs* and other fell creatures. Their protection of the Shire* made a peaceful hobbit* existence possible, a fact not often appreciated until first Bilbo,* then other hobbits, became involved in events in the wider world.

Children of Ilúvatar

This was the name given to elves* and humans, as both peoples were directly created by Ilúvatar,* rather than being the work of the Valar,* his demiurgic agents of creation. The dwarves* didn't have this title, as they were made by the Vala, Aulë,* though it was necessary for Ilúvatar to breathe life into them to make them personal beings.

Círdan

A mariner and shipbuilder (his name means, 'Ship-maker'), Círdan was among the wisest of the elves* in Middle-earth.* In the First Age* he was associated with the harbours of the Falas, to the west of Beleriand.* He was forced to withdraw to Arvernien, at the Mouths of the River Sirion,* where he provided a haven for fleeing elves and humans, including Elwing.* After the destruction of Beleriand he became Lord of the Grey Havens.* Círdan possessed one of the elven Rings, Narya,* which he humbly passed on to Gandalf.*

Cirith Gorgor

The haunted pass into Mordor* in *The Lord of the Rings*.‡

Cirith Ungol

The high pass into Mordor* used by Sam* and Frodo* in *The Lord of the Rings*.‡ Shelob's* Lair effectively protected the pass.

Company of the Ring

In *The Lord of the Rings*,‡ the fellowship which accompanied the Ring-bearer, Frodo,* on his perilous quest† to destroy it. The Company represented all the free peoples: elves,* dwarves,* hobbits,* and humans. Gandalf* also accompanied Frodo. The Company consisted of the hobbits Frodo, Sam,* Merry* and Pippin;* the Wood-elf Legolas*; the dwarf Gimli; and the men Aragorn* and Boromir.* The Company first lost Gandalf in

Moria,* and then later was divided at the death of Boromir, Sam and Frodo going on alone to Mordor.* They were reunited after the destruction of the Ring.*

Cuiviénen

In *The Silmarillion*,‡ a bay in the far east of Middle-earth* by the shores of which the elves* awoke, after being created by Ilúvatar.* The name means 'awakening-water' in Quenya.* From here the elves were called to their long journey† to the west.

Curufin

In *The Silmarillion*,‡ an elf,* and son of Fëanor,* who took the Oath of Fëanor* and thus came under the Doom of Mandos.*

Dale

This city-kingdom of mortals related to the Edain* was situated on the southern slopes of Erebor,* the Lonely Mountain. At the time of the events of *The Hobbit*‡ it was deserted, having been destroyed by Smaug,* the dragon,† its inhabitants fled to Esgaroth* (Lake-town). Bard* the bowman, a descendant of the old kings of Dale, rebuilt it after slaying the dragon. Relations thereafter with the dwarves* of Erebor were re-established. In the War of the Ring* Dale was besieged by Sauron's* forces, by which time it had grown in size and prosperity.

Dark elves

This sometimes refers to elves* in the First Age* who did not cross Belegaer,* the Great Sea, to Valinor,* and thus did not see the light† of the Two Trees.* Sometimes it refers more specifically to the elves at the very beginning who refused to join the westward march from Cuiviénen.*

Dead Marshes

In *The Lord of the Rings*,‡ an extensive area of marshland east of

Emyn Muil, encountered by Frodo* and Sam.* They are west of the battle plain of Dagorlad, and get their name from the fact that the marshes had encroached upon the graves of those slain in ancient battles. The faces of putrefying warriors can be glimpsed deep in its pools. The uncanny atmosphere is enhanced by peculiar, candle-like flames called 'candles of corpses'.

Dead men of Dunharrow

Men of the White Mountains of Gondor* at its founding swore allegiance to Isildur.* Influenced by Sauron* they refused a call to battle against Mordor.* As a result, they were cursed to remain as spirits in or near the White Mountains until Isildur's heir (revealed, in *The Lord of the Rings*‡ as Aragorn*) called upon them to fulfil their oath. Under Aragorn's authority they overwhelmed the Corsairs of Umbar* on the River Anduin* at Pelargir, a vital phase of the War of the Ring.*

Denethor

The final Steward of Gondor,* the southern kingdom of the exiled Númenoreans. As told in *The Lord of the Rings*,‡ he was suspicious of Gandalf,* as he was opposed to the crown of Gondor going to the heir of Isildur,* revealed as Aragorn.* He clung to power, instead of displaying the true stewardship exemplified in Gandalf.

He had married the tragic† Finduilas* of Dol Amroth on the southern coast. She had pined away for the sea, living in Minas Tirith.* Their children were the very different brothers, Boromir,* proud and ambitious like his father, and Faramir.* In his wisdom Denethor perceived that Sauron's* attack on Gondor would come in his lifetime. He started looking into the palantir* of Gondor to discern the Dark Lord's plans. He thus came under the influence of Sauron's subtle distortions, leading eventually to despair and madness.

Denethor is one of a number of tragic characters in the history of Middle-earth.*

Dior

In *The Silmarillion*,‡ son of Beren* and Lúthien,* the elf-maiden. He was father of Elwing* (mother of Elrond* and wife of Eärendil,* the mariner). After the murder of the elf-king Thingol,* he attempted to restore Doriath.* After the second deaths of Beren and Lúthien, he received the silmaril* set in the Nauglamir,* the necklace of the dwarves.* The jealous sons of Fëanor* murdered him in Menegroth.* Dior had the blood of three races: human, elven and Maiar,* flowing in him.

Dol Guldur

In the Third Age,* a fortress built by Sauron* in south-western Mirkwood.* In a background event to *The Hobbit*,‡ Gandalf* travelled to Dol Guldur to ascertain the identity of its ruler. After being driven out by the White Council,* Sauron fled to Mordor.* In the War of the Ring,* Dol Guldur was used as a stronghold by Sauron's forces.

Doom of Mandos (Doom of the Noldor)

The prophecy by one of the Valar,* Mandos,* of the tragic† events that would overtake the elves* who left Valinor* to return to Middle-earth* to recover the silmarils* stolen by Morgoth.* The prophecy was particularly directed at the House of Fëanor,* but encompassed elves and humans who became involved. The Doom followed Fëanor's dreadful oath to recover the gems, the kinslaying* of elves, and defiance of the will of the Valar. The curse or doom of Mandos works out in tragic events throughout the history of the First Age* in Middle-earth, in, for example, the tale of Beren and Lúthien, the elf-maiden.‡

Doriath

A great elven kingdom in Beleriand,* associated with many events of the First Age,* as recorded in *The Silmarillion*.‡ It was ruled by King Thingol* and Queen Melian.* Their beautiful daughter was

Lúthien,* called the Nightingale. To protect Doriath from the power of Morgoth,* Melian wove a magic barrier around the mainly wooded kingdom. By demanding of Beren* that he obtained a silmaril* in order to marry his daughter, Thingol enmeshed Doriath in the Doom of Mandos.* *The Lord of the Rings*‡ describes Lórien,* which was modelled upon Doriath by Galadriel.*

Dor-Lómin

An area north of Beleriand* between two mountain ranges running roughly north–south, the Ered Luin and the mountains of Mithrim, in Hithlum.* When elves* returned from Valinor* to Middle-earth,* Fingon controlled Dor-Lómin. It eventually became the home of the mannish House of Hador.* In the battles of Beleriand,* Morgoth* overran the area. Dor-Lómin is associated with the life of the hero,† Túrin Turambar.*

Dorthonion

A highland region north of Beleriand* in *The Silmarillion*.‡ Its name means 'land of pines' because of its great forests. As Morgoth* gained in ascendancy, Dorthonion was eventually abandoned by elves* and humans. Sauron* fled here after his encounter with Lúthien* and Huan.* Because of its ensuing corruption, the region was renamed Taur-nu-Fuin* ('forest-beneath-night'), the Mirkwood* of the First Age.*

Dúnedain; Dúnadan

See Edain;* Chieftains of the Dúnedain.*

Dunharrow

In *The Lord of the Rings*,‡ a high fortress and refuge in Rohan.*

Durin

In *The Silmarillion*,‡ one of the Seven Fathers of the dwarves,* who awoke at Ilúvatar's* command in Khazad-dûm.* He was the ancestor of Durin's Folk, who were the most significant family of the dwarves in the Third Age.*

Dwarves

In Tolkien's Middle-earth,* dwarves are one of the free peoples, especially created by Ilúvatar,* rather than being brought into existence by his agents, the Valar.* One of the Valar, Aulë,* did shape them, but could not give them personal life. Although the dwarves were not his concept, Ilúvatar had pity on Aulë, and gave his creation life. But the seven figures the Vala had shaped had to sleep until Ilúvatar awoke them. Chief among the seven was Durin.*

Designed by Aulë to resist the evils of Morgoth,* dwarves were short and hardy. Though proud, dwarves resisted evil.† Like their shaper, Aulë, dwarves were drawn to the substances of the earth – metals, minerals and precious stones. They were great craftsmen. A great temptation for them was possession.†

Dwarves lived long lives, not marrying as a rule until they were a hundred. They had their own, secret language.

In *The Hobbit*,‡ Bilbo* travelled with a party of dwarves, Thorin and Company,* to seek the dragon's† treasure. In *The Lord of the Rings*,‡ Gimli, the dwarf, is a member of the Company of the Ring.* His friendship with the elf, Legolas,* helps to heal an ancient enmity.

Eä

The material universe, or the world. In Elvish* Eä means simply 'It is' or 'Let it be', the word used by Ilúvatar* to bring the world into existence out of nothing. Creation itself is larger than Eä, as the Valar* and other angelic† orders are created beings, even though they are agents in the shaping of Eä.

Eärendil, the mariner

In *The Silmarillion*,‡ Eärendil is a central figure, with associations of Christ himself. After interceding on behalf of the elves* and people of Middle-earth,* in distress from the evil† of Morgoth,* he 'sailed out of the mists of the world into the seas of heaven with the Silmaril upon his brow'. His star in the sky was a sign of the providence† of Ilúvatar,* providing hope. The name 'Earendel' in the Old English poem 'Christ' provided an important seed for the growth of Tolkien's invented mythology. The story of his life and voyage is one of the earliest elements in Tolkien's fiction.

Edain

Strictly, this is the plural name for humans in Sindarin* Elvish.* In First-Age* Beleriand,* however, the name was associated with people of the Three Houses of the elf-friends, rather than humanity in general. This association carried through to the people of Númenor,* and their descendants in the Third Age* of Middle-earth,* such as Aragorn.* These were called Dúnedain,* 'Men of the West'. The Edain were enriched by marriages with elves,* as with Beren* and Lúthien,* and Aragorn and Arwen* (*see also* Elven quality†).

Edoras

In *The Lord of the Rings*,‡ the capital of Rohan,* situated on the River Snowbourn and containing the great feast-hall of Meduseld.

Elanor

A star-shaped yellow flower of Lórien,* appearing in the winter. Sam* and Rosie* Gamgee named their first child after the flower. Because of her beauty, Elanor Gamgee was called 'the Fair'.

Elbereth

The popular Sindarin* name for the Vala* Varda,* meaning 'star-queen'.
See also A Elbereth Gilthoniel.*

Eldar

Originally this term, meaning in Quenya* 'people of the stars', referred to all elves.* Later, it was used to refer to the Three Kindreds (the Vanyar,* Noldor* and Teleri*) who were summoned to the Great Journey† west from their birthplace in Cuiviénen* by the Vala,* Oromë.*

Elendil

Elendil the Tall was the son of Amandil,* leader of the faithful in Númenor.* When Númenor was destroyed he escaped with his sons Isildur* and Anárion* to Middle-earth,* where he founded the Númenorean realms Arnor* and Gondor.* At the end of the Second Age* he, with Gil-galad,* was killed during the overthrow of Sauron.*

Elrond

An elf* whose life spanned the Three Ages* of Middle-earth* chronicled in The Silmarillion,‡ The Lord of the Rings,‡ and other writings. Son of Eärendil* and Elwing,* he chose to be an elf, unlike his brother, and daughter Arwen* (who married Aragorn*). Tolkien's central theme of death† and immortality touches his life.

Elrond founded Rivendell* after the fall of Eregion* to Sauron.* He married Celebrian, daughter of Galadriel* and Celeborn.* Their children were Elladan, Elrohir and Arwen. Throughout the Third Age* Elrond helped the Dúnedain* of the north. He brought up Aragorn, a Chieftain of the Dúnedain.*

Elvish

The language of the elves,* invented by Tolkien and inspired in its chief variants by Finnish and Welsh. Many of the names of beings and places in Middle-earth* are Elvish in origin, which explains their aesthetic quality. The title of Tolkien's famous book, The Silmarillion,‡ derives from an Elvish word.

The chief variants of Elvish, variants accounted for historically and geographically by Tolkien, are Quenya,* and Sindarin.* Elvish enriched the speech of the Edain* (*see* Westron*).

Tolkien invented a number of languages in making Middle-earth (*see* Languages of Middle-earth*).

Elvish can be studied with the aid of Jim Allan's *An Introduction to Elvish* (1978), Ruth S. Noel's *The Languages of Middle-earth* (1980), and glossaries to the volumes of *The History of Middle-earth* and other unfinished material by Tolkien edited by his son, Christopher Tolkien.‡

Elwë

See Thingol.*

Elwing

In *The Silmarillion*,‡ daughter of Dior* and princess of Doriath,* who escaped there with the silmaril* after her parents were murdered by the sons of Fëanor.* She married Eärendil* at the Mouths of Sirion,* and they had two sons, Elrond* and Elros. While Eärendil was at sea the sons of Fëanor attacked, and Elwing cast herself into the ocean with the silmaril. Ulmo* the Vala* saved her by transforming her into a bird, allowing her to fly to her husband. The silmaril helped them to sail through the protective shadowy seas to Valinor.* Being half-elven she was allowed to choose the fate of an elf* or human, and chose the former. When Eärendil with the silmaril was allowed to sail in the sky, Elwing lived in a tower on the northern coast of Valinor, from where she flew as a bird to meet him as he drew near.

Ents

Herders who were originally given the task, by Yavanna,* of being guardians of the flora of Middle-earth.* Trees† were the chief among plant life and Ents described in *The Lord of the Rings*‡ resembled trees, though they had the power of speech and movement, and were about 14 feet tall.

Ents came into being around the same time as elves* and were taught to speak by them. In the First Age* Ents and Entwives* were found throughout Beleriand* and to the east. As time went on, male and female became separated, as Entwives favoured agriculture and gardens, and Ents tended the great forests. In the Third Age* Ents were associated with the Forest of Fangorn,* where they entered the War of the Ring* after meeting the hobbits,* Merry* and Pippin.*

Ents had their own slow language, reflecting the tree-like timescale of their being. Those other than Ents were unable to learn this complex language, with the exception of Tolkien himself. Ents also spoke Quenya,* but in an Entish style.

Entwives

Entwives were said to have taught humans the skills of agriculture. Tragically, their gardens were destroyed and they vanished before the end of the Second Age.* Ents* encountered during the events recorded in *The Lord of the Rings*‡ lamented the disappearance of the Entwives. Their loss is part of the poignant sense of fading and impermanence in the tales of Middle-earth,* particularly the tales of the Third Age* (*see* Death†).

Éowyn

In *The Lord of the Rings*,‡ a beautiful woman of Rohan,* niece of King Théoden.* She was golden-haired, slim and graceful. Her height allowed her to pass as a man when she disguised herself in order to fight in the great battle before Minas Tirith.* With the aid of Merry* she slew the Lord of the Nazgûl.* Wounded, she found healing† at the hands of Aragorn.* At first her heart had been lost in hopeless love for him, but she was won over, and her will to live restored, by Faramir.* After marrying him, she became Lady of Ithilien.*

Erebor

In *The Hobbit*,‡ a dwarf* kingdom under a mountain possessed by
Smaug,* the dragon.† Later the restored kingdom played a part in
the War of the Ring.*
See the Lonely Mountain.*

Ered Luin

The vast mountain-chain, the 'Blue Mountains', running north to
south which marked the eastern boundary of Beleriand* in the
First Age.* At that time the dwarf* cities of Belegost and Nogrod
were located there. The southernmost part of the Ered Luin survived the catastrophic changes in the terrain of the world at the
end of the First Age. They then lay to the west of Middle-earth,*
west of Arnor* and Eriador.*

Eregion

This 'Land of Holly' was called Hollin in Westron,* and lay at the
western feet of the Misty Mountains* in the Second Age,* when it
was a realm of Noldorin* elves.* The elven Rings* were made here.
Eregion lay between the rivers Glanduin and Bruinen. Moria* lay
nearby, connected by a tunnel travelled in a later Age by the
Company of the Ring.*

Eriador

The area between the Ered Luin* to the west and the Misty
Mountains* to the east, in which lay Arnor* and where later the
Shire* was settled.

Esgaroth

The Lake-town of *The Hobbit*,‡ where humans lived on the Long
Lake south of the Lonely Mountain.* It was an excellent commer-
cial centre, trading with the Woodland Realm and Erebor.*

Fair elves

In *The Silmarillion*,‡ these were the first group of elves* to set out on the Great Journey† to the west from Cuiviénen,* where they first awoke. They were golden-haired fairy beings from myth and folk-lore represented as elves in Tolkien's fiction.
See Fairy stories.†

Fall of Gondolin

The earliest part of *The Silmarillion*‡ in terms of composition, this tale tells of Morgoth's* invasion of the hidden elven city of Gondolin,* the heroism† of its defenders, and the escape of Tuor,* Eärendil,* and others.

Fangorn Forest

In *The Lord of the Rings*,‡ an ancient woodland east of the south-ern tip of the Misty Mountains,* and home of its guardian, the Ent* Fangorn, encountered by Merry* and Pippin.*

Faramir

In *The Lord of the Rings*,‡ brother of Boromir,* and son of Denethor,* Steward of Gondor.* A Dúnadan,* Faramir was Captain of the Rangers* of Ithilien* when he encountered the Ring-bearers Frodo* and Sam* on their quest† to destroy the One Ring.* Though a brave warrior, Faramir had a gentle and courteous disposition, like Aragorn* the ideal Christian hero.† He also loved music† and tales from the ancient days of Middle-earth.* While recovering from his wounds in the War of the Ring* he fell in love with Éowyn,* the battle-maiden of Rohan,* later marrying her.

Fëanor

In *The Silmarillion*,‡ an elven prince of the Noldor,* and genius in skill of mind and hands. His tragic† flaw was a quickness to anger, possession† and pride. His great inventions included adapting the Tengwar script of Elvish* and the making of the Silmarils,* incorporating the holy light† of the Two Trees.* When Morgoth* stole the Silmarils* and murdered his father, Fëanor decided to return to Middle-earth* in defiance of the wishes of the Valar.* He swore the dreadful oath of Fëanor,* which led to catastrophe for him, his household, and the region of Beleriand* (see Doom of Mandos*). One of his notorious deeds was the slaughter of fellow elves* at Alqualondë* (see Kinslaying*). Fëanor died after conflict with Morgoth's Balrogs.* His name in Sindarin* Elvish means 'spirit of fire'.

Finduilas

In The Silmarillion,‡ a Noldorin* princess of Nargothrond* who fell in love with the tragic† Túrin,* and was murdered by orcs* who captured her. Finduilas is also the name of the wife of Denethor.*

First Age

This is the Age of the great period of the elves,* though their creation preceded it. The First Age is dominated by events shaped by the existence of the Silmarils,* and by the theme of light† and darkness. The Silmarillion‡ concerns this Age, though, as published, the book contains material from later Ages, and from before the First Age.

The First Age came to an end with the Great Battle (see Battles of Beleriand*) and the defeat of Morgoth,* which resulted in the devastation of Beleriand* and northern Middle-earth.*

Firstborn, The

In The Silmarillion,‡ the name given to the elves,* created before the other Children of Ilúvatar,* humans. It particularly referred to the Eldar.*

Forelith

In The Lord of the Rings,‡ the sixth month of the Shire* Reckoning, approximating our June. Lith, or Lithe, is Mid-Year's Day in the Shire.

Foreyule

In *The Lord of the Rings*,‡ the last month of the Shire* Reckoning, approximating our December.

Fourth Age

In Tolkien's Middle-earth,* the Age which began the dominance of humans, and the virtual fading of the elves* and even hobbits* (who are human). The Christian era of the *evangelium* in which we now live comes after the Ages chronicled by *The Silmarillion*,‡ *The Hobbit*,‡ and *The Lord of the Rings*.‡ Many of Tolkien's stories are set beyond the Fourth Age, including *The Lost Road*,‡ *Farmer Giles of Ham*‡ and *Smith of Wootten Major*,‡ but usually were not intended to be part of his invented mythology. *The Lost Road* and *The Book of Lost Tales*† are exceptions (see *The History of Middle-earth*). The Fourth Age began with the passing of the Three Rings* after Sauron's* defeat. Most of the elves, especially those of the Eldar,* passed over the sea to Valinor.*

Frodo Baggins

See Baggins, Frodo.*

Galadriel

In Tolkien's mythology,† an elven princess and sister of Finrod Felagund. Galadriel's name in Sindarin* means 'Maiden crowned with gleaming hair'. She was given this name in her youth because she had long hair which glistened with gold but was also diffused with silver. At that time her disposition was like an Amazon (*see also* Haleth*), and when she took part in athletic events she bound up her hair as a crown.

With Elrond* and perhaps Glorfindel,* Galadriel is one of the significant figures from the First Age,* prominent in *The*

Silmarillion,‡ to appear in *The Lord of the Rings*.‡ Galadriel was implicated in the Noldorin* rebellion against the Valar.* Hence at first she was forbidden to return to Valinor* – the Valar only relented and let her return at end of Third Age.* When in Middle-earth* she at first lived with her brother on Tol Sirion* – when he went to Nargo-thrond* she moved to Doriath.* There she was taught by Queen Melian.* In a later Age, she modelled Lórien* on Doriath.

It was in Doriath that she married Celeborn.* She remained with him in Middle-earth after the First Age.

In the Second Age* Galadriel lived for a while in Lindon and Eregion* before founding Lórien. She became keeper of the one of the elven Rings,* Nenya, the Ring of Water.

A significant moral moment is the temptation of Galadriel when offered the One Ring* by Frodo,* in *The Lord of the Rings*. She contemplated the possibility of successfully wielding the Ring against Sauron* (*see* Evil†).

For some readers, the devotion of Sam* and Gimli to Galadriel undeniably evokes the veneration for Mary, the mother of Jesus that Roman Catholics have. Tolkien was a devout member of that denomination.

In a letter in 1971 Tolkien commented on the religious association of Galadriel:

> I think it is true that I owe much of this character to Christian and Catholic teaching and imagination about Mary, but actually Galadriel was a penitent: in her youth a leader in the rebellion against the Valar (the angelic guardians). At the end of the First Age she proudly refused forgiveness or permission to return. She was pardoned because of her resistance to the final and overwhelming temptation to take the Ring for herself.

Also significant is Galadriel's desire for the uttermost West of

Valinor. This desire was fulfilled when she was allowed to go over the sea with the Ring-bearers. Her longing was what C.S. Lewis called 'joy'† or *sehnsucht*, characteristic of so much of his writing, a concept taken up by Tolkien in his essay 'On Fairy Stories'.‡ Such longing is captured in Galadriel's song,† which also laments the eventual passing of Lórien.

Something of the development of Galadriel's important place in the history of Middle-earth can be seen in *Unfinished Tales*.‡

Gamgee, Samwise ('Sam')

In *The Lord of the Rings*,‡ the loyal companion of the Ring-bearer, Frodo Baggins* and the real hero† of the quest.† He was chosen as one of the Companions of the Ring,* a hobbit* of the Shire* like Frodo. Bilbo* in earlier years had taught him his letters and put in his head a love and longing for elves.* Samwise is a translation into Old English of his name in Hobbitish,* and means 'Half-wit' (which is fitting for a shrewd, honest, and heroic figure considered a fool by the great and powerful). Even Tolkien's attitude to Sam is at times condescending. Like Christ himself, Sam is a fool-figure.

In a letter to his son Christopher,‡ Christmas Eve 1944, Tolkien speaks revealingly of Sam: 'Cert.[ainly] Sam is the most closely drawn character [in *The Lord of the Rings*], the successor to Bilbo of the first book, the genuine hobbit. Frodo is not so interesting, because he has to be highminded, and has (as it were) a vocation.' Elsewhere (letter 131) Tolkien calls Sam 'the chief hero'. Tolkien is not here downplaying Frodo's deep significance in the tale, but rather pointing out the contrasting functions of the two hobbits. In many respects, Sam is squire to Frodo as lord, following an ancient courtesy that Tolkien admired.

Sam has an acute sense, awakened by the events of the quest, of what Tolkien calls 'the seamless web of story'. He is an essential part of the narrative frame of *The Lord of the Rings* and thus the older tales of *The Silmarillion*.‡ Sam senses, because of an intuitive feeling of providence,† that he and Frodo are part of a larger story (*see* Story, Tolkien's theology of†). He also is integral to the structure of the book in representing homeliness (*see* Nature†). His love for Rosie* is an 'untold story', yet regarded as an essential backdrop to the heroic story. Tolkien writes in a letter probably sent in 1951:

> I think the simple 'rustic' love of Sam and his Rosie (nowhere elaborated) is absolutely essential to the study of his (the chief hero's) character, and to the theme of the relation of ordinary life (breathing, eating, working, begetting) and quests, sacrifice, causes, and the 'longing for Elves', and sheer beauty.

Gandalf

In *The Hobbit*‡ and *The Lord of the Rings*,‡ Gandalf appears as an old man. He is a wizard,† one of the Maiar* sent by the Valar* to Middle-earth* in the Third Age* to encourage the resistance to Sauron.* In his youth in Valinor* he was called Olorin (letter 325, in Tolkien's *Letters*‡).

In his fatal conflict with the Balrog* in Moria* he is one of the supreme examples of sacrifice† in Tolkien's writings. In laying down his life, he gave up (as he thought) the chance to play his central part in the resistance to Sauron when those who opposed him were at their most vulnerable. His sacrifice was accepted and he was allowed to return to Middle-earth in a resurrected body.

Faithful to his calling as a wizard, Gandalf is a prime mover in the fight against Sauron. On his coronation Aragorn* says of Gandalf: 'he has been the mover of all that has been accomplished, and this is his victory'.

Gandalf is also important to the narrative of *The Hobbit* and *The Lord of the Rings*. This is because he interprets the place of providence† in events. For example, he reveals the key part that the pity of Frodo* and Sam* for Gollum* played in the unfolding of events. He also foresaw what could be accomplished by the 'foolish' act of sending weak hobbits* into the stronghold of Sauron (*see* Hero†).

Gandalf himself was a Ring-bearer. He bore Narya,* the Ring of fire, the Kindler, which aspect of himself he represented to the hobbits in a childlike way as a love of fireworks.

Geography of Middle-earth

See Chapter 5: How *The Lord of the Rings* Relates to *The Silmarillion*.

Gil-galad

The last High King of the Noldorian* elves* in Middle-earth.* His name in Sindarin* means 'Star of Radiance'. After the end of the First Age* he remained in Lindon. With Elendil* he lead the Last Alliance of Men and Elves against Sauron* when he grew to power again after the destruction of Númenor.* Though Sauron was defeated, Gil-galad was burnt to death by his heat. Sam* recites part of a lay called 'The Fall of Gil-galad', translated by Bilbo Baggins.*

Glorfindel

In *The Silmarillion*,‡ a noble elf* of Gondolin* who fell to his death in combat with a Balrog* after escaping Morgoth's* sack of the city. His name means 'golden-haired' in Sindarin.* Tolkien suggests that an elf of the same name, who appears in the Third Age* in *The Lord of the Rings*‡ was, almost certainly, a reincarnation of the same person. That Glorfindel seemed to be the second most important elf, after Elrond,* in Rivendell.* He fought the Nazgûl,* protecting Frodo* and his companions as they drew near to Rivendell.

God

See God;† Ilúvatar;* Providence;† Natural Theology, Tolkien and;† Christianity, Tolkien and.†

Goldberry

In *The Lord of the Rings*,‡ the River-daughter, child of the River-woman of the Withywindle,* which ran through the Old Forest,* to the east of the Shire.* She was the wife of Tom Bombadil.* Her race is not clear. As a Maia,* Tom could marry one of another race (as the Maia Melian* married an elf,* and her daughter, Lúthien,* married a human). She shared Tom's affinity with nature,† symbolizing the hippie ideal in the 1960s, when *The Lord of the Rings* had a cult following. The courtship and marriage of Tom and Goldberry is described in *The Adventures of Tom Bombadil*.‡

Gollum

In *The Lord of the Rings*,‡ he was once a hobbit* who bore the marks of long years underground† guarding, yet possessed by, the One Ring* which he called 'My precious', and which he had deluded himself into thinking was a birthday present to him.

He originally had been a Stoor* hobbit, before hobbits migrated westwards over the Misty Mountains* and settled in the Shire.* His original name was Smeagol. He had acquired the Ring by murdering his cousin Deagol, who found it while fishing in the River Anduin.* The name Gollum was given to him because of his filthy habit of noisily clearing his throat.

After possessing the Ring, Gollum hid for centuries in the roots of the Misty Mountains. Seemingly by luck (*see* Providence†) Bilbo Baggins* stumbled across the underground lake where Gollum dwelt (as recorded in *The Hobbit*‡). After losing the Ring to its new bearer, Gollum ventured out into unfamiliar daylight to seek out Bilbo, falling into Sauron's* hands. Anxious to discover the Ring for himself, Sauron found the clue from Gollum that it lay in the Shire. The events after this, culminating in the War of the Ring,* are chronicled in *The Lord of the Rings*.

Gollum picked up the trail of Frodo,* the new Ring-bearer, and the Company of the Ring* before they entered Moria.* After Frodo and Sam* parted from the Company Gollum fell into their hands and led them towards Mordor.* Treacherously, he guided them into Shelob's* Lair, where the quest† to destroy the Ring was nearly foiled. Later, when Frodo failed to cast the Ring into the Cracks of Doom, Gollum seized the Ring but fell into the fires of Mount Doom with it.

Gollum is of crucial importance to the movement and resolution of events. This is not only because of the contrast between his ravished appearance after centuries possessed by the Ring, and the appearance of a normal, well-rounded hobbit. He is also important morally because of pity shown to him first by Bilbo, then Frodo and, finally, the less soft-hearted Sam. Their pity proves to be a key action in the outworking of providence. The character of Gollum also reveals Tolkien's concern for repentance in human life. Despite his depravity, a side of Gollum struggles to rise above the overwhelming demands of the Ring which possesses him. There are times in the story when it seems possible that Gollum will be saved. He retains the moral character of a hobbit. The two sides of his nature are so marked that Sam, characteristically, dubs them Slinker and Stinker. The former, expressed in his fawning attitude to Frodo, showed hope of something better, despite Sam's cynicism.

Gondolin

In *The Silmarillion*,‡ a great city whose name in Sindarin* means 'The Hidden Rock'. It was built in a secret and protected realm by the elf-king Turgon,* surrounded by the Encircling Mountains. For centuries it lay hidden from Morgoth* who eventually sacked it with the help of Balrogs,* orcs,* and dragons.† Among the survivors were Tuor,* Idril* and the young Eärendil.*

Gondor

Founded in the Second Age* by Elendil,* the realm of Gondor plays a significant part in the events chronicled in *The Lord of the Rings*.‡ At its founding it was the South Kingdom in Middle-earth,* the North Kingdom being Arnor,* of which only ruins remained in Frodo's* day.

Great Council
See White Council.*

Green-elves
In *The Silmarillion*,‡ elves* who remained in Ossiriand,* to the east of Beleriand.* They were skilled woodmen who lived secretly. The Green-elves tended to wear green, and loved to sing. The bow was their favoured weapon.

Grey-elves
See Sindar.*

Grey Havens
A town and harbour founded by Círdan* after the destruction of Beleriand.* Those leaving Middle-earth* for the uttermost West sailed from there, like Bilbo* and Frodo* in *The Lord of the Rings*.‡

Grima
See Wormtongue.*

Hador
In *The Silmarillion*,‡ the greatest chieftain among humans in the First Age.* He was given the dominion of Dor-Lómin,* gathering together the Third House of the Edain.*

Haladin
In *The Silmarillion*,‡ the second group of humans to enter Beleriand.* They lived in the Forest of Brethil.* They were granted habitation here by King Thingol* of Doriath* in return for guarding the region, especially the Crossings of Teiglin. Túrin Turambar* dwelt with them for a time, becoming their leader.

Haleth

In *The Silmarillion*,‡ she was the first chief of the Haladin,* leading them to Brethil* to settle. Haleth was a renowned Amazon, who had a select bodyguard of women (*see also* Galadriel*).

Halflings

See Hobbits.*

Halimath

In the reckoning of the Shire,* the ninth month. It is approximately September. It is from the Old English *halig-monath*, holy-month – the month of sacrifice.†

Hallow of Eru

In Númenor,* the sole temple, to be found on the top of Menel-tarma. It had no roof. As devotion to Ilúvatar* (Eru) declined, worship at the Hallow was neglected. Ar-Pharazon finally banned it altogether. After the overwhelming of Númenor* by the sea it was thought that the Hallow rose above the waves.

The Hallow is a rare reference to religious practice in Tolkien's Middle-earth* (*see* Christianity, Tolkien and†).

Halls of Mandos (Houses of the Dead)

In *The Silmarillion*,‡ a waiting place for the spirits of elves* and mortals after death. Lúthien,* in the tale of Beren and Lúthien, the elf-maiden,‡ came here to plead for her lover, Beren.* The Halls of Mandos are situated on the far western shores of Aman.*

Haradrim

In Middle-earth,* the people of Harad (meaning 'the South'), the area south of Mordor.* They fought for Sauron* during the War of the Ring,* some of their number using elephants in battle. They have some similarity to the Calormenes in C.S. Lewis'‡ *The Chronicles of Narnia*.

Harfoots

The most numerous of the three branches of hobbits.* They were the first to migrate over the Misty Mountains* from the River Anduin* region. They persisted with the custom of living underground† longer than the other types of hobbit.

Helcaraxë

The strait separating Aman* from Middle-earth* in *The Silmarillion*‡ before the great change in the world after the destruction of Númenor.* Many of the elves* returning to Middle-earth crossed here after the theft of the Silmarils* by Morgoth.*

It was also referred to as 'the Grinding Ice'.

High elves

In *The Silmarillion*,‡ the name given to elves* of Aman* and to elves who dwelt at some time there.

History of Middle-earth

Strictly, Middle-earth* is only part of the world, or Eä.* Before the change in the world, after the destruction of Númenor,* the Undying Lands of the West, including Valinor,* were physically part of the world. The history of elves* and humans incorporates events in Valinor. The history can be divided into four Ages (*see* Chapter 5: How *The Lord of the Rings* Relates to *The Silmarillion*).

Much of Tolkien's invention concerned the history, annals, languages, chronology, and geography of Middle-earth. He was concerned to make an inwardly consistent sub-creation.† There were a number of major tales which stood (or were intended to stand) independently of the history, with that history as an imaginatively appealing backdrop. The tales were those of Beren and Lúthien, the elf-maiden,‡ Túrin Turambar,* Tuor* and the Fall of

Gondolin,* the Voyage of Eärendil,* the Mariner, *The Hobbit*‡ and *The Lord of the Rings*.‡ Tolkien may of course have intended to create others.

Tolkien also invented a beautiful cosmological myth, portraying events before the creation of the world (*see* 'Ainulindalë'‡).

Hithlum

In *The Silmarillion*,‡ the region to the north-west of Beleriand,* to the south of which was Dor-Lómin* (associated with Túrin Turambar*). The name, which is Sindarin,* means 'Land of Mist'.

Hobbitish

In *The Lord of the Rings*,‡ a dialect of Westron* (or Common Speech) belonging to hobbits* settled in the Shire.* It has many resemblances to the speech of humans of the Anduin* region, to which the people of Rohan* were related. Tolkien revealed dialect differences in the style of English into which he 'translated' them. Ideally, some would have been represented in Old English.

Hobbiton

A village in the Shire* made famous by events recounted in *The Lord of the Rings*.‡ Hobbiton was the home of Bilbo* and Frodo* Baggins, as well as Sam Gamgee.* Its features such as Bagshot Row, the Mill, and the Ivy Bush pub, are part of its homeliness.

Hobbits

Many people have been acquainted with hobbits through J.R.R. Tolkien's children's story, *The Hobbit*.‡ The title of that book refers to its hero,† Mr Bilbo Baggins.* A critic in the *New Statesman* remarked of Tolkien: 'It is a triumph that the genus Hobbit, which he himself has invented, rings just as real as the time-hallowed genera of Goblin, Troll, and Elf.' C.S. Lewis‡ believed that the hobbits 'are perhaps a myth that only an Englishman (or, should we add, a Dutchman?) could have created'. Instead of a creation of character as we find in novels, much of what we know of Bilbo, Frodo,* Sam* and other hobbits comes from our acquaintance with them in character as hobbits, as we are familiar with Gandalf* in character as a wizard,† or Treebeard* in character as an Ent.* Tolkien sustains the character of these different races with great skill.

Bilbo's house was a typical dwelling place of a wealthy hobbit. It was not a worm-filled, dirty, damp hole, but a comfortable, many-roomed underground† home. Its hall, which connected all the rooms, had 'panelled walls, and floors tiled and carpeted, provided with polished chairs, and lots and lots of pegs for hats and coats – the hobbit was fond of visitors'. Hobbits generally liked to be thought respectable, not having adventures or behaving in an unexpected way.

At the time of *The Hobbit* and *The Lord of the Rings*‡ in the Third Age* hobbits mainly lived in the Shire,* but they had migrated from the east, from the other side of the Misty Mountains,* in the Vale of Anduin. Originally, they were closely related to humankind, created in the First Age.* Gollum* was originally a Stoor* hobbit of the Anduin* region.

Hobbits such as Bilbo and Frodo and their contemporaries spoke Hobbitish,* a provincial form of Westron,* the Common Speech. They were called a variety of names by other races, such as Halfling or, in Rohirric,* *holbytla* ('hole-builder'). The term 'hobbit' is Tolkien's English equivalent for their name for themselves, *kuduk*.

Hobbits are a little people, about half the height of humans, and even smaller than the bearded dwarves.* Male hobbits themselves have no beards (though Stoors have down on their faces) and are inclined to be rather fat in the stomach, but not as much as the dwarves. They dress in bright colours (chiefly green and yellow), and wear no shoes – for, as Tolkien tells us, 'their feet grow natural leathery soles and thick warm brown hair like the stuff on their heads (which is curly)'. Also they have 'long clever brown fingers, good-natured faces, and laugh deep fruity laughs (especially after dinner, which they have twice a day when they can get it).'

Nowadays, one could be forgiven for thinking that the race is extinct. They are now much less numerous, and are able to quickly hide when a human comes blundering along. Hobbits recover quickly from falls or bruises, as well as having a fund of sayings that they consider wise. Some hobbits reveal a gift for lyrics and poetry, as evidenced in the collection gleaned from the Red Book of Westmarch,* *The Adventures of Tom Bombadil.*‡

Bilbo Baggins was undoubtedly one of the most scholarly of the hobbits, being a main contributor to the Red Book, which was composed by hobbits. In attributing this as his source for *The Hobbit* and *The Lord of the Rings*, Tolkien was able to account for the style and perspective of their narration. It also provided him with some kind of solution to the vexed question of the narrative framework of *The Silmarillion.*‡ Attached to the Red Book were a number of other chronicles, including the three volumes of Bilbo's translations from the Elvish,* which, as translations, retained the high style which makes *The Silmarillion* so different a narrative to *The Hobbit* and *The Lord of the Rings*. One could imagine a hobbit chronicler treating a tale such as that of Beren* and Lúthien‡ in the humbler, homelier style of *The Lord of the Rings*, and creating a similar masterpiece. But, alas, no such chronicle survives.

Huan

In *The Silmarillion*,‡ the noble wolfhound of Valinor* given to Celegorm* by the Vala* Oromë.* He features in the tale of Beren and Lúthien the elf-maiden,‡ killing the foul werewolf, Carcharoth.* Huan had much of the nature of an elf,* being ageless and tireless. Three times he was allowed to speak.

Húrin

In *The Silmarillion*,‡ the father of the tragic Túrin* and Nienor.* Captured by Morgoth,* he was set upon Thangorodrim* for many years to view the outworkings of Morgoth's curse on his family. What he saw was twisted by the malice and deceit of the enemy of elves* and humans. After his release he unintentionally gave Morgoth a clue as to the whereabouts of the hidden kingdom of Gondolin.* Húrin recovered the blessed Nauglamir,* which he brought to King Thingol* in Doriath,* where Queen Melian* exerted her healing† power to free him from Morgoth's deceits.

Idril

In *The Silmarillion*,‡ the elven daughter of King Turgon* of Gondolin.* In one of only three marriages of elves* and humans, she chose Tuor,* one of the Edain.* Their son was Eärendil.* The family escaped the fall of Gondolin to the Mouths of Sirion,* in Arvernien in the south of Beleriand.* When Tuor became old, she sailed with him into the Uttermost West. The line of Gondolin passed to their son, Eärendil.

Ilúvatar

See God.†

Imrahil

In *The Lord of the Rings*,‡ Prince of Dol Amroth, in southern Gondor.* He played an important part in the War of the Ring.* During Faramir's* illness, after the suicide of the Steward* Denethor,* he ruled Minas Tirith.*

Isengard

In *The Lord of the Rings*,‡ the stronghold of the wizard† Saruman.* There a great tower, Orthanc,* lay in the centre of a broad plain, which was surrounded by a natural circle of stone wall. The only gate into Isengard faced south. Isengard was built by men of Gondor* in its golden age. Later, Saruman was given permission to dwell there, after which he fortified it, replacing grass and trees† with stone and technology (*see* Magic†). Secretly, orcs* and wolves were brought there to bolster Saruman's increasing power and desire for domination. His stronghold was destroyed by Ents,* led by Fangorn, at the time of the War of the Ring.*

Isildur

A Dúnadan* of Númenor* referred to in *The Lord of the Rings*‡ on account of his cutting the One Ring* from Sauron's* hand, and then losing it in the River Anduin* while fleeing orcs* who killed him. The lost Ring was eventually found by Gollum's* cousin, whom Gollum murdered for it.

Isildur was the older son of Elendil,* the leader of the faithful in Númenor. He bravely stole a fruit of the threatened Tree† Nimloth* and thus preserved the line of the White Tree when he escaped the drowning of the great island. He helped to found the Númenorean realms in exile, Gondor* and Arnor.*

Istari

See Wizards.†

Ithilien

In *The Lord of the Rings*,‡ an area of Gondor* between the River Anduin* and the western mountain range of Mordor,* the Mountains of Shadow. Here the Ring-bearer, Frodo,* with Sam* and Gollum,* encountered Faramir.* Because the influence of Sauron* had not been long in the region, it still retained its beauty at the time of the War of the Ring.*

Ivrin

In *The Silmarillion*,‡ a lake at the source of the River Narog, to the north of Beleriand.* There were beautiful falls here. Ulmo,* the Vala,* guarded the purity of the water. However, the area was polluted and desecrated by Glaurung as the dragon† moved south to ravish Nargothrond.*

Khazad-dûm

Also called Moria,* the greatest of the dwarf* realms, carved under the Misty Mountains* in the First Age.* It consisted of many vast halls on various levels. In the Second Age* a connecting tunnel was made to Eregion.* *The Lord of the Rings*‡ records how the Company of the Ring* disturbed a Balrog* deep underneath Khazad-dûm. Gandalf* sacrificed† his life fighting the monster.

Kíli

In *The Hobbit*,‡ a member of the company of dwarves* for which Bilbo Baggins* was the official burglar. He was nephew of Thorin Oakenshield* and, with his brother Fili, died defending Thorin's body during the great Battle of the Five Armies. Tolkien obtained his name from the Poetic Edda.

Kinslaying

In *The Silmarillion*,‡ the slaying of the elves* of Alqualondë* by the Noldor,* led by the rebellious Fëanor.* They refused to give ships to the Noldor to return to Middle-earth.* One consequence of the kinslaying was the alienation of Thingol* and Doriath* from the family of Fëanor.

See also Doom of Mandos.*

Kortirion

See Warwick.‡

Lamps of the Valar

In *The Silmarillion*,‡ two great globes set on top of great pillars of stone in the north and south of Middle-earth* by the Valar* to light the world. The malicious destruction of the lamps by Morgoth* (Melkor) marked the end of the spring of the world.

See Light.†

Languages of Middle-earth
See Adûnaic;* Black Speech;* Elvish;* Hobbitish;* Philology, Tolkien and;† Quenya;* Rohirric;* Sindarin;* Westron.*

Last Battle, The
In Tolkien's mythology,† the final conflict against evil† at the end of the world, an end which will mark a new beginning.
See Apocalyptic, Tolkien and.†

Laurelin
In *The Silmarillion*,‡ one of the Two Trees* of Valinor.* She was also called the Golden Tree, and her name means 'the song of gold' in Elvish.* Her light-green leaves were edged with gold, her flowers were dazzling yellow, and her dew seemed like a golden rain.

Legolas
In *The Lord of the Rings*,‡ an elf* of the Woodland Realm, son of King Thranduil,* who was a member of the Company of the Ring.* His friendship with Gimli the dwarf* symbolized the resolution of an ancient animosity between the two races. When Legolas first saw the sea in southern Gondor* it awoke a longing for the Elvinhome in the uttermost west (*see* Joy†). After the passing of Aragorn,* Legolas and Gimli sailed together to the west on the Straight Road.*

Legolas and a number of the woodland elves were notable for restoring the land of Ithilien,* despoiled in the War of the Ring.*

Lembas
In Tolkien's Middle-earth,* the waybread of the elves.* In Sindarin* Elvish* this means journey- or way-bread; in Quenya* it means 'life-bread'. Some readers have seen a sacramental echo in the function of lembas (*see* Christianity, Tolkien and†). Many travellers were sustained by it, including Frodo* and Sam* in *The Lord of the Rings*.‡

Lonely Mountain

In *The Hobbit*, a mountain east of Mirkwood* under which lay the abandoned dwarf kingdom of Erebor,* in which Smaug* the dragon† had his lair.

Lórien

In *The Lord of the Rings*,‡ the elvish* realm of Celeborn* and Galadriel* between the rivers Celebrant and Anduin.* It was modelled upon Doriath* of the First Age,* where Galadriel learnt of Melian.* It is also called LothLórien ('Lórien of the blossom'). Lórien was one of a few elvish areas left in Middle-earth* in the Third Age* (*see also* Grey Havens*; Rivendell*). It best preserved the beauty and timelessness of Valinor.* The chief city of Lórien was called Caras Galadon.*

The Lost Road

See The Straight Road.*

LothLórien

See Lórien.*

Lúthien

In *The Silmarillion*,‡ the elven daughter of King Thingol* and Queen Melian* in Doriath,* the most beautiful of elf* and human. She had great powers, including music,† and courage. The story of her sacrificial† love for Beren* the mortal is recorded both in *The Silmarillion* as published, and in an unfinished poetic version published in *The Lays of Beleriand*.* Hers was the most significant union of an elf with a human being and illustrates Tolkien's central theme of immortality and death.†

See Chapter 5: How *The Lord of the Rings* Relates to *The Silmarillion*.

Maedhros

In *The Silmarillion*,‡ the eldest son of Fëanor,* a Noldorin* elf.*

He is one of Tolkien's tragic heroes† (*see* Tragedy†). He resisted the excesses of his father and brothers, even though he swore the Oath of Fëanor.* Morgoth* captured him and cruelly hung him upon Thangorodrim* by his right wrist. He was rescued by his friend, Fingon, with the help of the great eagle,† Thorondor.* Maedhros cleverly resisted the onslaughts of Morgoth. After the passing of Beren* and Lúthien* Maedhros succumbed to the Oath of Fëanor. This culminated in his stealing a Silmaril,* along with Maglor* his brother. Suffering from his moral guilt, and the physical pain of the Silmaril burning his hand, Maedhros threw himself and the gem into a volcanic chasm.

Maglor

In *The Silmarillion*,‡ a Noldorin* elf* and son of Fëanor.* Though he swore the Oath of Fëanor,* he later tried, unsuccessfully, to reverse his claim to the Silmarils.* His brother Maedhros* persuaded him to join in stealing the Silmarils. He cast the tormenting gem into the sea in remorse. Maglor was one of the great singers (*see* Music†) among the Eldar.*

Maiar

In *The Silmarillion*,‡ angelic† beings, or Ainur,* of lesser degree than the Valar.* The singular form is Maia. They stewarded the world under the direction of the Valar.

The loyal of the Maiar included Olórin (Gandalf*), Melian,* and Tom Bombadil.* They were capable of various incarnations.

Those who rebelled against Ilúvatar* (God†), with Morgoth* (Melkor), expressed degrees of depravity, and included Sauron* (once striking in appearance) and the Balrogs.*

Mandos

In *The Silmarillion*,‡ one of the Valar,* who impassively kept the Houses of the Dead (the Halls of Mandos*). He judged the fates of elves* and humans in knowledge of the will of Ilúvatar* (God†).

He is only recorded as being moved to pity by the plea of Lúthien*
for Beren.*
See also Doom of Mandos.*

Manwë

In *The Silmarillion*,‡ the chief of the angelic† Ainur,* brother of
the fallen Melkor (Morgoth*), and husband of Varda.* Of the
Valar* he had the greatest understanding of the will and designs
of Ilúvatar* (God†). He was particularly concerned with the ideas
of air, clouds and wind, and with the birds of the air, eagles†
being especially significant. He is Lord of the World and the West.

Melian

In *The Silmarillion*,‡ one of the Maiar,* who took on human form
for love of the elven-king, Thingol.* The two of them founded
Doriath,* and had a single child, Lúthien.* After the passing of
Lúthien, who chose mortality for love of Beren,* and the murder
of Thingol, Melian abandoned Middle-earth* and her human form.

Melkor

See Morgoth.*

Menegroth

The underground† halls of the elven-king Thingol* in Doriath,*
also called the Thousand Caves. Menegroth was built in a rocky
hill beside the river Esgalduin, accessible by a stone bridge.

Meriadoc ('Merry') Brandybuck

In *The Lord of the Rings*,‡ one of the Company of the Ring;* a
hobbit* of the Shire.* Merry was a friend of the young Frodo
Baggins,* growing up in Buckland.* He accompanied him from
Bag End, when Frodo departed with the Ring.* When the Company was divided by an orc* attack, Merry and Pippin* were captured. They escaped into Fangorn Forest,* and there encountered

Ents.* This eventually led to reunion with others in the Company. Merry took service with King Théoden,* rode with Éowyn* to battle, and in it Merry and Éowyn killed the dread Lord of the Nazgûl.* Both found healing† at the hands of Aragorn.* After the War of the Ring,* Merry in later years became Master of Buckland. He wrote several scholarly works, such as *Old Words* and *Names in the Shire*.

Michel Delving

A town in the Shire,* essentially the capital, and located in the West-farthing. It was the seat of the mayor, the Shire's main dignitary.

Middle-earth

Tolkien's sub-created world (*see* Sub-creation†) that features in *The Silmarillion*,‡ *The Hobbit*‡ and *The Lord of the Rings*.‡ Middle-earth can refer to the whole world, or only the landmass east of the great sea of Belegaer.* The world of the First Age* seems to be flat – Tolkien envisaged a complex cosmology. The blessed realm of Aman,* west of the Great Sea, could be reached by sea from the east, from Beleriand* and other regions. This became increasingly difficult, because of the disobedience of the Noldor,* the Elves† swayed by Fëanor.*

In the Second Age,* after the destruction of Númenor,* the shape of the world changed. It became the sphere we know. Aman was removed from the physical geography of the world, though still a real place.

Middle-earth is the planned habitation of humankind. Though elves awoke here they were called on the great journey† to Aman, to be with the Valar.* Those who stayed in Middle-earth, or returned to it from Aman, enriched the life and language of humanity (*see* Elven quality†). Eventually, most elves passed from Middle-earth, but left their mark genetically on humans, most especially through the marriage of the elf-maiden Lúthien* to the mortal Beren.*

The Atlas of Middle-earth provides a guide to the geographies of Tolkien's world.

Minas Tirith

The name means 'tower of guard'. In *The Silmarillion*,‡ Minas Tirith is a fortress built on the river island of Tol Sirion* by Finrod, later occupied by Sauron.* In *The Lord of the Rings*,‡ Minas Tirith is the great and beautiful city of Gondor,* having the significance of Byzantium in Christendom. It combined strength with architectural beauty. Minas Tirith was built on seven levels, and contained many features, such as the Houses of Healing.

Mirkwood

In *The Hobbit*,‡ a great forest to the east of the Misty Mountains* and the River Anduin.* In earlier times it had been called Greenwood the Great – until the shadow of Sauron* fell on it. Like Dorthonion* in the First Age,* it became a place of evil. Mirkwood was polluted with great spiders, the presence of orcs,* and other terrors. Bilbo,* with Thorin and the Company,* passed through it in the quest† for dragon's† treasure. After the War of the Ring,* Mirkwood was cleansed and restored, and renamed Eryn Lasgalen, 'wood of green leaves'.

Misty Mountains

A major feature of the geography of Middle-earth* in the Third Age.* The Misty Mountains were a great chain of mountains running from north to south like a spine. They ran about 900 miles, from the Northern Waste to the Gap of Rohan.* In *The Lord of the Rings*,‡ the Company of the Ring* are unable to cross the mountains because of a fierce snow storm, and go underneath via Moria.* In *The Hobbit*,‡ Bilbo* and the dwarves* with him cross through by orc* tunnels. Bilbo encounters Gollum* far underground.
See Underground places and journeys.†

Mithril

A valuable metal that was both light and strong, and which shone like silver. It was jealously prized by the dwarves,* and could only be found in Khazad-dûm,* where it provided the basis for the dwarf-region's economy.

Morannon

The Black Gate leading to Mordor.* It had one great iron gate, with three huge doors.

Mordor

The name means 'black land' because of the effects of its possession† by Sauron.* Lying to the east of the lower reaches of the River Anduin,* Mordor is bounded on three sides by mountain chains. Sauron possessed Mordor in the Second Age.* He left it for a long period during his sojourn in Númenor.* After his defeat, Gondor* drove out the evil inhabitants of Mordor and built strongholds to prevent their return. In the Third Age,* the Nazgûl* entered Mordor and prepared for the return of Sauron, then hidden in Dol Guldur* (where he was at the time of the events in *The Hobbit*‡). *The Lord of the Rings*‡ tells of the War of the Ring,* and the heroic quest† to destroy it in the very heart of Mordor, at Mount Doom.*

Morgoth

This name meaning 'the Black Enemy', was given to the Fallen Vala,* Melkor, by Fëanor,* after he had stolen the Silmarils* and helped to extinguish the light† of the Two Trees.*

Morgoth is an equivalent to the biblical Satan, or Lucifer, who was originally an angel† of high rank who rebelled against God.† Satan figures large in John Milton's poem, *Paradise Lost*. Milton captures the greatness of the angel, which explains the extent of the havoc he wrought after his fall.† In Tolkien, the focus is on the appalling malice of Morgoth, and the effect of this malice on events concerning elves* and humans (and even the Valar).

Although the emphases of Milton and Tolkien are different, their theology and explanation of evil† is very close.

Morgoth figures in *The Silmarillion*,‡ being cast out of the world at the end of the First Age.* In the Second* and Third Ages* his place is taken by his less powerful, but more subtly evil, lieutenant, Sauron.*

In Tolkien's mythology,† Morgoth (Melkor) was the first of the Ainur.* He was the brother of Manwë,* of the Valar. He became jealous of his maker, Ilúvatar,* seeking the secret of the creation principle, rather than merely being an agent of creation. His rebellion introduced discord into the original music† of creation (*see* 'Ainulindalë'‡). Morgoth (Melkor) set himself in opposition to Ilúvatar and the Valar. When the world was made he particularly hated the Children of Ilúvatar* – elves and humans.

Morgoth used darkness and cold as a weapon, extinguishing the light† of the Two Lamps and using Ungoliant* to devour the light of the Two Trees.* The latter deed was done after Morgoth had been in chains for a vast period of time, and had only been released by the Valar because he seemed repentant. After seizing the Silmarils,* Morgoth returned to the icy northern wastes of Middle-earth,* to Angband.* Here he planned the domination of Beleriand,* breeding orcs* and other monsters (*see* Battles of Beleriand*). One of the greatest deeds in resistance to him was the stealing back of a Silmaril from his Iron Crown by Beren* and Lúthien.* Morgoth showed particular malice towards the Children of Húrin.*

Fëanor* the elf had some of Morgoth's characteristics, and his rebellion against the wishes of the Valar, when he swore his dreadful oath after Morgoth's stealing of the Silmarils, led to the Doom of Mandos.* The outworking of this judgment greatly aided Morgoth's purposes, and led to the eventual destruction of Beleriand.

Moria
See Khazad-dûm.*

Mount Doom

In elvish called Orodruin (mountain of red flame), a volcano in Mordor.* It was named Mount Doom by the people of Gondor* at the end of the Second Age, during an eruption. Here Sauron* made the One Ring,* and it was to here that Frodo* and Sam* made their way to return the Ring to its fire, the only way that the Ring and its power could be unmade.

Nan Dungortheb

In *The Silmarillion*,‡ this 'valley of dreadful death' lay between Taur-nu-Fuin,* to the north, and Doriath,* to the south. Ungoliant* possessed this region after darkening the Two Trees,* and, after her, her offspring and other terrible creatures continued its horror. Beren* crossed the region on his way to Doriath, and this was considered an heroic deed because of the dangers. Such a presence of spiders is echoed, on a lesser scale, in Mirkwood,* many centuries later, as recounted in *The Hobbit*.‡

Nargothrond

In *The Silmarillion*,‡ a great underground† fortress, consisting of many halls, beside the River Narog, and founded by Finrod Felagund, the elven-king. The name was also used to refer to the realm of the king, extending east and west of the river. Nargothrond was impregnable until Túrin* persuaded the elves* to build an access bridge over the river. Glaurung the dragon† crossed this stone bridge to rout the elven caverns.

Narya

One of the Three Rings* of the elves,† known as the 'Ring of fire', or 'the Red Ring'. Its bearer was Círdan,* until he passed it on to Gandalf.*

Nauglamir

This is 'the Necklace of the Dwarves' spoken of in *The Silmarillion*.‡

Set with many jewels, it was made for Finrod Felagund by the dwarves.* Húrin* brought it out of Nargothrond* to King Thingol* in Doriath.* Thingol hired dwarves to refashion it, setting the Silmaril* in it that Beren* and Lúthien* had wrestled from Morgoth.*

Nazgûl

In *The Lord of the Rings*,‡ spirits of men enslaved to the Nine Rings,* and chief servants of Sauron.* The men – three of them from Númenor* – had been given the Rings by Sauron in the Second Age.* In the Third Age,* the chief of the Nazgûl was the Witch-king. The eight others prepared Mordor* for Sauron. The Nazgûl were also the Black Riders, sent to the Shire* by the Dark Lord. After the destruction of their black horses at the Ford of Bruinen, they later appeared mounted on large flying beasts. The chief of the Nazgûl was killed by Merry* and Éowyn* during the battle before Minas Tirith,* and the others disintegrated when the Ring was destroyed at Mount Doom.*

Nienor

In *The Silmarillion*,‡ the tragic sister of Túrin.* After a spell is cast upon her by Glaurung the dragon† she loses her memory. Not knowing she is his sister, Túrin marries her, after naming her Níniel. These 'twists of fate' are fashioned by the malice of Sauron* against Húrin,* their father.

Nimloth

The White Tree of Númenor,* from which a fruit is secretly taken by Isildur* before the tree† is wickedly cut down. The fruit is carried to Middle-earth,* and hence the line of the tree is preserved in Gondor.* Nimloth itself was a seedling of the white tree, Celeborn.*

Nine Rings

The Rings of Power† given to humans after being made by the Noldorin* smiths of Eregion.* With the forging of the One Ring,* Sauron* controlled these Rings, enslaving their bearers, who became the Nazgûl.*

Níniel

The name given to Nienor* by Túrin,* unaware that she was his sister.

Nogrod

In *The Silmarillion*,‡ the name of one of two cities of the dwarves* in the Blue Mountains, east of Beleriand.*

Noldor

Elves,* the second group of the Eldar* on the westward journey from Cuiviénen,* led by Finwe. They had a thirst for knowledge, and great skill in craftsmanship – symbolizing high culture (*see* Elven quality†). Noldor means 'knowledgeable'. To the Noldor belonged the family of Fëanor,* who became caught in the Doom of Mandos.* Fëanor's creation of the Silmarils* ranked with the work of the Valar.* Galadriel* also belonged to the Noldor.

Númenor

In *The Silmarillion*,‡ a great island in the middle of the sea of Belegaer.* It lay between Aman* and Middle-earth.* Númenor, shaped like a star, was given as a home to the Edain* by the Valar* at the end of the First Age.* The gift was given as a reward for their faithfulness and courage in the wars against Morgoth.* It is equivalent to Atlantis.

In his *Letters*, Tolkien vividly explained to a publisher how Númenor was the setting for a prohibition and a fall.†

The Númenoreans dwell within sight of the easternmost 'immortal' land, Eressea . . . but they remained mortal, even though rewarded by a triple, or more than a triple, span of years. Their reward is their undoing – or the means of their temptation. Their long life aids their achievements in art and wisdom, but breeds a possessive attitude to these things, and desire awakes for more time for their enjoyment. Foreseeing this in part, the gods [Valar] laid a Ban on the Númenoreans from the beginning . . . They must not set foot on 'immortal' lands . . . (letter 131)

When the ban is broken, the Valar lay down their delegated powers over the world and call directly to God† (Ilúvatar*), who allows them to destroy Númenor and change the shape of the world. Only a faithful remnant escape to Middle-earth.

Oath of Fëanor

The Silmarillion‡ recounts the revolt of the Noldor* against the wishes of the guardian Valar* in the First Age.* This began with the far-reaching oath taken by Fëanor* and his sons. They swore everlasting darkness on themselves if they failed to hound anyone who stole or kept a Silmaril* from them. The Doom of Mandos* was a direct consequence of the oath, and many of the tragic† events in Middle-earth* were shaped by this oath. The effects of the oath embody Tolkien's characteristic theme of the fall.† Part of the meaning of the history of the First Age is the outworking of the oath in events.

Old Forest

In The Lord of the Rings,‡ a remnant of a great forest which had once covered most of Eriador.* It lay to the east of the Shire,* between Buckland* and the Barrow-downs. At the heart of the forest was the malevolent figure of Old Man Willow. The

Withywindle flowed through the forest. Tom Bombadil* had great power over the forest, and poems about him are set in the old forest and nearby (*see The Adventures of Tom Bombadil‡*).

Frodo* and his companions journey through the forest after leaving the Shire.

Olorin
See Gandalf.*

One Ring
Also called the Great Ring, or Ruling Ring. This is the Ring treacherously made by Sauron* to control the other Rings: the Three, the Seven and the Nine. The Three Rings* of the elves* were, however, kept from his power, and he was unable to control the Seven Rings* of the dwarves.* The story of the Ring shapes the events chronicled in *The Lord of the Rings*.‡ After the original downfall of Sauron at the end of the Second Age,* Isildur* took possession of the Ring but lost it in the River Anduin.* There it lay for centuries, until possessed, after a murder, by Gollum.* He bore it for centuries until Bilbo Baggins* stumbled into his part of the underground caverns north in the Misty Mountains,* as told in *The Hobbit*.‡ *The Lord of the Rings* records how Bilbo reluctantly dispossessed himself of the Ring, passing it to Frodo.* Frodo took on the task of the Ring's destruction in the very heart of Mordor,* the only way its power of evil† could be stopped for ever.
See Rings of Power.†

Orcs
A race bred by Morgoth* purposely for his evil,† and hence having no moral choice. Because Morgoth was incapable of creating life, it seems that he made use of captured elves* that he had tortured for this genetic engineering. Orcs had different names in various languages; hobbits* called them goblins. Morgoth made use of orcs

in his attempts to dominate and suppress Beleriand.* After his downfall, and the destruction of Beleriand, orcs survived in other parts of Middle-earth.* In the Second* and Third Ages,* Sauron* used them in his service. The conception of the orcs in *The Hobbit*,‡ a children's book, is reminiscent of George MacDonald's‡ goblins (as in *The Princess and the Goblin*). The orcs of *The Silmarillion*‡ and *The Lord of the Rings*‡ are darker and crueller. As the elves symbolize what is high and noble in human life, the orcs represent what is base, twisted, insensitive and cruel.

It is beyond the scope of this book to outline a sociology of orcs, but there were various types and tribes. Not all orcs were loyal to Sauron; some served Saruman.*

Further reading
David Day, *A Tolkien Bestiary* (1979).

Orodreth

Elven-king of Nargothrond* after the death of his brother, Finrod Felagund. His daughter, Finduilas,* fell in love with the mortal Túrin.*

Oromë

In *The Silmarillion*,‡ one of the Valar,* the great hunter who discovered the awakened elves* and led them westwards on their Great Journey† from Cuiviénen.*

Orthanc

The stronghold built by men of Númenor* in the Circle of Isengard,* and possessed by Saruman.* It was built of four forked pillars of unbreakable black stone. Orthanc towered 500 feet above the surrounding plain.

Ossiriand

In *The Silmarillion*,‡ an area of east Beleriand* the name of which means 'Land of Seven Rivers', after its seven rivers (Gelion and its tributaries). Its many woods included elms. Beren* and Lúthien* lived here after their return from the dead. In later Ages* the region was known as Lindon.

Overlithe
In the Shire* Reckoning this was leap-day, occurring every fourth year with the exception of the last in the century. It was a special holiday, and occurred after Mid-Year's Day.

Palantíri
These were eight crystal globes, through which could be seen events and places far off in time and space. In conjunction, the stones could therefore be used for communication. These seeing-stones were made by the Noldor* in Aman.* Like the Silmarils* and the Rings,* the Palantíri have great symbolic power in the tales of Middle-earth* (*see* Symbolism†). The master-stone was kept in Tol Eressëa.* The seven remaining stones were brought to Middle-earth at the fall of Númenor,* and located at various places. One stone, in the Tower Hills, west of the Shire,* was guarded by the Eldar.* Unlike the others, it looked only to Aman, and served as a reminder to the elves* of the Undying Lands. Sauron* gained pos-session of a palantir when Osgiliath was captured by his forces. When both Saruman* and Denethor* made use of other Palantíri, Sauron twisted their wills and distorted their visions gained through it. The stone from Orthanc,* used by Saruman, was recovered after Wormtongue* threw it out of the tower. By this stone, Aragorn,* its rightful user, was able to gain intelligence of the movements of Sauron's forces. In later years Aragorn as king used it to aid his reign.

Pelennor
A fertile fenced land in Gondor* surrounding Minas Tirith.* Here the Battle of Pelennor Fields was fought during the War of the Ring.*

Peregrin ('Pippin') Took

In *The Lord of the Rings*,‡ he is one of the Company of the Ring,*
a hobbit* of the Shire.* Pippin was a boyhood friend of Frodo
Baggins* in Buckland.* During the War of the Ring* he entered into
the service of Denethor,* and saved Faramir* from his madness.

Phial of Galadriel

A jar of crystal given as a gift to Frodo* by the Lady Galadriel*
during his quest† to destroy the One Ring.* The jar contained the
light†† of Eärendil* captured in the Mirror of Galadriel. Because
of its source, light from the phial brought hope and courage to a
bearer who had faith. With the phial, Frodo resisted the attraction
of the Ring, and Sam* was able to confront the terror of Shelob.*
The phial has a sacramental value in the tale of *The Lord of the
Rings*‡ (*see* Christianity, Tolkien and†).

The Prancing Pony

In *The Lord of the Rings*,‡ the inn at Bree* at which Frodo* and his
friends stayed on their way to Rivendell.* It was run by Barliman
Butterbar, the scatter-brained friend of Gandalf.*

Quenya

A major form of Elvish* used in Aman,* probably close to the
original language taught by the Valar.* Quenya shared its ancestry
with Sindarin* Elvish. Both diverged in grammar, vocabulary and
sound, but Quenya was less dynamic, not being exposed to the
same extent of geographical and historical influences. Quenya owes
its inspiration to Tolkien's love of Finnish. An example revealing
the great beauty of Quenya is the song, *Namarie*, set to music by
Donald Swann (*see The Road Goes Ever On*‡). Tolkien's use of
Quenya throughout his stories of Middle-earth* in names, quota-
tions, and fragments of song, help to give a numinous† quality
that achieves great beauty.

Radagast

One of the wizards,† and called Radagast the Brown. His responsibilities included the welfare of animals. He was particularly friendly with birds. He lived in the Anduin* region, near Mirkwood.*

Rangers of the North

The name given to the Dúnedain* of the north, of the lost kingdom of Arnor,* who guarded the Shire* and the larger region of Eriador.* They were led by the Chieftains of the Dúnedain,* heirs of Isildur.* In the time of *The Lord of the Rings*,‡ this was Aragorn.*

The Red Book of Westmarch

This book was so named because of its red leather covers, and because it was preserved in the Shire* in Westmarch, after the War of the Ring.* It was written in by Bilbo* and Frodo* Baggins, and Sam Gamgee,* as well as others. Its subject was the events recorded in *The Hobbit*‡ and *The Lord of the Rings*,‡ and was Tolkien's supposed source.

With the Red Book were the three volumes of translations from the Elvish,* by Bilbo, the supposed source of *The Silmarillion*.‡ Many copies of the Red Book, and presumably, the translations, were made.

Ring

See Rings of Power.†

Ring of Barahir

An elven-ring given by King Finrod Felagund to Barahir, father of Beren,* in gratitude. It was a pledge of help in time of need, taken up by Beren, who bore the ring after his father's death.

The ring was treasured and passed on through the Ages, until it became one of the heirlooms of the north-kingdom, inherited by Aragorn.*

Rivendell

An elven dwelling, remnant of the great, protected elven kingdoms of Nargothrond* and Doriath* in the First Age* of Middle-earth.* It was founded in the Second Age* by Elrond* in the foothills of the Misty Mountains,* in a hidden, deep-cloven valley. Rivendell lay between the rivers Hoarwell and Loudwater. Its Elvish* name was Imladris. In *The Hobbit*,‡ Rivendell is described as 'The Last Homely House East of the Sea', a place of refuge for any of the faithful, not just elves.* Bilbo* spent many years here translating the Elvish tales of *The Silmarillion.*‡

The Hobbit tries to capture the special essence of Elrond's Rivendell: 'His house was perfect, whether you liked food, or sleep, or work, or storytelling, or singing, or just sitting and thinking best, or a pleasant mixture of them all. Evil things did not come into that valley' (Chapter III).

Roäc

The chief of the friendly ravens of Erebor,* like the eagles,† agents of providence.† Roäc informed Thorin* of the death of Smaug.*

Rohan

Kingdom of the horsemen – the Rohirrim – in southern Middle-earth.* Its people raised horses on the country's large plains. The capital was Edoras,* below ancient Dunharrow. Rohan was originally a province of Gondor,* and traditionally had close links with it. At the time of the events recorded in *The Lord of the Rings*,‡ Théoden* was king of Rohan.

Rohirric

In *The Lord of the Rings*,‡ the language used by the people of Rohan.* It is related to the languages belonging to the men of the Anduin* region. Like Westron* Rohirric was descended from Adûnaic,* and in fact is an archaic form of Westron. There were similarities with the dialect of Westron used in the Shire* by hobbits.* In representing Rohirric in English translation, it was natural for Tolkien to draw on Old English or archaic English.

Rosie Gamgee (née Cotton)

Rose, from the Shire,* married Sam Gamgee* in *The Lord of the Rings*.‡ Tolkien was enjoying a joke here, as 'Gamgee' in the West Midlands of his childhood was a household term for cotton wool, after a certain Dr Gamgee from Birmingham‡ who had invented 'gamgee-tissue', a surgical dressing made from cotton wool.

Rosie and Sam had 13 children, including Elanor* the Fair.

Rúmil

In the First Age* of Middle-earth,* a wise scholar of Tirion* who, it is said, wrote the 'Ainulindalë'.‡ He also invented the first writing system. He plays an important part in the earliest versions of *The Silmarillion*.‡

Runes

An alphabet, the 'cirith' was first created in Beleriand* for inscriptions, and brief memorials on stone or wood. This purpose explains its angular shapes. It was later characteristically adopted and modified by dwarves,* and was particularly associated with Moria.* Tolkien drew upon the runes of ancient North Germanic tribes. Their use may have been associated with magical powers.* Runes may date back to the second century BC or later. The earliest remaining runic inscriptions come from Denmark and Schleswig, and belong between the third and sixth century AD. Later runes have been found in Norway and Sweden, and there are also a number of Anglo-Saxon runic inscriptions.

Saruman

One of the wizards† sent to Middle-earth* to aid the faithful resisting Sauron.* He was originally the chief of the Order, until

desire for possession† of the One Ring* brought about his downfall. Centuries before the events recorded in *The Lord of the Rings*,‡
he had taken over the ancient stronghold of Isengard.* Among
his many evils was his misleading of the White Council,* his
employment of orcs,* his manipulation of King Théoden* of
Rohan,* and his control of the Shire.* He brought about his own
destruction by trying to capture Frodo,* the Ring-bearer, with an
orc band. They captured only Merry* and Pippin,* who escaped
into Fangorn Forest* and won the help of Treebeard* and his
Ents.*

Sauron

The greatest of Morgoth's* servants, his deeds encompass three
Ages of Middle-earth,* until his final downfall with the War of the
Rings.* In origin he is one of the Maiar,* the lesser Ainur,* the
same order of being as Gandalf.*

He appears in the tale of Beren* and Lúthien,* figures strongly
in the Fall† of Númenor,* creates the One Ring* to rule the Rings
of Power.† He lost the Ring to the ill-fated Isildur,* but, by near
the end of the Third Age,* has consolidated his power enough to
attempt to dominate Middle-earth, as his master, Morgoth, had
attempted long before to enslave Beleriand.*

Sauron is a more subtle image of incarnate evil† than Morgoth.
Before being caught in the destruction of Númenor, he was able
to assume a fair appearance, helping him to win over the minds
of elves* and humans. Sauron is particularly associated with a lust
for power and possession.† He very nearly succeeded in seducing
the elves of Eregion* to the 'magic' of technocracy – what Tolkien
called 'machinery'. In a letter, Tolkien remarked: 'At Eregion great
work began and the Elves came their nearest to falling to "magic"
and machinery.'

Sea elves
See Teleri.*

Second Age

In the history of Middle-earth,* this is the period of Númenor* and the exile of elves* to Tol Eressëa* from the devastation of Beleriand.* Here they built Avallónë, and planted Celeborn,* a seedling of Galathilion. Tolkien describes it as a dark age of the world.

The themes of the Second Age, according to Tolkien, are:

1 The delaying elves who lingered in Middle-earth;
2 Sauron's* growth into a new Dark Lord, master and god of humankind, replacing the banished Morgoth;*
3 The civilization of Númenor (Atlantis).

The period is mainly dealt with annalistically or historically, as in the Akallabêth,* published in *The Silmarillion*.‡ There are very few tales, none comparing with stories like *The Tale of Beren and Lúthien*, the elf-maiden.‡

In *Unfinished Tales*‡ is an incomplete tale, 'Aldarion and Erendis: The Mariner's Wife', as well as a description of the island of Númenor. Had Tolkien persisted with *The Lost Road* or 'The Notion Club Papers'‡ many tales might have opened up.

Second music of Ilúvatar

This is the theme which is to be sung after the end of the world by the Ainur* and humankind. The Valar* do not know what this music will be, or what role will be played by elves* and dwarves.* *See also* Apocalyptic, Tolkien and.‡

Seven Rings

The Rings of Power† of the dwarves,* referred to in the rhyme on the One Ring,* revealed in *The Lord of the Rings*.‡ They had metal bands, set with single gems.

Shadowfax

An untamed silver grey horse of King Theoden's* chosen by Gandalf* to carry him through many adventures and over vast distances. He was the most princely horse of Rohan,* and notable for his stamina. Gandalf rode him without saddle or bridle. When the wizard passed westwards over the sea, after the destruction of the Ring,† Shadowfax accompanied him.

Shelob

A monstrous spider, possibly bred by Ungoliant* in Nan Dungortheb* in the First Age.* She escaped the destruction of Beleriand* and made her way south. Making a den in Cirith Ungol,* she preyed on humans, elves* and orcs,* providing a guard for that route into Mordor.* Gollum* treacherously led Frodo* and Sam* into her lair, but Shelob was blinded by the courageous Sam.

The Shire

A region of Eriador* in Middle-earth,* the home of hobbits,* settled in the Third Age.* Hobbits lived comfortably in its four Farthings. Its chief town was Michel Delving.* Bilbo Baggins* lived in Bag End, Hobbiton,* where he was joined by Frodo* when Bilbo adopted him after the adventures chronicled in *The Hobbit*.‡ Frodo had grown up in Buckland.*

Tolkien was attached to the West Midlands, and tried to convey the quality of life in turn-of-the-century Worcestershire and Warwickshire in his creation of the Shire.

See also Sarehole Mill;‡ Chapter 5: How *The Lord of the Rings* Relates to *The Silmarillion*.

Silmarils

The beautiful gems forged by Fëanor* which captured the holy light† of the Two Trees,* and which gave their name to *The Silmarillion*,‡ for which they provided the unifying motif. (*See* Chapter 5: How *The Lord of the Rings* Relates to *The Silmarillion*.)

Silvan elves

These were elves* other than the Eldar,* who were not enriched by the westward journey† to Aman.* They lived in forests or mountains. At the time of the events of *The Hobbit*‡ and *The Lord of the Rings*‡ they lived in places such as the Woodland Realm (whence came Legolas*) or Lórien* which were ruled by Eldar such as Galadriel* and Celeborn,* or Thranduil.* They were also known as the wood-elves, or the woodland elves.

Sindar

These, also called Grey-elves, lived in Beleriand,* and did not complete the Great Journey to the uttermost West. Their chief habitation was the kingdom of Doriath,* ruled by Thingol* and Melian.* They spoke a major variant of Elvish,* Sindarin.*

Sindarin

A major form of Elvish* used by Sindarin or Grey-elves. It had a common ancestry with Quenya* Elvish, but both diverged in grammar, vocabulary and sound. Sindarin owes its inspiration to Tolkien's love of Welsh, which it structurally resembles. The changes in Elvish which resulted in Sindarin are accounted for in terms of geography and history by Tolkien. The main factor was that the Sindarin elves remained in Beleriand* rather than completing the Great Journey to Aman.* Historically, Fëanor's* rebellion against the Valar,* and the kinslaying,* alienated Thingol* of Doriath* from the Quenya-speaking elves of Valinor.* Sindarin enriched the mannish language which became Westron.*

Further reading

Jim Allan, *An Introduction to Elvish* (1978).
Ruth S. Noel, *The Languages of Tolkien's Middle-earth* (1980).

Sirion

The major river of Beleriand* in *The Silmarillion*.‡ Its name means 'River' in Sindarin* Elvish.* The Sirion's main tributaries were the Teiglin, Esgalduin, Aros, and Narog.

Smaug

A winged dragon† who appears in *The Hobbit*.‡ Smaug hoarded treasure stolen from the dwarves* and the people of Dale,* including the Arkenstone.* Bilbo Baggins* is indirectly responsible for his death, by discovering the weak point in his scaly armour.

Spiders

See Shelob;* Ungoliant.*

Stewards

In the absence of kings to reign, stewards ruled Gondor. Originally they were stewards to the king. At the time of the War of the Ring* Denethor* ruled. When Aragorn* returned to rule as King Elessar, Faramir,* the heir of Denethor, became his steward.

Stoors

One of three varieties of hobbit,* the one that stayed longest in the Anduin* region before crossing the Misty Mountains.* At the time of the events of *The Lord of the Rings*,‡ stoors were to be found in the Marish and Buckland.* They liked flat lands and riversides and were the only hobbits to enjoy watery pursuits such as swimming, boating and fishing.

Straight Road

Also called the Lost Road. Even before the changing of the world, it was difficult to sail from Middle-earth* to Aman,* the Uttermost West. After the change, when the world became a sphere, and the seas bent, some elven ships were allowed to pass beyond the world to the undying lands. They used the straight road. Tolkien employed the idea of a lost road in early formulations of his mythology,† involving the voyage of the mariner Aelfwine* to Tol Eressëa,* where he hears the tales of the First Age.*
See also The Lost Road and Other Writings.‡

Strider

See Aragorn.*

Taniquetil

In *The Silmarillion*,‡ the highest mountain in the world, located in Aman* on the borders of the sea. The Valar* Manwë* and Varda* have their halls on its summit. Some of the elves* – some of the Vanyar* – live on its slopes.

Tar-

A prefix added to names to denote kings, and queens who ruled, and who took Quenya* names, in Númenor* in the Second Age* of Middle-earth.*

Taur-nu-Fuin

The name given to the forested region of Dorthonian* after Morgoth* brought evil and terror to it. Beren,* and his father Barahir, were among the last of men to remain here. Beleg found Gwindor here, resulting in Túrin's* rescue from the orcs.* Taur-nu-Fuin in some ways resembled Mirkwood.*

Teleri

In *The Silmarillion*,‡ the third and largest group of elves* known as the Eldar.* In Quenya* Elvish* 'teleri' means 'last' or 'hindmost'. They trailed behind during the Great Journey† to the uttermost West, Aman,* and only reluctantly left the shores of Middle-earth.* The Teleri had a great love of the sea, and eventually settled in the beautiful city of Alqualondë. Fëanor* turned against them for refusing to help him in his rebellion against the wishes of the Valar,* and the dreadful kinslaying* took place.

The Teleri were taught the art of ship-building by the Vala, Osse.

Telperion

One of the Two Trees of Valinor,* known also as the White Tree.

The upper surfaces of his leaves were dark green, and the lower were shimmering silver. Varda* made the stars from Telperion's dews, and the moon from his final flower.

Thangorodrim

In *The Silmarillion*,‡ a great mountain with three peaks made by Morgoth* above Angband.* He made the mountain out of the slag from his mines. Like Mount Doom, it was a volcano, its smoke visible from a large distance. The mountain was destroyed when the dragon,† Ancalagon,* fell upon it. Húrin,* father of Túrin,* was set high on the slopes of Thangorodrim by Morgoth for 28 years, so that he could see the outworkings of Morgoth's curse against him on his family.

Théoden

In *The Lord of the Rings*,‡ the seventeenth king of Rohan.* He had been deceived by Saruman* for many years through his counsellor, Grima (Wormtongue*). The spell was broken by, and Théoden found healing† through, Gandalf.* Théoden then joined his forces with Gondor* against Sauron.* He was killed by the Lord of the Nazgûl* in the Battle of Pelennor Fields (*see* War of the Ring*).

Thingol

The popular name (Sindarin* elvish,* 'grey cloak') given to Elwë, a great elven lord who married the Maia* Melian.* King Thingol was the father of Lúthien,* who from Melian had angelic blood in her elven frame, accounting for her remarkable grace and beauty.

Third Age

This Age of Middle-earth* was reckoned from the first defeat of Sauron,* when Gil-galad* died, to the War of the Ring,* when Sauron was defeated for a second and seemingly final time. At the end of the Age the Ring-bearers and the greatest of the elves* passed over the sea to the uttermost West. The period was called by elves the Fading Years, as it marked the end of their dominance, and the beginning of the dominance of humankind. Much of the history of the Age concerns the mannish kingdoms of Arnor* and Gondor* and, unexpectedly, the Shire* of the hobbits,* distant relations of humans.

Third House of the Edain

In *The Silmarillion*,‡ the last and probably the largest group of the Edain* to enter Beleriand.* Eventually, they consolidated under Hador* in Dor-Lómin.* They were renowned for their courage in resisting Morgoth,* and heroes† such as Túrin,* Tuor* and Eärendil* belonged to the Third House. In Dor-Lómin both Sindarin* and an early form of Adûnaic* were spoken.

Thorin Oakenshield

In *The Hobbit*,‡ the dwarf* king who led the party, Thorin and Company,* to recover the treasure hoarded by Smaug,* the dragon.† He grew to respect the hobbit,* Bilbo Baggins.* The king died in the Battle of the Five Armies. He was called Oakenshield because, in his youth, he had fought bravely in the Battle of Azanulbizar, the greatest battle between dwarves and orcs,* and had used an oak-branch as a shield and club.

Thorin and Company

The Company, in *The Hobbit*,‡ led by Thorin Oakenshield* to recover treasure from Smaug,* the dragon† in Erebor.* Bilbo Baggins* was employed as their burglar. The remainder of the Company were dwarves*: Thorin, Balin, Dwalin, Fili, Kíli,* Dori, Ori, Nori, Oin, Gloin, Bifur, Bofur, and Bombur. Gandalf* was with them for some of their journey.†

Thorondor

In *The Silmarillion*‡ the lord of the eagles† helping to protect elves* and humans. Part of his role was the guarding of Gondolin.*

Among his many great deeds was the rescue of Beren* and Lúthien* as they fled from Morgoth* after stealing back a Silmaril.*

Thráin II

A dwarf* king captured by Sauron* and imprisoned in Dol Guldur.* One of the seven Rings* was extracted from him after long torture. Gandalf* found him before he died, and the king gave him the key to the Side-door of Erebor,* under the Lonely Mountain.* This key allowed Thorin and Company* access to Smaug's* hoard in *The Hobbit*.‡

Thranduil

In *The Hobbit*,‡ the elven-king of the Woodland Realm. He captured Thorin Oakenshield* and his dwarves,* but Bilbo* rescued them. In the Battle of the Five Armies he led the elven army. He also fought in the War of the Ring* against Sauron's* forces. Legolas,* of the Company of the Ring,* was his son.

Three Rings

These were the Rings of Power† belonging to the elves.* Though they were made without Sauron's* help, they could be controlled by the One Ring.* When the Ring was destroyed, they lost their power.

Unlike the other rings, their power did not lie in control and domination. Rather, their power lay in building, understanding and healing.† The Three Rings were called Vilya, Nenya and Narya.* Nenya was worn by Galadriel,* and Narya by Gandalf.*

Thrimidge

In the Reckoning of the Shire* this was the fifth month, approximating our May.

Tinúviel

Sindarin* Elvish* for 'twilight-maiden', a poetic name for the nightingale. Beren* gave Lúthien* this name when he first heard her singing in Doriath.*

Tirion

In *The Silmarillion*,‡ the first habitation of elves* in Eldamar, and its main city. It was built on the hill of Túna,* having white walls and crystal stairs. It was set in the great ravine in the great mountains of the Pelori, through which passed the light of the Two Trees.*

Tol Eressëa

In *The Silmarillion*,‡ a large island in the Bay of Eldamar, off Valinor.* Its western shore received the light of the Two Trees.* The Teleri* lived here for a long time. At the end of the First Age* many elves* settled on the island, building Avallónë. In the Second Age* there was communion between the elves of Tol Eressëa and the people of Númenor.*

Tol Sirion

In *The Silmarillion*,‡ a beautiful green island of the River Sirion,* where the river flows through the Pass of Sirion. Finrod Felagund built a fortress here which was eventually captured by Sauron,* and renamed Tol-in-Gaurhoth. When Finrod and Beren* were imprisoned here, Finrod was murdered by Sauron's wolf. Lúthien* cast out Sauron and broke the tower.

Tower of Amon Sul

See Weathertop.*

Trolls

A variety of troll, the Stone-troll, figures dramatically in *The Hobbit*.‡ There seem to have been four types in all, each large and wicked. Trolls originated in the First Age,* bred by Morgoth,* perhaps based on Ents,* just as orcs* were debased elves.*

Tulkas

One of the Valar,* noted for his strength. He valiantly opposed Morgoth* (Melkor).

Túna

In *The Silmarillion*,‡ the high green hill in the ravine through the high mountains of the Pelori in Aman.* The beautiful city of Tirion* was built on it.

Tuor

The Silmarillion‡ records that the man, Tuor, was fostered by the Grey-elves* of Mithrim. He was given a message by the Vala* Ulmo* for the hidden kingdom of Gondolin.* There he married the elf-maiden, Idril.* With her, and their son Eärendil,* he escaped the fall of Gondolin.*

Túrin Turambar

His is one of the central stories of *The Silmarillion*‡ (*see* Chapter 5: How *The Lord of the Rings* Relates to *The Silmarillion*). He was a dragon-slayer and tragic hero† of the First Age* of Middle-earth* (*see* Tragedy†). Tolkien never completed his plans for telling the story of Túrin, but unfinished versions exist in poetry and prose.

Further reading

J.R.R. Tolkien:
The Book of Lost Tales, 2, chapter II.
The Lays of Beleriand, chapter I.
The Shaping of Middle-earth, 'The Quenta', sections 12–13.
The Silmarillion, chapter 21.
Unfinished Tales, Part One, chapter II.

Turgon

In *The Silmarillion*‡ the king of the hidden kingdom of Gondolin.* Though he opposed Fëanor's* plan to pursue Morgoth* when he stole the Silmarils,* Turgon became one of the exiles from Aman.* When in Middle-earth* he settled at Vinyamar, but was led to the site where he founded Gondolin. Though a wise leader, Turgon ignored the warning sent by Ulmo* through Tuor,* leading to the downfall of Gondolin. Turgon was the father of Idril* and grand-father of Eärendil.*

The Two Trees

In *The Silmarillion*,‡ the two trees of Valinor,* Telperion* and Laurelin,* one white and one golden. They lit up the world, and their glory was such that the sun and moon were made out of their dying light.

See also Light;† Tree.†

Ulmo

In *The Silmarillion*,‡ one of the Valar,* called Lord of Waters and King of the Sea. In him, providential† care for elves* and humans is often revealed, by dreams, appearances and the very music† of the waters of Middle-earth.* This is particularly so with Turgon,* but also with Tuor,* Elwing,* and others.

Umbar

In Middle-earth,* a coastal area in Harad that contained a natural harbour. It changed hands many times. At the time of *The Lord of the Rings*‡ Umbar was in the hands of enemy Corsairs, but in the Fourth Age* came under the control of Gondor* once again.

Ungoliant

In *The Silmarillion*,‡ the monstrous spider who, with Morgoth* (Melkor), destroyed the Two Trees* of Valinor.* *The Lord of the Rings*‡ records that, Ages later, Shelob* was 'the last child of Ungoliant to trouble the unhappy world'. Ungoliant may have been one of the fallen Maiar.*

Uruk-hai

In *The Lord of the Rings*,‡ a stronger kind of orc* bred by Sauron,* and used both by him and by the traitor Saruman.*

Utumno

In *The Silmarillion*,‡ Morgoth's* first great stronghold in the icy north of Middle-earth,* and destroyed by the power of the Valar.*

Vairë

In *The Silmarillion*,‡ one of the Valar.* She was known as 'the Weaver', because she wove the tapestries that adorned the walls of the halls of Mandos,* her husband. The tapestries told the story of all the events in the creation of Ilúvatar.*

Valacirca

In Middle-earth,* the name of the constellation of the Great Bear, 'The Sickle of the Valar'. The seven stars were shaped by Varda* to prepare for the awakening of the elves* and as a challenge to Morgoth* (Melkor), foreboding his end.

Valar

In *The Silmarillion*,‡ the powers, or 'those with power', who entered the world (Eä*) at the beginning of creation, and thus time. They are angelic† beings, or Ainur,* demiurgic agents of Ilúvatar* (God†). They function as guardians and governors of the world (both the world of nature† and of elves† and humankind). The Valar have some similarity with gods in mythologies† such as those of the north, yet are unique as a mythology in being created and derived rather than divine creators. (For the reasons for Tolkien's theology, *see* Christianity, Tolkien and†.) The Valar take on human or elvish appearance, like a person dressing rather than an incarnation. One of the Valar, Melkor, fell into evil, becoming known as Morgoth.*

Some of the Valar were given titles in Middle-earth*:

Manwë*	–	Lord of the Air
Yavanna*	–	The Giver of Fruits
Tulkas*	–	The Valiant
Aulë*	–	The Master of Crafts
Varda*	–	Queen of the Stars (Elbereth*)
Mandos* (Namo)	–	Keeper of the Houses of the Dead
Vairë*	–	The Weaver
Oromë*	–	Lord of Trees†
Ulmo*	–	Lord of Waters
Vána*	–	The Ever-Young

Valimar

Also known as Valmar. In *The Silmarillion*,‡ the city of the Valar* in Valinor.* It can also be used to refer to Valinor as a whole.

Valinor

In *The Silmarillion*,‡ the land of the Valar* in Aman,* westwards beyond the great mountains of the Pelori.

Vána

In *The Silmarillion*,‡ one of the Valar,* sister of Yavanna* and wife of Oromë.* She was known as the Ever-Young, caring for birds and flowers, and having gardens with golden flowers in Valinor.*

Vanyar

The foremost group of elves* on the westward journey† from Cuiviénen,* in *The Silmarillion*.‡

Varda

The most beloved of the Valar* in Middle-earth,* and wife of Manwë.* Also known as Elbereth,* and Snow-white, she kindled the stars, and dwelt with Manwë on Mount Taniquetil (see Taniquetil*). Varda was particularly concerned with light,† setting the star

Eärendil* in the sky, and aiding Sam* in Shelob's* lair with the Phial of Galadriel.*

Vingilot

In *The Silmarillion*,‡ the name of the ship of Eärendil,* meaning 'Foam-flower' in Quenya* Elvish.*

Voronwë

An elf* of Gondolin* in *The Silmarillion*.‡ He was the only survivor from a ship sent into the west for help, and saved by Ulmo* to help Tuor* find Gondolin. His name means 'The Steadfast' in Quenya* Elvish.*

War of the Ring

The great battle between the forces of Sauron* and those of the faithful at the end of the Third Age* of Middle-earth,* as chronicled in *The Lord of the Rings*.‡ The battle was won by the heroism (*see* Hero†) of Frodo Baggins* and Sam Gamgee,* who slipped into Mordor* under the dreadful eye of Sauron* and destroyed the Ring. Key battles in the war included those at Helm's Deep and at the Pelennor Fields by Minas Tirith.*

Wars

See Battles of Beleriand*; War of the Ring.*

Weathertop

The edge of the Weather Hills closest to The Great East Road leading from Bree* to Rivendell.* Here Frodo and the other hobbits encountered the ruins of the ancient watchtower of Amon Sûl, and found recent traces of Gandalf.*

Westron

In Tolkien's mythology† of Middle-earth,* the language of humankind which, in Númenor,* was called Adûnaic.* It goes back to the ancient world, before human beings migrated to the land north of Middle-earth, Beleriand,* which sank beneath the waves at the end of the First Age.*

Originally, humans learnt much of Elvish* from the Dark Elves* who stayed behind east of the Misty Mountains* when others emigrated west to Valinor.* This deeply influenced the development of their language. Then many tribes moved to Beleriand, and there elves and humans had much to do with each other. To this period belongs the story of Beren* and Lúthien,* and the tragedy of Túrin Turambar.* At the end of the First Age, the island of Númenor was given to humankind – at least, the Dúnedain* – to live, and Westron continued to develop. The Númenoreans were great mariners and colonizers, spreading their, at first, benign civilization, and Westron with it, as the language of trade and culture. They continued to use Elvish also, as a language of ceremony and tradition, in which the great cosmology and history of the elves and other peoples was recorded.

As Númenor became corrupt, attempts were made to suppress the use of Elvish, but the faithful continued to use it and remember the great Elvish mythology.† After the destruction of Númenor, the faithful remnant established Arnor* and Gondor* in the north and south of Middle-earth. Elendil* was their leader. The common speech they spoke was enriched with Elvish words, often calling themselves the names of Elvish and human heroes† from the First Age. As the use of Westron spread through Middle-earth, it increased in diversity.

Tolkien represents Westron with English in *The Lord of the Rings*,‡ varying his style to match some of its range and diversity. The speech of the hobbits* is represented quite differently from that of the noble people of Gondor, who were steeped in the traditions of elves and Númenor. He retains this device in *The Silmarillion*,‡ where the high Elvish style is represented by deliberate archaisms of syntax and vocabulary. He intends to suggest the Elvish source of *The Silmarillion*, and the hobbitish* writing of *The Hobbit*‡ and *The Lord of the Rings* (*see* The Red Book of Westmarch*).

White Council
In *The Lord of the Rings*‡ we learn of this Council of the wise. It was summoned by Elrond to plan a strategy in opposition to Sauron,* as his threat upon peace grew.

Winterfilth
In the Shire* Reckoning, the tenth month, equivalent to October. Its name refers to the filling or completing of the days before winter (from 'winter-fylleth').

Withywindle
A river encountered by Frodo* and his hobbit* companions as they made their perilous way through the Old Forest.* It rose in the Barrow Downs* and flowed through the forest on its way to join the Brandywine below Buckland.* It also features in *The Adventures of Tom Bombadil*.‡

Wormtongue
In *The Lord of the Rings*,‡ the nickname of King Théoden's* treacherous counsellor, Grima,* who was in league with Saruman* to control Théoden, and to pass on intelligence to the wizard.†

Woses
At the time of the events recorded in *The Lord of the Rings*,‡ these were primitive men living in Druadan Forest. They helped the Riders of Rohan* to move secretly through the Forest on their way to join the forces against Sauron.*

Yavanna
In *The Silmarillion*,‡ one of the Valar,* elder sister of Vána* and wife of Aulë.* Her name means 'giver of fruits'. Yavanna watched

over the flora of the world, and planted the first seeds of all plants. Her greatest work was the creation of the Two Trees.* Sometimes she appeared as a tree† reaching to the heavens.

Years of the Trees

In *The Silmarillion*,‡ before the rising of the sun and moon, time was measured according to the blooming of the Two Trees* in Valinor* (Aman*). Years were longer than solar years.

Yuledays

In the Shire* Reckoning, the first and last days of the year, belonging to no month.

Part Four

A Look Behind Tolkien's Life and Work

SEVEN

KEY THEMES, CONCEPTS AND IMAGES IN TOLKIEN

Allegory

An extended metaphor, or sustained personification. In literature, a figurative narrative or description which conveys a hidden meaning, often moral. Key examples in English literature are John Bunyan's *The Pilgrim's Progress* and Edmund Spenser's *Faerie Queene*. Tolkien's short story *Leaf by Niggle*‡ is an allegory.

When *The Lord of the Rings*‡ first appeared some interpreted the One Ring* as meaning the atomic bomb. Apart from the fact that the Ring was conceived before the bomb existed or was known about as a possibility, such an interpretation is wrong in treating the work as an allegory. Tolkien pointed out that such an interpretation confused meaning with applicability. In his Foreword, he writes:

> I much prefer history, true or feigned, with its varied applica-
> bility to the thought and experience of readers. I think that
> many confuse 'applicability' with 'allegory'; but the one resides
> in the freedom of the reader, and the other in the purposed
> domination of the author.

Angels

As an orthodox Christian like C.S. Lewis‡ or John Bunyan, J.R.R. Tolkien believed in the literal existence of angels. They appear historically, for example, in the Gospels, at the annunciation of Christ. For imaginative force and freshness he, like Bunyan and Lewis, avoids the term, 'angel'. Whereas Bunyan, in *The Pilgrim's*

Progress, uses 'Shining Ones', and Lewis, in his *Cosmic Trilogy*, employs the terms, 'Oyarsa' and 'eldila', Tolkien writes of the Valar* and Maiar.* He wished to capture the imaginative vitality of the Old Norse or Olympian gods, yet to portray beings acceptable to someone who believes in 'The Blessed Trinity'. The Valar and Maiar represent the activity of God† (Ilúvatar*). Tolkien's is not a deistic world (*see* Natural theology, Tolkien and†).

The Valar and Maiar are partly modelled on biblical angels. The biblical angels are witnesses of creation, whereas the Valar participate in making the world (even though they are distinct creations of God themselves). The nearest biblical equivalent to the Valar is the personification of Wisdom in Proverbs 8. Like biblical angels (e.g. Abraham's visitors) the Maiar can take on human (or human-like) form, as with Gandalf,* Melian,* Sauron* in Númenor,* and Tom Bombadil.* The intermarriage of Melian and the elvish King Thingol echoes the marriages of 'Sons of God' and daughters of men in Genesis 6. The Valar also take on appearances at will (as Ulmo,* for example, appears to Tuor*).

As in the Bible, there are fallen angels: Sauron, Morgoth* or Melkor (equivalent to Lucifer), and the balrogs.* There seems no equivalent of ordinary demons. The orcs* don't seem to be capable of moral choice (being bred into evil by Morgoth, originally from captured elves*). Also like biblical angels, the Valar can be militant, as at the end of the First Age,* when Morgoth and his forces are overcome by their intervention.

In Tolkien, unlike in the Bible, the Valar are more like intermediaries between God (Ilúvatar) and the beings of Middle-earth.* They also have a demiurgic role in creation, like God in Plato's myth of *Timaeus*. It is interesting that C.S. Lewis, and the puritan, John Bunyan, do not have an intermediary role for angelic beings. God directly and personally communicates (as in Christ and Aslan, the creator-lion of Narnia) as well as using messengers and angelic interpreters. In Tolkien, angels have a subtle and pervasive role in providence,† working in and behind events. One of the functions of Gandalf the Maia is that of interpreting providential events.

Elves, who symbolically represent an aspect of humankind, have some angelic qualities. Their elvish quality† enters human life and history through example and intermarriage (such as the marriage of Beren* and the elf-maiden Lúthien*). Angels have made a number of appearances in contemporary fiction, as in C.S. Lewis' *The Screwtape Letters* and *The Cosmic Trilogy*, Harry Blamires' *Highway to Heaven*, and Frank Peretti's colourful *This Present Darkness*. Tolkien's famous forerunners include John Milton (*Paradise Lost*) and Dante (*The Divine Comedy*). They also include the unjustly neglected John Macgowan, and his *Infernal Conference*; or *Dialogues of the Devil*.

Tolkien seems to be inspired by momentous sections of the Bible that portray the unseen world behind human history, for instance, the scene in the heavenly court at the beginning of the book of Job, or the portrayal of Wisdom in Proverbs. In total, though *The Lord of the Rings* is a heroic romance, and the tales are the main interest of *The Silmarillion*‡ and accounts of the Second Age,* Tolkien's work on the Three Ages of Middle-earth may perhaps be seen as a modern apocalypse. Biblical apocalyptic is grounded in the Hebrew imagination. Tolkien, however, based his fictional overview of time and history on a northern European imagination.

See also Apocalypse, Tolkien and.†

Apocalypse, Tolkien and

The purpose of sub-creation,† according to Tolkien, is to 'survey the depths of space and time'. Whereas his friend C.S. Lewis‡ explored space in his science fiction, *The Cosmic Trilogy*, Tolkien surveyed time in his invented mythology† of Middle-earth.*

Tolkien's history of the Three Ages of Middle-earth might be seen as a modern apocalypse – an unveiling of hidden realities.

The biblical apocalyptic books and passages are grounded on a Hebrew imagination in a near Eastern setting. Tolkien is grounded in a northern European imagination. His purpose is fictional, rather than historical and prophetic.

Apocalyptic writing in the Bible provides hope and consolation† in hard times (a glimpse, for Tolkien, of the *evangelium*). 'Apocalyptics flourished in times of national crisis', according to a Bible dictionary. Tolkien, like his fellow Inklings,‡ saw the modern world as in crisis. This sense of crisis is vividly portrayed in C.S. Lewis' book, *The Abolition of Man*. The purpose of apocalypse is to reveal the hand of God in history. It can also be cosmological, revealing mysteries of the cosmos. Both these elements are true of Tolkien's writings (*see* Providence;† 'Ainulindalë'‡). Biblical apocalypse is concerned with the problem of evil† and suffering. Tolkien, too, in his writings, is intensely aware of evil.

In *Tolkien and the Silmarillion*, Clyde S. Kilby points out that

There is evidence that, had his story continued to its full and concluding end the ubiquitous evil of such as Morgoth and Sauron would have ceased. He intended a final glorious eventuality similar to the one described in the Book of Revelation with the true Telperion reappearing, the earth remade, the lands lying under the waves lifted up, the Silmarils recovered, Eärendil returned to earth, the Two Trees rekindled in their original light and life-giving power, and the mountains of the Pelori levelled so that the light should go out over all the earth – yes, and the dead be raised and the original purposes of Eru executed (pages 64–65).

Tolkien's apocalyptic element may be one of the reasons for his popularity, and why he seems so contemporary. There is strong evidence that western culture is now in deep crisis, and Tolkien has rediscovered or refreshed symbols that point to hope in this present darkness.

See also Death;† Angels.†

Christianity, Tolkien and

According to Paul Kocher, Tolkien was inspired and guided on his way by the mythology of Denmark, Germany, Norway, and especially Iceland (*see* Myth;† Imagination†). The Norse pantheon of gods was headed by Odin. This is particularly clear as embodied in the Icelandic Elder Edda and Younger Edda, and the Icelandic sagas. As a Christian, Tolkien rejected much of the Norse world outlook, but admired its imaginative power. Those elements that he could transform into Christian meaning, he kept. Of course, he rejected the idea of a polytheistic assembly of gods. Also, he rejected its concept of fate, which conditioned not only humans, but also the gods. Instead, he attempted to portray a biblical vision of providence.† This was a central theme of his fiction. Equally central was a passionate portrayal of free will, which also rejected fate. Although Norse-Icelandic mythology has a void or chaos at the beginning of creation, this is not the biblical creation out of nothing, *ex nihilo*, to which Tolkien was committed. So there is a sharp distinction here between Tolkien's invented mythology and that of the Old Norse peoples.

Paul Kocher points out that Tolkien also rejected the Norse idea of the ending of the world in the Twilight of the gods (Ragnarok). Yet, imaginatively, he retains the northern atmosphere of heroic endurance, as in the elves* enduring the Doom of Mandos,* or the stoicism of the great army of the west advancing to the gates of Mordor.* Tolkien has, in place of the Twilight of the gods, suggestions of a Last Battle at the end of a later Age* of Middle-earth* that is full of the Christian hope of the end of the world.

Tolkien sets *The Silmarillion*‡ in a pre-Christian age (like the author of *Beowulf*, so it can't express the full hope of Christianity, only prefigure it). According to Kocher, its theme is 'Morgoth's implanting of the seeds of evil in the hearts of Elves and Men, which will bear evil fruit until the last days'. In this outworking of the theme of evil,† Sauron* plays a crucial role in the first Three Ages of the world of Middle-earth.

An important element in the embodiment of Christian meaning in Tolkien's fiction comes from his theory of sub-creation.† *The Silmarillion, The Lord of the Rings,*‡ and even *The Hobbit*‡ are attempts at sub-creation, and as such try to 'survey the depths of space and time'. Tolkien is particularly concerned with time, and Christian apocalypse. That is, his theme is to reveal the essential meaning behind human history. Pre-eminently like the biblical book of Revelation, he is concerned to bring hope and consolation† in dark and difficult days.

To appreciate the freshness and depth of Christian meaning in Tolkien's work, he can be compared with John Milton, the author of the epic poem, *Paradise Lost*. It could be argued that the legacy of Milton's work is with us still, in science fiction and fantasy. There are important parallels between Tolkien's fiction and Milton's great work – both are a study of evil, and a defence of God's ways to humankind. In Tolkien, Morgoth,* and his servant Sauron, are of central importance, as Satan is in *Paradise Lost*. The very title of Tolkien's popular trilogy refers to Sauron, the dark lord of the rings. As also in Milton's work, the theme of fall† from grace (disgrace) into sin or chosen wickedness predominates.

Clyde S. Kilby was able to spend much of the summer of 1966 working with Tolkien on the unfinished *Silmarillion*, and asked him many questions concerning the underlying meanings of his work. In his little book, *Tolkien and the Silmarillion*, he discusses Tolkien as a Christian writer. Kilby describes him as a Tridentine Roman Catholic, a convinced supernaturalist. He believed in a personal yet infinite God who could answer prayer. He and his wife believed that one of their sons had been healed of a heart complaint. Talking to Tolkien had been a major factor in the conversion of C.S. Lewis‡ to Christianity. Tolkien had a high view of Mary the mother of Jesus. His own faith was tied up with that of his mother, who had been ostracized for her faith. He believed that this was a factor in her death. He lost her before his teens. Kilby also mentions Tolkien's work on *The Jerusalem Bible*.

Although the name of God doesn't appear in Tolkien's fiction (there he is called Ilúvatar*), it is full of Christian meaning. Tolkien spoke to Clyde Kilby, for instance, of the invocations in *A Elbereth Gilthoniel*.* The Professor characteristically wrote in *The Road Goes Ever On*:‡ 'These and other references to religion in *The Lord of the Rings* are frequently overlooked.' The meaning, in fact, is implicit rather than explicit. It is incarnate in the whole world of the story. Tolkien deliberately avoided cultic or other explicit references to religion. His interest was in theology, philosophy and cosmology – the elements which make Christianity a world outlook rather than merely a matter of private and public religious experience. It was part of Tolkien's view of humankind as sub-creator, in God's image, that human sub-creations would be like all possible worlds created by God in having a moral and religious character or 'nature'.†

Before and since Tolkien's death there have been numerous articles and books on the meaning of his fiction. Kilby records Tolkien's favourable reaction to an essay sent him from Australia, concerned with the themes of kingship, priesthood and prophecy in *The Lord of the Rings*. He endorsed the spirit of the essay, in finding Christian meaning in his work, even though, as he remarked, it displayed the tendency of such scholarly analysis to suggest that it was a conscious schema for him as he wrote. He didn't deliberately try to insert Christian meaning into his work – a point over which he disagreed with C.S. Lewis, in whose fantasy he felt the Christianity was too explicit. A fruitful way of considering Christian meaning in Tolkien is in terms of his commitment to a natural theology.† C.S. Lewis, in his book, *Miracles*, emphasized the importance of presuppositions or our preunderstanding in approaching historical and natural events. Tolkien, on the contrary, finds real history and natural events a reliable guide to truth in themselves. Whereas traditional natural theology concentrates on the revelation of God in nature and cosmology, Tolkien particularly finds inevitable theology revealed in language and story, or myth.

Clyde Kilby points out that Tolkien believed in the *anima naturaliter christiana*, 'the sense of God and responsibility to Him inborn in mankind'. This sense is both reflected in language and story and reinforced by them.

Tolkien's thinking about this inevitable structure of the language of story is most clearly found in his essay, 'On Fairy Stories'.‡ Here he finds the attributes of escape,† recovery† and consolation.† Consolation, particularly, is loaded with Christian meaning, focused on the *evangelium*. This structure of story is vindicated by the greatest story of all, told in the biblical Gospels. This has the story qualities of escape, recovery and consolation, yet is, astoundingly, true in the real world, in actual human history.

The inspiration for Tolkien's fiction came from such Christian works of medieval English literature as *Beowulf* and *Christ*. One sentence in the latter in particular inspired the tale of Eärendil* the mariner. The line was *Eala Earendel engla beorhtast ofer middengeard monnum sended*. Commenting on this sentence in a letter to Clyde Kilby, Tolkien declared: 'These are Cynewulf's words from which ultimately sprang the whole of my mythology.' Tolkien gave a literal translation of the line to Kilby: 'Here Earendel, brightest of angels, sent from God to men.'

As well as his natural theology, Tolkien was deeply inspired by, or at least found himself using parallels with, biblical imagery. Kilby is useful in pointing out some of these biblical associations. A study of them would take a whole book. These associations include biblical imagery of trees,† the fall of humankind and some angels,† the personification of Wisdom in Proverbs 8, and the biblical portrayal of heroism.† In a letter to W.H. Auden‡ (in 1965), Tolkien commented on *The Lord of the Rings* in relation to Christian theology: 'I don't feel under any obligation to make my story fit with formalized Christian theology, though I actually intended it to be consonant with Christian thought and belief.'

See also Story, Tolkien's theology of.†

Further reading
Clyde S. Kilby, *Tolkien and the Silmarillion* (1976).
Paul H. Kocher, *A Reader's Guide to the Silmarillion* (1980).

Consolation

Tolkien believed that consolation was a central quality of good fantasy or fairy tale – the kind of story he wrote in *The Lord of the Rings*‡ or the tale of Beren* and Lúthien,* the elf-maiden'.‡ The quality is related to that of escape† (but not escapism). There are things 'grim and terrible to fly from', says Tolkien. 'These are hunger, thirst, poverty, pain, sorrow, injustice, death.' But even when people are fortunate enough not to face such extremes 'there are ancient limitations from which fairy stories offer a sort of escape, and old ambitions and desires (touching the very root of fantasy) to which they offer a kind of satisfaction and consolation'. Some include the desire 'to visit, free as a fish, the deep sea' or to fly among the clouds. There are also primordial desires to survey the depths of space and time (*see* Sub-creation†) and to converse with animals.

The desire for talking animals comes from a sense of separation from nature,† from the fall.† C.S. Lewis‡ tried to define such a desire like this:

> We do not want merely to see beauty...We want something else which can hardly be put into words – to be united with the beauty we see, to pass into it, to receive it into ourselves, to bathe in it, to become part of it. That is why we have peopled air and earth and water with gods and goddesses and nymphs and elves.

The oldest desire of course, Tolkien points out, is to escape death.† This desire is a common characteristic of the fairy stories of human beings. Elves* would be concerned to escape deathlessness. Tolkien feels however that the consolation of fairy stories has a more important aspect than 'the imaginative satisfaction of ancient desires'. This is the consolation of the Happy Ending. He coins the term, eucatastrophe, for this ending. Just as tragedy† is the true form of drama, its highest function, eucatastrophe is the true form of the fairy tale.

Such eucatastrophe, the sudden 'turn' in the story, 'is not essentially "escapist" or "fugitive". In its fairy tale – or otherworld – setting, it is a sudden and miraculous grace: never to be counted on to return.' This is not to deny or make light of sorrow and failure, for their possibility 'is necessary to the joy of deliverance'. What is denied, says Tolkien, is 'universal final defeat'. This denial is 'evangelium, giving a fleeting glimpse of Joy, Joy beyond the walls of the world, poignant as grief'. This joy† 'rends indeed the very web of story, and lets a gleam come through'.

The source of joy and consolation is objective (as it was for Tolkien's friend C.S. Lewis). Reality itself is the grounding of the meaning of such stories. In his essay on fairy stories, Tolkien explicitly links consolation with the Christian gospel (*see* Christianity, Tolkien and†).

See also Fairy stories;† Apocalyptic, Tolkien and.†

Death

Tolkien commented, in his essay on fairy stories, that 'Death is the theme that most inspired George MacDonald'. Though Tolkien was impatient with MacDonald,‡ he owes a great deal to him. There are affinities between 'good death' in MacDonald (in, for instance, his *Phantastes, Lilith* and *At the Back of the North Wind*), and Tolkien. Death is also a theme which greatly inspired Tolkien, and is central to his mythology† of Middle-earth.* Much of his thinking about the theme is found in his published *Letters*,‡ where he often patiently explained his fiction to those who wrote to him with enquiries.

Centrally, Tolkien saw 'mortality' as a special gift of God† to human beings. While this would be 'bad theology' in the primary world, in his invented world the idea helped to elucidate truth, and was, he believed, a legitimate basis for legends. In biological terms, explained Tolkien, elves* and humankind are one race – they are capable of intermarriage. Biologically, however, there would also be some difference accounting for the fact that one was immortal and one was not. Elves have certain aspects of human beings (*see* Elven quality†), as well as freedoms and powers humans desire. 'The beauty and peril and sorrow of these things is exhibited in them.'

Tolkien's invention of a mortality–immortality contrast opens up all kinds of imaginative possibilities, for example, sacrifice† in Lúthien's* momentous choice of mortality for the sake of Beren.* Her choice, and efforts to have that choice, exhibit some of the meaning of her love. Centuries later, long after the death of the once immortal maiden, the most beautiful to walk the earth, Arwen* makes a similar choice in order to be one with the mortal Aragorn.*

Another variation in the theme of death is the allowance made to the Númenoreans of a triple span of mortal life. This increased life-span is integral to the plot of *The Lord of the Rings*‡ where much is made of Aragorn's longevity as the last flowering of the Númenoreans. For the faithful, this served to deepen their sense of identity as created beings who would expect to die eventually, and to pass on to a greater, but still human, fulfilment. A good Númenorean died of free will, letting his or her life go, as Aragorn did. But for the rebels, seduced by the malice of Sauron,* there was a deepening fear of death, which led to their ill-fated attempt to occupy the Undying Lands of the West.

Sauron's deceit was that the lands had a magical property of deathlessness. In fact, it was only the beings – the Valar,* Maiar,* and elves – who were the immortal of the land, conferring blessing on it.

Time, of course, is fundamental in relation to mortality. Here other imaginative possibilities are played out by Tolkien. A person such as Galadriel* has an existence which spans Three Ages of

Middle-earth. In contrast, humans with a short life-span would be willing to lay down their lives fighting the enemy, Morgoth.* The elves of the Third Age* in particular were conscious of the increasing burden of immortality, as they experienced the gradual fading and decline of their race in Middle-earth, making way for the domination of humankind. Yet other imaginative possibilities arise. Though death is a gift to human beings, healing† and escape† from death are desirable. Such healing and escape provide a vivid image of the very heart of human life – the timelessness and transcendence of our relationship with God and with other human beings.

Escape from death, and healing, are constant themes in Tolkien's tales of Middle-earth. Frodo* and Faramir* are near death, Frodo on several occasions. Gandalf* (though a Maia) sacrifices his physical life for his friends, but is sent back to complete his work in a transformed body. The Ring-bearers Bilbo* and Frodo, and eventually Sam,* are allowed to pass over into the Undying Lands of the west for proper healing and rest (though eventually even they would die, or be changed, like the biblical Enoch and Elijah). Such healing and escape from death provide what Tolkien calls consolation.†

Descent into the underworld
See Underground places and journeys.†

Dragons
Bred by Morgoth,* these evil† beings brought terror to Beleriand* and elsewhere, as chronicled in *The Silmarillion*.‡ In *The Hobbit*,‡ Bilbo* encounters the winged dragon, Smaug,* in Erebor.*

In his essay, 'Beowulf: The Monsters and the Critics',‡ Tolkien paints a vivid picture of the symbolism† of the dragon as an enemy more evil than any human foe. The Beowulf poem is something new, 'a measure and interpretation' of all northern legends of dragons. He explains:

Beowulf's dragon, if one wishes really to criticize, is not to be blamed for being a dragon, but rather for not being dragon enough, plain pure fairy-story dragon. There are in the poem some vivid touches of the right kind . . . in which this dragon is real worm, with a bestial life and thought of his own, but the conception, none the less, approaches *draconitas* rather than *draco*: a personification of malice, greed, destruction (the evil side of heroic life), and of the undiscriminating cruelty of fortune that distinguishes not good or bad (the evil aspect of all life). But for Beowulf, the poem, that is as it should be. In this poem the balance is nice, but it is preserved. The large symbolism is near the surface, but it does not break through, nor become allegory. Something more significant than a standard hero, a man faced with a foe more evil than any human enemy of house or realm, is before us, and yet incarnate in time, walking in heroic history, and treading the named lands of the North.

In the human beings of Middle-earth,* such as elves,* hobbits* and humans, there can also be a dragon-like quality. It could be presented as a psychological state, the 'Dragon-complex' (to invent a name for it). The quality is that of possession,† possessiveness. A dragon like Smaug embodies possessiveness vividly in his great, but useless, hoard. But possessiveness applies to knowledge, power over others, and many other areas. Fallen creatures like Fëanor,* Morgoth, and Sauron* are characterized by the Dragon-complex, the lust to possess. The Silmarils* (and later, for the Dark Lord, the Ring*) symbolize this lust.

As a foil to this complex are creatures who have no desire to possess, or who are lost in their joy in creating. They include Ilúvatar* himself, father of all, Aulë* the Vala,* Sam* (over whom the Ring has little power), and Tom Bombadil.*

Tolkien could be criticized for attributing such evil to dragons which, like orcs,* were bred for wickedness, and hence had no moral choice. Human beings are wrong to be dragon-like, bestial, but a dragon is a dragon. However, as symbolic embodiments of nameless evil they have great imaginative power.

Eagles

Eagles play an important part in the events of Middle-earth,* and are associated with the providence† of Ilúvatar,* the creator of all. They were brought into being by Manwë* and Yavanna* at the very beginning. They were noble, immense creatures (the wing-span of Thorondor* was 180 feet), large enough to carry humans and hobbits.* Their providential acts included the protection of Gondolin,* the rescue of Beren* and Lúthien* after they stole back a Silmaril* from Morgoth,* the protection of Tuor* and other sur-vivors of the Fall of Gondolin,* the fight against winged dragons† at the end of the First Age,* aiding Bilbo Baggins* and Thorin's* dwarves* in the events recounted in *The Hobbit*,‡ and the rescue of Sam* and Frodo* from the slopes of Mount Doom. Eagle-shaped clouds presaged the destruction of Númenor.* In the story of Aldarion* and Erendis, in *Unfinished Tales*,‡ there is the sign of an eagle on Aldarion's ship.

Elven quality

In his invented mythology† of Middle-earth,* Tolkien intended that his elves* were an extended metaphor of a key aspect of human nature. This 'elven quality' in human life was a central pre-occupation of Tolkien's. Elves, like dwarves,* hobbits,* and the like, 'partially represent' human beings (Letter 131, in *Letters*‡).

The idea of embodying qualities in fiction was one he shared with his friend, C.S. Lewis.‡ Lewis for instance wished to embody or make incarnate the quality of joy.† Both men were imagina-tively struck with the quality of 'northernness'. Both incorporated events and situations which had a quality of the numinous.† In the previous century, George MacDonald,‡ whom Lewis regarded as his 'master', was also preoccupied with the capture of qualities in fiction, particularly fantasy. The quality of holiness, for example, is so tangible in his *Phantastes* that Lewis described it as baptizing his imagination† long before he became a confessing Christian.

In Tolkien's mythology, and also in other fiction (such as *Smith of Wootten Major*‡) elves represent what is high and noble in human beings. In particular, they represent the arts. In their highest form, Tolkien regarded the arts as sub-creation,† work done in the image of God† and his created world. The elves may in fact be taken as a metaphor of human culture, highlighting its meaning. They were to teach their arts and crafts to human beings (Letter 131, *Letters*‡).

Tolkien's depiction of the ideal in human life could well be interpreted as Platonic and elitist. However, in my view, his depiction is ultimately rescued from such an interpretation by two key factors, though there is undoubtedly a Platonic element in Tolkien (coming from his embrace of the medieval world). The first factor is that Tolkien balances the 'elven' side of human nature with the homely. Like MacDonald and Lewis, he founds his fantasy on the ordinary and on homeliness (*see* Nature†). The second factor is that Tolkien conscientiously tried to make his invention consonant with Christian belief. In the orthodox Christianity† of Tolkien, the material world is a real creation of God's, where Christ's incarnation and continued (though glorified) humanity are central.

Though in later life, Tolkien disliked MacDonald's fantasy, there is in fact a deep affinity between the two writers below the surface. His reaction to MacDonald was a creative one, as was his reaction to some of Lewis' fiction (for example, *The Chronicles of Narnia*, which he regarded as too allegorical). The recurring figure of the Wise Woman or the Great-Great-Grandmother in MacDonald's fairy stories for children represents the same kind of 'elven' or faerie quality as Tolkien's elves. How does Tolkien move from inventing a race of elves in a story to presenting them as an extended metaphor of human life and culture?

In Tolkien's tales of the First Age* of Middle-earth, the subject of *The Silmarillion*‡ proper, the elves are dominant. As the Second* and Third Ages* progress the elves decline and fade. In 'The Later

Annals of Valinor' (in *The Lost Road*) it is recorded: 'The Sun was set as a sign of the waning of the Elves, but the Moon cherisheth their memory.' However, key tales (such as that of Beren* and Lúthien* the elf-maiden‡) record intermarriages between elves and humans which introduce the elven quality dramatically into human history. For instance, Eärendil,* an ideal human being and Christ-figure, is the son of a human, Tuor,* and an elf, Idril.*

Tolkien comments:

> The contact of Men and Elves already foreshadows the history of the later Ages, and a recurrent theme is the idea that in Men (as they are now) there is a strand of 'blood' and inheritance, derived from the Elves, and that the art and poetry of Men is largely dependent on it, or modified by it. (Letter 131)

By the time of the Fourth Age* – our own, where mythology such as Tolkien's has moved into history – the elven quality mainly persists in human form. The three Ages recorded in Tolkien's Middle-earth stories and annals are pre-Christian. Our present Fourth Age and beyond is the Christian era, where the elven quality is perhaps now pre-eminently a spiritual one, associated with Christianity, the grace of the gospel (or *evangelium*), and the presence of the Holy Spirit. Tolkien inclines to a 'spiritual' view of art.

The previous paragraph may make Tolkien's aims seem more ambitious than they were. He was largely concerned with making a 'mythology for England', with his mythology providing an imagined history. He was trying to compensate for the destruction of a rich literature in Old English. Surviving texts like *Beowulf* give a hint of what might have existed. Meanwhile words and phrases gave tantalizing clues to a missing mythology, such as the word 'Earendel' in the text of *Christ*. In the unfinished story, 'The Lost Road', it is supposed that certain Old English words point back to a forgotten language. This is the language of Tolkien's invention, Elvish,* which he feigned was more discovery than invention.

In a secondary way, Tolkien embodied the same 'elven quality' in human figures. This embodiment is more complex because humans are subject to the 'gift of Ilúvatar', death,† whereas elves are immortal. The Númenorean humans, though, were granted a life-span far exceeding the normal. They were, however, to view death positively (it had no association of punishment for rebellion against God, as in actual history). Death was meant to highlight the eternal quality within themselves, which carried the promise of continuing life in the future in the plan of Ilúvatar.* The good Númenoreans were in fact enriched by their acceptance of providence.† In culture, laws and the arts, theirs was a great civilization, a standard for all human society.

Tolkien, like C.S. Lewis, was persuaded by the view of their mutual friend, Owen Barfield,‡ that language and symbolism† have become increasingly abstract through history. In Tolkien's beginning, there are real elves (and a real Númenorean civilization). Now there is merely an 'elven quality' to human life, which some can see clearly and others fail to perceive at all. In all the abstraction, there has been a real loss. He sees such a loss restored by the *evangelium*, as he points out in his seminal essay, 'On Fairy Stories'. Tolkien concludes: 'God is the Lord, of angels, and of man – and of Elves. Legend and history have met and fused.'

Tolkien saw the 'elven quality' embodied and made real in the incarnation, death and resurrection of Christ. It may reveal itself at any time in ordinary mortals. Though not so ordinary, Clyde Kilby saw such a quality in Tolkien when he spent some weeks working with him. He wrote, after his death:

He had the life of a mortal man, a little more than threescore years and ten. Yet he had Elvish immortality too, as thousands know from acquiring a measure of it themselves through his works. Tolkien was 'otherworldly' in the best sense of that term . . .

Whether Tolkien will survive as a significant literary figure is a question no one can presently answer. What many of us know

now with great assurance is that he survives deeply and joyously in us.

Aragorn* expressed the hope that Tolkien was intent in capturing through his 'elvishness'. As Aragorn lay dying he said to his wife Arwen,* an elf who had taken Lúthien's* choice of human mortality: 'Behold! we are not bound for ever to the circles of the world, and beyond them is more than memory.'
See also Fairy stories.†

Elves

In his *Letters†* (letter 181) Tolkien describes the 'mythology'† of Middle-earth* as being 'elf-centred'. The mythology is embodied in *The Silmarillion,*‡ which concerns the First Age.* The elvish framework of *The Silmarillion* particularly shows up where it is compared with *The Hobbit,*‡ and *The Lord of the Rings,*‡ both of which could be said to be hobbit-centred, the narrative being composed by hobbits.*

In his essay, 'On Fairy Stories'‡ (*see* Fairy stories†), Tolkien speaks of the relationship between what he called sub-creation,† and faerie, which is 'the realm or state where faeries have their being'. As elves* belong to faerie, their conception lies at the very centre of Tolkien's fiction.

In terms of the story, elves are, like humans, the Children of Ilúvatar.* They are not part of the creation fashioned through the agency of the Valar,* but direct creations of God.† They are personal, thinking, speaking and creative beings.

The elves awoke at Cuiviénen.* They soon divided into two groups: the Eldar,* who took part in the great journey westwards at the summons of the Valar, and those who refused the call.

The First Age* was the golden age of the elves. In the later Ages they were a remnant in Middle-earth, tending to gather in small elven-realms, or refuges. As they faded humans gradually became ascendant.

Elves resembled humans (*see* Elven quality†), and could marry with them, as the elf-maiden Lúthien* did with Beren.* They were however immortal, tied for ever to this world.

The varieties of elves resulted from the fundamental early division into two groups. Some varieties were the Vanyar,* the Noldor,* the Teleri,* and the Sindar.*
See also Death.†

Escape
See Fairy stories.†

Eucatastrophe
See Consolation.†

Evil
The Lord of the Rings,‡ according to Tom Shippey, attempts to reconcile two views of evil, the Manichaeist (associated with Boethius) and the Judeo-Christian (represented by Augustine). One is a subjective view of evil, and the other objective. The Augustinian view can be called subjective in the sense that evil is a negation, not being in itself. For Augustine, all God's creation was pronounced by him to be good.

Tolkien, believes Shippey, tries to take account of both sides, each of which is true to our experience. He sees this happening with the symbol of the Ring* borne by Frodo.* It is an objective reality, the power† of which is to be resisted. It also however appeals subjectively to a person's weakness. For instance, the Ring appeals to possessiveness in Bilbo,* fear in Frodo, patriotism in Boromir,* and pity in Gandalf.*

But is Tolkien's portrayal of the objective reality of evil through the Ring Manichaeist? Such a view sees evil as part of the very nature of the universe. Tolkien's Ring, however, is not the creation of Ilúvatar,* but of a creature, Sauron,* a Maia.* The description of Manichaeist might be more true of Tolkien's cosmological myth. In this, the fall† of Melkor, or Morgoth,* takes place before the creation of the world. In his music† of creation, on which the making of the world is founded, Ilúvatar incorporates the discord of evil as a lesser theme, ultimately overcome in the conduct of the music. This might show a lack of reconciliation of good and evil in Tolkien's thinking. Such a lack could suggest Manichaeism. However, the whole beautiful myth of the creation music of the 'Ainulindalë'‡ actually rejects a dualism of good and evil. A greater problem, philosophically and theologically, is the existence of the Valar* before creation. This conflicts with Tolkien's depiction of the Valar as angels, servants of Ilúvatar, rather than deities. This can be reconciled by seeing the world, Ea,* within which is Middle-earth,* as only part of creation, the larger reality of which includes the being of the Valar.

In achieving a realistic tension between subjective and objective evil, Tolkien's fertile imagination creates many embodiments of evil – balrogs,* dragons,† orcs,* the fallen Vala, Morgoth, and his servant, the Maia Sauron, the ringwraiths (see Nazgûl*), spiders such as Shelob* or Ungoliant,* werewolves and trolls.*

John Milton, in his great epic, *Paradise Lost*, has often been charged with unwittingly making Satan the hero† of his poem. To fallen human beings, evil is fatally attractive, and bad characters are easier to create in fiction than good. Are evil beings such as Morgoth, Sauron or Saruman,* and elves* and humans who fall into evil like Fëanor* and Denethor,* more convincing than Gandalf, Aragorn,* Frodo, Beren* or Galadriel? Colin Manlove tends to find the moral struggles of Frodo lacking in depth, but many would not agree with him. Good beings as well as evil are ably created by Tolkien, as well as the objective aspects of both good and evil. We are delighted by the vision of Valinor,* the earlier days of Númenor,* or Rivendell,* and the goodness of Lúthien,* Aragorn or Frodo. We understand the tragedy† of Fëanor, Túrin* or Boromir.

Set against evil in Tolkien's world are many elements, but rarely physical force (as in the overthrow of Morgoth at the end of the

First Age,* the destruction of Númenor, or Gandalf's fight with the balrog). One important element is healing.† Another is art, in many forms of creativity, such as song.† Another is the renunciation of possession.† A further element is sacrifice.† Underlying them all is faith in providence,† hope in the ultimate happy ending even if a person does not live to see it.

Because of his theology of Middle-earth, Tolkien is able to portray evil as utterly real, without falling into a dualism of good and evil. The many occasions of tragedy within his tales (pre-eminently in the story of Túrin) emphasize the reality of evil in the world, evil originated by the fall of Melkor (Morgoth).

Evil is only possible to creatures capable of creativity and free will. The orcs, to the contrary, are programmed to inflict evil, tools rather than agents of Morgoth and Sauron.

Much of Tolkien's invented mythology concerns creativity and art, the foundation of language and culture. The making of the world by the demiurgic Valar, the fashioning of the Silmarils,* and the forging of the Rings, shape all events. For Tolkien, a study of evil necessarily has to do with the use and misuse of creativity and free will. Both salvation and damnation involve moral choices. Thus evil is indivisible: its implications are applicable to the real world, as well as to Tolkien's invented, secondary world (itself one example of creativity).

Further reading

Paul H. Kocher, *A Reader's Guide to 'The Silmarillion'* (1980).
C.N. Manlove, *Modern Fantasy: Five Studies* (1975).
T.A. Shippey, *The Road to Middle-earth* (1982).

Fairy stories

J.R.R. Tolkien's lecture 'On Fairy Stories'‡ (1939) is the key source for thinking and theology behind his creation of Middle-earth* and its stories. He links God† and humanity in two related ways. In the first, he, as an orthodox Christian, sees humankind – male and female – as being made in the image of God. This makes a qualitative difference between humans and all other things which exist in the universe. Our ability to speak, love and create fantasy originates in this imageness of God. The second way Tolkien links God and humanity is in similarities that exist by necessity between the universe of God's making and human making. Human making derives, that is, from our being in God's image.

The actual course of Tolkien's essay does not so starkly highlight these two related links between God and humanity, but they underlie both the essay and Tolkien's fiction. 'On Fairy Stories' was originally given as a lecture at St Andrews University. It is concerned to rehabilitate the idea of the fairy story, which had been relegated to children's literature, and fantasy in general. To regard fairy stories as trivial, suitable only for telling to children, failed to do justice either to such stories or to real children.

The Professor, who had by then written much of *The Silmarillion*,‡ and published *The Hobbit*,‡ attempted to set out a structure which belonged to good fairy tales and fantasies. This structure demonstrated that fairy tales were worthy of serious attention.

Fairy tales, he pointed out, were stories about faerie: 'the realm or state where fairies have their being'. Listeners who had read his essay, 'Beowulf: The Monsters or the Critics',‡ may have noticed a similarity here with Tolkien's portrayal of the Old English poem. Tolkien had spoken of the poet making his theme 'incarnate in the world of history and geography'. Fairy tales were fantasy, allowing their hearers or readers to move from the details of their limited experience to 'survey the depths of space and time'. The successful fairy story in fact was 'sub-creation',† the ultimate achievement of fantasy, the highest art, deriving its power from human language itself. The successful writer of fairy story 'makes a Secondary World which your mind can enter. Inside it, what he relates is "true": it accords with the laws of that world.' In addition to offering a Secondary World, with an 'inner consistency of reality', a good fairy tale has three other key structural features. In the first place, it helps to bring about in the reader what Tolkien called recovery† – that is, the restoration of a true view of the meaning of ordinary and humble things which make up human life and reality such as love, thought, trees,† hills and food. (*See also* Healing.†) Second, the good fairy story offers escape† from one's narrow and distorted view of reality and meaning. This is the escape of the prisoner rather than the flight of the deserter. Third, the good story offers consolation,† leading to joy† (what C.S. Lewis‡ called *sehnsucht*).

The consolation, argued Tolkien, only had meaning because good stories pointed to the greatest story of all. This story had all the structural features of a fairy tale, myth, or great story, with the additional feature of being true in actual human history. This was the Gospel, the story of God himself coming to earth as a humble human being, a king, like Aragorn,* in disguise, a seeming fool, like Frodo* and Sam,* the greatest storyteller entering his own story.

Tolkien's fundamental idea of the consolation is related to his view of nature,† which was deeply theological. He saw nature in terms of a natural theology† which was sacramental. His own created elves* – which are the central concern of *The Silmarillion*, and his invented languages – were natural creatures, or, at least, their destinies were tied up with the natural world. Elves are his name for fairies, and thus are central to this essay. His main fiction, like this essay, was concerned to rehabilitate the fairy tale, and to provide consolation for his readers. The three features of recovery, escape and consolation, focus on the effect that good fairy tales have on their readers. The effect of a work of literature on its reader is an important dimension of literary meaning. C.S. Lewis explored such effects in relation to story in his *An Experiment in Criticism*. His ideas in this late book were hammered out in meetings of the Inklings,‡ and Tolkien would have been in substantial agreement with them. Thus, to explore the themes of Tolkien's essay and fiction further, it is important to read this book of Lewis. *See also* Myth;† Story, Tolkien's theology of.†

Fall

Tolkien isolates the theme of fall as one of the central concerns of his mythology† of Middle-earth.* His theology of the fall is taken from the Bible (*see* Christianity, Tolkien and†), but he shapes it according to his artistic purposes.

There is no direct equivalent of the biblical fall of humankind and some angels† as (1) Tolkien is writing fiction; and (2) there are races other than humans. Fall is experienced in both aspects of the human, however, the elvish and the mannish. Elves† are not fallen as a race, and only rarely turn to wickedness individually, so they have no original sin. The position of humans is different. Tolkien introduces the idea of Re-formation to cover the good human beings in his tales of Middle-earth. These are distinguished from Black Númenoreans (Númenor* has its own, second fall), and other wicked people, such as the Haradrim.* Tolkien explains:

> Men have 'fallen' – any legends put in the form of supposed ancient history of this actual world of ours must accept that – but the peoples of the west, the good side are Re-formed. That is they are the descendants of Men that tried to repent and fled Westward from the domination of the Prime Dark Lord, and his false worship, and by contrast with the Elves renewed (and enlarged) their knowledge of the truth and the nature of the World.

In this way Tolkien pictures a pagan, pre-Christian, naturally monotheistic group of people. To them has been revealed part of God's purposes, inklings of what is to come in the gospel story, a revelation to which they have faithfully responded according to their light. C.S. Lewis‡ makes a similar exploration of what might be called enlightened paganism, on a smaller scale, in his beautiful historical novel, *Till We Have Faces*.

The fall in the garden of Eden does not come into Tolkien's tales – it happens off-stage, as it were. Tolkien regarded the events of Eden as part of actual human history, accounting for the darkness of the world. In his fantasy, he explored the fall theme primarily in the fall of Morgoth* (Melkor) before the making of the world, and in the disobedience of the Númenoreans in breaking the Ban of the Valar* against setting foot on the shores of the Undying Lands.

These moral falls, which, like the fall of Lucifer and the fall of Adam, are related, account for the separation of elves and humans (*see* Elvish quality†). More dramatically, they account for the destruction of Beleriand* and Númenor,* and the change in the shape of the world, making it normally impossible to reach the Uttermost West, the lost Eden. On an individual scale, the story of Túrin* explores the effects of evil on a good man who has a tragic† flaw. Other explorations include the fall of Saruman* and the more tragic Denethor,* and the corrosive effect of the One Ring* on Gollum,* and to a lesser extent, on Bilbo* and Frodo.* There is denial of fall, too, in the faithful of Númenor like Elendil,* and those that refuse possession† of the Ring such as Gandalf* and Galadriel.*

Although original sin is muted in the good humans of Middle-earth, there is a powerful image of it in the orcs* (who, like elves, symbolize an aspect of human beings). Orcs were bred into evil by Morgoth, originally from captured elves (as the Maiar* do not have the power to create conscious beings). They were programmed by this breeding, and thus had no moral choice. Their inability to do good is applicable to the concept of original sin. In speaking of human beings in relation to fall and to sin, Tolkien argued that we are still moral, free-willed beings, to whom is revealed something of God's purposes (*see* Natural theology, Tolkien and†). As he wrote to C.S. Lewis, in the poem 'Mythopoeia':‡

> Although now long estranged,
> Man is not wholly lost nor wholly changed.
> Dis-graced he may be, yet is not de-throned,
> and keeps the rags of lordship once he owned . . .

See also Evil.†

God

In *The Silmarillion*,‡ the name of God, creator of the world, is Ilúvatar* (also called Eru, 'The One'). Ilúvatar means 'Father of All'. The 'Ainulindalë'‡ records how, when he created the angelic† beings, he revealed to them the themes of creation in music.† As his agents they helped to realize the vision in the making of the world.

Though superficially, God seems absent from the events of Middle-earth,* in fact its history is the outworking of the themes of the music at the beginning of creation. Consequently, providence† is a constant reality throughout the tales of Middle-earth. The presence of the will of Ilúvatar, the creator, emphasizes Tolkien's idea of sub-creation.† In reading the fiction, the reader is aware of the mind and will of the teller and maker of the tale (Tolkien). In making and telling stories, Tolkien believed, we exercise a God-given right to be a sub-creator. If done with skill and integrity, our creation parallels the primary world. It is part of 'the seamless web of story'. The human creator as imitator parallels the divine creator, though on a sub-scale.

In Tolkien's mythology,† elves* and humans are called 'the Children of Ilúvatar'* as they were the special and direct creations of God, not the handiwork of the demiurgic angels. Their destiny had an element of mystery to it. The elves were to be for ever tied up with the world, whereas the destiny of mortals beyond death was to be greater.

These sorts of theological and philosophical themes constantly preoccupied Tolkien as he invented his mythology. They contributed to his inability to complete his work.

See also Christianity, Tolkien and;† Natural theology, Tolkien and.†

Healing

As a counter to the ever-present effects of evil† and the fall† in Tolkien's fiction is the persistence of this theme. Healing powers are often a quality of gifted people, whether Maiar,* elves* or humans – such as Melian,* Gandalf,* Lúthien,* Beleg (in the tale of Túrin Turambar*), or Aragorn.* It is also a property of certain places such as the Pools of Ivrin, Lórien* or Fangorn Forest.* Healing can also be instituted as an expression of care, as in the Houses of Healing in Minas Tirith.*

When Beren* was grey and exhausted by his journey to Doriath* across the Nan Dungortheb* the sight of Lúthien's beauty, and her singing, brought healing to him – the power of romantic love – 'Enchantment healed his weary feet' (*The Fellowship of the Ring*, I, 11).

Lúthien's healing powers are often exercised, as when she healed Beren of the evil wound he received from Carcharoth.* Her greatest healing deed was when, by her sacrifice,† she brought Beren back from the dead.

One of the principal healers in *The Lord of the Rings*‡ is the future king, Aragorn. The power of healing was part of his true kingship, a kingship that was Christ-like (*see* Christianity, Tolkien and†). One of his ancient names was Envinyatar, the Renewer. His healing hands are laid on Faramir,* the Lady Éowyn* and the hobbit,* Merry.* The healing process took great skill and persistence. In this restoration an old prophecy was fulfilled:

> Life to the dying
> In the king's hand lying!

Hero(ism)

Modern fiction tends to concern itself with the anti-hero, rather than the hero, as traditionally understood. Tolkien's choice of fantasy however, and in particular heroic romance such as *The Lord of the Rings*,‡ allows a use of the hero. Traditional heroes are expected by the reader, as part of the genre.

Tolkien, however, knew his readership, and knew that he could not write like the author of *The Odyssey*, *Morte d'Arthur*, or *Beowulf*. The original audience for these works believed that evil† could be dealt with by a superhero. A hero like that today would be an unconvincing picture-strip hero like Indiana Jones or James Bond, where believability depends on action.

Tolkien's concept of heroism deserves careful study. He has been able (for those who can enter his imaginary world) to create convincing heroes that are more biblical than superhuman. In Tolkien's Middle-earth,* ultimately the meek inherit the world.

C.S. Lewis‡ puts his finger on the main characteristic of heroism in Tolkien's mythology,† that apparent foolishness is the method of providence,† that imagination† wins over brute strength. The model of heroism is a God† who becomes a humble carpenter.

In his review of *The Fellowship of the Ring*, Lewis observed:

> Almost the central theme of the book is the contrast between the Hobbits (or 'the Shire') and the appalling destiny to which some of them are called, the terrifying discovery that the humdrum happiness of the Shire, which they had taken for granted as something normal, is in reality a sort of local and temporal accident, that its existence depends on being protected by powers which Hobbits dare not imagine, that any Hobbit may find himself forced out of the Shire and caught up in that high conflict. More strangely still, the event of that conflict between strongest things may come to depend on him, who is almost the weakest.

Sam* the hobbit* is the 'chief hero' (as Tolkien calls him) of *The Lord of the Rings*. In a letter to his son, Christopher, in 1944, Tolkien wrote that, certainly, 'Sam is the most closely drawn character, the successor to Bilbo of the first book, the genuine hobbit. Frodo is not so interesting, because he has to be highminded, and has (as it were) a vocation.' Frodo,* however, despite this disclaimer, is a central hero, not least in his persistence in pursuing his long quest† to reach Mordor* and Mount Doom.

In both *The Hobbit*‡ and *The Lord of the Rings*, the ways of providence, often managed and interpreted by Gandalf,* are to use unheroic, humble figures like Bilbo,* Frodo, Sam and Merry,* in a heroic manner. The world is to be saved by humble, ordinary people, not by the mighty, powerful and wise. But there are 'heroic' heroes as well, with qualities that redefine greatness. Aragorn* is a figure who can stand with the great heroes of legend. Yet he is marked by gentleness, humility, and a gift of healing.† Though the setting is pre-Christian, he is a Christian hero and king. In him high qualities more often than not associated with the elves* are softened and humanized.

Significantly, Tolkien's heroes are not autonomous, and individualistic. (Where they are, as in Túrin,* this is accounted a tragic† flaw.) They are helped by providence, and by Gandalf the wizard;† Frodo is helped by Sam, Beren* by Lúthien.* The virtue of healing, redressing the effects of the fall† and thus striking a blow against the enemy, is a constant theme in the tales of Middle-earth. One can think of the healing hands of Melian,* Aragorn, Gandalf, Lúthien, and many others. Aragorn combines many heroic qualities. He is a Christ-like true king, whose return is heralded in ancient prophecy. He is healer, guardian (as Ranger*) and wise man as well as warrior, whose command even the dead acknowledge. That he is more than just a good king can be seen by contrast with Théoden.* Théoden gives leadership in battle, and expresses love and fatherliness to his warriors. But Aragorn excels him by being primarily a healer.

Stewardship is also a heroic quality valued in Tolkien's world. So is sacrifice.† Aragorn and the free defenders of Minas Tirith* are willing to sacrifice their lives in hopeless battle to distract Sauron's* attention from Frodo, the Ring-bearer, and Sam. Frodo and Sam are willing to give their lives to destroy the Ring.* Lúthien and Arwen* are willing to renounce natural immortality for love of humans, sharing their fate beyond death.†

Servanthood and loyalty are also heroic qualities. Aragorn for years serves the hobbits as unappreciated guardian, with other Rangers. Sam serves Frodo, helping him achieve his task. Even Gollum* serves the purposes of providence.

Another aspect of the hero in Tolkien, helpfully set out by Jane Chance Nitzsche, is the 'elf-knight' as a figure of Christ. Tolkien, Nitzsche demonstrates, takes his symbolism† here from Edmund Spenser's *The Faerie Queene*, and from the imagery of Christ as knight in the *Ancrene Wisse*. Here knights or heroes have an elven quality† of goodness. For Tolkien, the elves symbolize the higher, desirable side of human nature, and he felt that he was picking up this tradition from Spenser and the author of the *Ancrene Wisse*.

The later idea of elves and fairies as dainty, diminutive figures Tolkien regarded with distaste as being degenerate. It led to George MacDonald's‡ fantasies eventually falling into disfavour with Tolkien, even though his debt to the Scotsman is great. MacDonald, for example, represents elvishness through the recurring figure of the wise woman, or Great-Great-Grandmother. For him, as for Tolkien, this elvish quality represented what is noble in human nature. As with Tolkien, the greatness of this quality is often feminine. For MacDonald's wise women there are Tolkien's Galadriel* and Lúthien. On the even higher level of the Valar* and the Maiar* there are Varda* (Elbereth) and Queen Melian.

According to Jane Nitzsche, in Tolkien, the Christian symbolism of the faery hero or faery king comes strongly in his story, *Smith of Wootton Major*.‡ She again finds Tolkien's inspiration in the *Ancrene Wisse*. She writes of Smith in Tolkien's story:

Here suffering is valuable because God may reward it – may 'turn towards it with His grace, and make the heart pure and clear-sighted, and this no one may achieve who is tainted with vices or with an earthly love of worldly things, for this taint affects the eyes of the heart so badly that it cannot recognize God or rejoice in the sight of him'... This quotation from 'Love', the seventh section of the Ancrene Wisse, beautifully summarizes the pure spiritual condition of the child Smith. Because free of vice and filled with charity he is 'graced' with the gift of the star, his passport into the other world of Faerie, but one which simultaneously endows him with a recovery of insight and perception because of his visits to the other world. And the love of Smith for his family and for his fellow man and ultimately for God stems from a pure heart: 'A pure heart, as St. Bernard says, effects two things: it makes you do all that you do either for the love of God alone, or for the good of others for His sake'..., an Augustinian pronouncement springing from the pages of the Ancrene Wisse (*Tolkien's Art*, page 67).

The Faery King in disguise – Alf (=Elf) – serves as a humble apprentice to the graceless Nokes, and thus is able to pass the star of inheritance to the worthy Smith. Thereafter Smith has an elven quality.

Homeliness
See Nature.‡

Imagination
In Tolkien, imagination is an integrating concept, affecting both his thought and fiction. The same is true of C.S. Lewis,‡ his friend, and the nineteenth-century author, George MacDonald,‡ whose ideas on the imagination anticipated those of Lewis and Tolkien. Laying the foundation for many of Tolkien's ideas was the romantic poet and thinker Samuel Taylor Coleridge.

Central to Coleridge's radical view of the imagination was the importance of metaphor, and 'the perception of similitude in dissimiltude'. At its best and most natural, imagination is expressed in language. Metaphor is imagination in action.

The mind, believed Coleridge, is active in making sense of the world. The mind imposes itself on reality, shaping it. Imagination has a central role, therefore, in knowledge, shaping and adapting it. The poet is the epitome of this process, using a 'synthetic and magical power' which Coleridge calls imagination.

The imagination is 'esemplastic', unifying and shaping. Its pattern, sharply revealed in poetry, is set out by Coleridge in his *Biographia Literaria* (1817):

This power, first put into action by the will and understanding, and retained under their irremissive, though gentle and unnoticed control . . . , reveals itself in the balance or reconcilement of opposite or discordant qualities: of sameness, with difference; of the general with the concrete; the idea with the image; the individual with the representative; the sense of novelty and freshness with old and familiar objects; a more than usual state of emotion with more than usual order; judgement ever awake and steady self-possession with enthusiasm and feeling profound or vehement; and while it blends and harmonizes the natural and the artificial, still subordinates art to nature; the manner to the matter; and our admiration of the poet to our sympathy with the poetry.

Like Tolkien, Coleridge tries to distinguish a primary and secondary imagination. The primary imagination is concerned with, and operates in, the primary or 'ordinary' world. The secondary imagination, employing language and metaphor, reworks and reshapes this primary or ordinary world. It captures the inscape, rather than visual surface, of reality. Tolkien sees the most exalted function of imagination as sub-creation† in linguistic form, creating, if successful, a secondary world.

Coleridge's thought is subtle and complex. Though not as powerful a thinker as Coleridge, George MacDonald explored the concept of the imagination in great depths, particularly in his essays, 'The Imagination: Its Functions and Its Culture' (1867) and 'The Fantastic Imagination' (1882). His views remarkably foreshadow those of Tolkien and C.S. Lewis, and are worked out creatively in his fantasies. For example, in *The Princess and Curdie* (1882) he creates a convincing secondary world. This can be seen especially in the city of Gwyntystorm, which has a distinct atmosphere, and in the varied country regions that lie between it and the ancient Queen's castle. It is also possible to map Fairy Land in *Phantastes*.

MacDonald does not tie imagination to language like Tolkien and Coleridge, but like Tolkien he sees the foundation for understanding it in the relationship between God† and his creation. Though he does not use the word, MacDonald sees the product of human imagination as 'sub-creation'. 'The imagination of man is made in the image of the imagination of God. Everything of man must have been of God first.' MacDonald sees the human imagination as living and moving and having its being in the imagination of God.

The human being is not creative in a primary sense. 'Indeed, a man is rather *being thought* than *thinking*, when a new thought arises in his mind . . . He did not create it.' Even the forms by which humans reveal their thoughts are not created by them in a primary sense; they belong to nature.†

MacDonald had a scientific training, and is remarkably modern in pointing out the importance of imagination in science. He also, like Lewis and Tolkien, values metaphor highly: 'All words . . ., belonging to the inner world of the mind, are of the imagination, are originally poetic.' He claims that in both the arts and sciences, imagination is central to knowledge: 'We dare to claim for the true, childlike, humble imagination, such an inward oneness with the laws of the universe that it possesses in itself an insight into the very nature of things.'

A central function of the imagination (an idea developed by C.S. Lewis) is the making of meaning. This making is strictly subordinate to the primary meanings put into his created reality by God. However, in 'the new arrangement of thought and figure . . . the new meaning contained is presented as it never was before'. He writes:

> Every new embodiment of a known truth must be a new and wider revelation. No man is capable of seeing for himself the whole of any truth: he needs it echoed back to him from every soul in the universe; and still its centre is hid in the Father of Lights.

He sees the operation of the imagination as choosing, gathering, and vitally combining the material of a new revelation.

> Such embodiments are not the result of the man's intention, or of the operation of his conscious nature. His feeling is that they are given to him; that from the vast unknown, where time and space are not, they suddenly appear in luminous writing upon the wall of his consciousness.

That there is always more to a work of art than the producer himself perceived while producing it, seemed to MacDonald a strong reason for 'attributing to it a larger origin than the man alone – for saying at the last, that the inspiration of the Almighty shaped its ends'. Somewhat similar ideas are found in Tolkien (*see* Natural Theology, Tolkien and†).

MacDonald's view of the imagination is squarely based on the view that all meanings are put into reality by their primary creator, God. All meaning refers to him, and thus is objective rather than subjective. He expresses this view eloquently in the following passage, anticipating Tolkien and C.S. Lewis:

One difference between God's work and man's is, that, while God's work cannot mean more than he meant, man's must mean more than he meant. For in everything that God has made, there is layer upon layer of ascending significance; also he expresses the same thought in higher and higher kinds of that thought: it is God's things, his embodied thoughts, which alone a man has to use, modified and adapted to his own purposes, for the expression of his thoughts; therefore he cannot help his words and figures falling into such combinations in the mind of another as he had himself not foreseen, so many are the thoughts allied to every other thought, so many are the relations involved in every figure, so many the facts hinted in every symbol. A man may well himself discover truth in what he wrote; for he was dealing all the time with things that came from thoughts beyond his own.

Intuitively, MacDonald dwells upon the importance of meaning. The question of meaning (both of reality itself and of language) is central in the twentieth century. It is a key theme running throughout the writings of C.S. Lewis, who was influenced by the ideas of Tolkien, and had much in common with him (*see* the Inklings‡). For Lewis, meaning was intimately tied up both with the role of the imagination, and with the fact that the entire universe is a dependent creation of God. He saw reason as the organ of truth, and imagination as the organ of meaning. Reason and imagination each had their own integrity. He particularly stressed the dependence of even the most abstract of thinking upon imagination.

C.S. Lewis, like Tolkien, believed that in some tangible sense the products of imagination in the arts could be true. Myth† could become fact. In writing fantasies such as *The Chronicles of Narnia* and *The Hobbit*.‡ they felt that they were discovering inevitable realities that were not the product of theories of the conscious mind (even though rational control is not relinquished in the making of good fantasy). It was this attitude which prompted both men to create consistent secondary worlds, or sub-creations, like Middle-earth* and Perelandra.

Tolkien's view of the imagination centres around his idea of sub-creation. This is most clearly set out in a famous essay, 'On Fairy Stories',‡ and reveals his affinity with the ideas of Coleridge, MacDonald and Lewis. There he speaks of creating secondary worlds with an 'inner consistency of reality', and of the relationship between works of imagination and truth. He also stresses the central importance of human language. It was typical of him to write elsewhere in a similar vein: 'Language has both strengthened imagination and been freed by it.'

See also Philology, Tolkien and;† Story, Tolkien's theology of.†

Immortality
See Death.†

Journey
See The Road;† Quest.†

Joy
In the stories of Middle-earth* the sea is a constant symbol† of longing. Over the sea in the west lay the Undying Lands, the blessed realm. As in the writings of C.S. Lewis,‡ such yearning is a pointer to joy and human fulfilment. Tolkien refers to the quality of joy in his essay, 'On Fairy Stories'.‡ It is a key feature of such stories, he believes, related to the happy ending, or eucatastrophe, part of the consolation† they endow. Tolkien believes that joy in the story marks the presence of grace from the primary world. 'It denies (in the face of much evidence, if you will) universal final defeat and in so far is *evangelium*, giving a fleeting glimpse of Joy, Joy beyond the walls of the world, poignant as grief.' He adds: 'In such stories when the sudden "turn" comes we get a piercing

glimpse of joy, and heart's desire, that for a moment passes outside the frame, rends indeed the very web of story, and lets a gleam come through.'

In an epilogue to the essay, Tolkien gives more consideration to the quality of joy, linking it to the Gospel narratives, which have all the qualities of an other-worldly, fairy story, while at the same time being primary world history. This doubleness intensifies the quality of joy, identifying its objective source.

Tolkien's friend, C.S. Lewis, explored the quality of joy, both in his quest,† which led to his Christian conversion, and in his writings. The two men were very much at one in seeking to define and embody this quality, so Lewis' view deserves some mention.

Joy, thought Lewis, inspired the creation of fantasy. The creation of another world is an attempt to reconcile human beings and the real world. It tries to embody the fulfilment of imaginative longing. Imaginative worlds, wonderlands, are 'regions of the spirit'. Such worlds of the numinous† may be found within science fiction, poetry, fairy stories, novels, myths, even within a phrase or sentence. Lewis claimed in *Of This and Other Worlds*: 'To construct plausible and moving "other worlds" you must draw on the only real "other world" we know, that of the spirit.'

In a dissertation, *The Dialectic of Desire*, Corbin Carnell explored the theme of joy in Lewis' work. He argued that Lewis illuminates a state of mind which has been a recurrent theme in literature. This is the compulsive quest 'which brings with it both fleeting joy and the sad realization that one is yet separated from what is desired'. Joy, for C.S. Lewis, is the key both to the nature of human beings and their creator (whom Lewis called 'the glad creator').

C.S. Lewis saw this unquenchable longing as a sure sign that no part of the created world, and thus no aspect of human experience, is capable of fulfilling fallen humankind. We are dominated by a homelessness, and yet by a keen sense of what home means.

For Lewis, joy is a foretaste of ultimate reality, heaven itself or, the same thing, our world or home as it was meant to be, unspoilt by the fall† of humankind, and one day to be remade. 'Joy', wrote C.S. Lewis, 'is the serious business of Heaven'.

In Tolkien, there is not only the quality of joy linked to the sudden turn in the story, the sense of eucatastrophe, but also this joy as inconsolable longing, in Lewis' sense. Dominating the entire cycle of his tales of Middle-earth is a longing to obtain the Undying Lands of the Uttermost West. The yearning is often symbolized by a desire for the sea, which lay to the west of Middle-earth, and over which lay Valinor,* even if by a hidden road.

Such longing is sharply portrayed in Galadriel,* who, since the rebellion of the Noldor,* had been forbidden to return to the west from Middle-earth. Her longing is poignantly captured in her song. Though a wood-elf, Legolas* grows to long for the sea and the west. In *The Silmarillion*,‡ Turgon* of Gondolin* instructs mariners to seek a way to the west in the hope that the Valar,* the lords of the west, might help him. One of them, Voronwë,* is gripped by the longing of his people, and, in the purposes of providence,† leads Tuor* to Gondolin. On a more homely level, Sam* is gripped with longing for all things elvish before he is chosen to aid Frodo* in the quest to destroy the One Ring.*

Last Battle, The

In Tolkien's mythology,† the final conflict against evil† at the end of the world, an end which will mark a new beginning.
See Apocalyptic, Tolkien and.†

Light

Light, and its contrast with darkness, is a key motif in Tolkien's mythology† of Middle-earth.* Through the tales he builds up a precise and careful meaning to light. Rather than a modern, New Age, meaning or, say, an intellectual concept of humanistic enlightenment, Tolkien's inspiration and model is biblical (*see* Christianity, Tolkien and†).

Verlyn Flieger has made a major study of the relationship of light, language and biblical content in Tolkien. In *Splintered Light: Logos and Language in Tolkien's World* (1983) she writes that *The Silmarillion*‡

> is a vast, fantasy mythology with the familiar mythological themes – gods and men, creation, transgression, love, war, heroism, and doom. But more than anything else, and more than most mythologies, it is a story about light. Images of light in all stages – brilliant, dim, whole, refracted – pervade the songs and stories of Tolkien's fictive world, a world peopled by sub-creators whose interactions with the light shape Middle-earth and their own destinies. Tolkien's use of light in *The Silmarillion* derives from his Christian belief . . .

Clyde Kilby, who was able to discuss Tolkien's fiction with him, speaks of the contrast of light and darkness always being emphasized in *The Lord of the Rings*.‡ In *Tolkien and the Silmarillion*, Clyde Kilby points out some of the many affinities between Tolkien's and the biblical imagination.† This affinity is startlingly evident in the case of the creation of light. As in the Bible, in Tolkien light is created before the existence of the sun and moon. The sun and moon are creatures, not deities.

Light itself is associated, Flieger points out, with the divine Logos, the light of the world, Christ himself. We see by him. Light in Tolkien's world is a sign of providence,† accomplished by the agency of the Valar,* and defiled by the primal enemy of elvish and human life, Melkor (or Morgoth*), the equivalent of Lucifer, who became darkened as Satan.

As in George MacDonald's‡ beautiful children's story, 'The Day Boy and the Night Girl', gradations of light are employed symbolically. Tolkien shows the process of the fall† by a diminution of the light. First there are the Two Lamps,* lighting the whole world, then the Two Trees,* lighting only the Undying Lands, and then the vastly diminished light of sun and moon, made from tiny vestiges of the light of the Trees. In MacDonald's story there is a beautiful description of how the Night Girl sees at night by light of moon and star – the only reality she knows. True reality is known only gradually. First there is dim light of night, then broad daylight, then the deeper light of true reality.

Other famous uses of the image of light include Plato's myth of the cave – where those in it have known only flickering representations of true forms in the world outside – and the dialogue between the green witch and Puddleglum, with the children, in her Underworld, in *The Silver Chair* by C.S. Lewis.‡ There she tries to persuade them that the sun and the world it shines upon doesn't exist; it is a fantasy based around the existence of lamps which light her gloomy world.

The abiding image of light in Tolkien's world is the Two Trees, extinguished by the visible darkness of Ungoliant.* Some of the light of the Trees had, however, been captured in the Silmarils* fashioned by Fëanor.* Fëanor's desire to recover the Silmarils, stolen by Morgoth, is a prime element in the events of the First Age* of Middle-earth.

As part of the theme of gradation and splintering of light, Tolkien creates the beautiful period of twilight in Middle-earth before the rising of sun and moon (the time when humans appear). The elves,* created in the twilight, looked upon and saw the dazzling stars, associated with Varda.* They are called to the light that exists in the Undying Lands – the light of the Two Trees. Consequently, they journey in quest† of those lands, some unwillingly. Not all complete the journey, but remain in Middle-earth, in the twilight. This division affects the history, and thus the language, of the elves, Quenya* being the language of the elves of Valinor,* and Sindarin,* the speech of those in Middle-earth.

Tolkien's portrayal of the twilight is haunted with a sense of the numinous†, and the presence of Varda. *A Elbereth Gilthoniel** is an elvish hymn or prayer to her. After the rising of the sun and moon, the stars in the night sky continued to comfort and give hope to those faithful to Ilúvatar.* The Seven Stars, the Sickle of the Valar, had been placed in the sky by Varda as a sign of the ultimate defeat of Morgoth.

As well as the delicate symbolism† of the gradation of light, darkness is a powerful image in Tolkien, again biblical, of all that is the enemy of human life in its full purpose. From the darkness that moved with the arachnid Ungoliant to the blackness of Shelob's* Lair, from the burning black of Morgoth's hands by the Silmarils he clutched to the threat of the Black Riders* in the long-protected Shire,* darkness is present through the tales as a palpable image of evil. Sam* in Mordor,* well-versed in the history of Middle-earth, was able to see that 'in the end the Shadow was only a small and passing thing: there was light and beauty for ever beyond its reach'.

A powerful image related to that of light is fire. In *The Silmarillion* we learn that there is a Secret Fire at the heart of real (rather than only envisaged) being. The Secret Fire has its biblical equivalent in the Holy Spirit. Gandalf* (who goes in title from 'the Grey' to 'the White') declares himself the servant of the Secret Fire, and bears the Ring of Fire, Narya.* This Ring* was passed on to Gandalf by Círdan* when the wizard† arrived in Middle-earth:

'Take this ring, Master,' he said, 'for your labours will be heavy; but it will support you in the weariness that you have taken upon yourself. For this is the Ring of Fire, and with it you may rekindle hearts in a world that grows chill.'

Fëanor, like Gandalf, is associated with fire. His name, given to him by his mother, is prophetic, and means 'Spirit of fire'. He is the epitome of elvish creativity and craftsmanship. Yet instead of being a servant of the Secret Fire like Gandalf, he desired possession† of it, like Morgoth before him. Thus he was unwilling to give back the Silmarils after the destruction of the Two Trees so that their light might be used. His pride in his achievement led him to foolishly pursue Morgoth into Middle-earth, which led to the exile of the Noldor.*

A very early part of Tolkien's invented mythology, the story of Eärendil,* displays the theme of light with great power. In Eärendil, the human who became the brightest star in the night sky over Middle-earth, Tolkien succeeded in making a Christ-figure, a prefigurement of the Saviour. The light came from the Silmaril on Eärendil's brow, as a sign of hope to the faithful in the world below. The story of Eärendil the intercessor was inspired by the Old English word, 'Earendel', in the poem, *Christ*.

Loyalty

We have only to think of Sam's* loyalty to Frodo* to realize that this is an important quality in Tolkien's world of Middle-earth.* This is a quality Tolkien was glad to borrow from medieval literature. He explored many permutations of loyalty, some good, some bad.

The negative aspect of loyalty is considered in *The Homecoming of Beorhtnoth Beorhthelm's Son‡* (*see The Tolkien Reader‡*). In *The Lord of the Rings*,‡ Denethor,* Steward of Gondor,* preferred his elder son Boromir,* even dead, to the younger, Faramir,* because of Boromir's loyalty to him. 'Boromir was loyal to me and no wizard's pupil. He would have remembered his father's need, and would not have squandered what fortune gave. He would have brought me a mighty gift.' On the positive side, there is not only Sam's loyalty to Frodo, but Merry's* to King Théoden,* and Pippin's* to Denethor, as well as the bizarre and fascinating loyalty that Gollum* has to Frodo, a loyalty that might possibly, it is hinted, have been his redemption. There is, also, Gandalf's* loyalty to the workings of goodness in providence.† He is able to declare that he is servant of the Secret Fire, the divine creativity behind all things that have been made.

Loyalty is most of all associated in Tolkien with heroism.† In figures such as Frodo and Sam, and in Beren* and Lúthien* of old, there is sacrifice† for the sake of others, as a basic principle of goodness and setting the world right. Tolkien appreciated this quality in the world of Beowulf. In his famous essay, 'Beowulf: The Monsters and the Critics',‡ he observes: 'Man, alien in a hostile world, engaged in a struggle which he cannot win while the world lasts, is assured that his foes are the foes also of Dryhten [God], that his courage noble in itself is also the highest loyalty.'

Magic
See Possession and Power.†

Mortality
See Death.†

Music
Music and song are a central theme running through Tolkien's tales of Middle-earth.* His mythology† begins with the 'Ainulindalë'‡, the music of the Ainur.* Before the creation of the world, its character and development is expressed in music. The presence of evil† in the world is prefigured in a discord introduced by Morgoth* (Melkor), a discord which Ilúvatar* is able to harness into a greater ultimate harmony. *The Hobbit*‡ and *The Lord of the Rings*‡ are replete with songs, songs integral to the story. Tolkien wrote major sections of *The Silmarillion*‡ in verse which, though not song, is closer to music than prose is, which is true of all poetry. Modern composers such as Donald Swann and Stephen Oliver have been able to set songs from Middle-earth to music with great effect. A love of song is characteristic of elves* and hobbits.* Tom Bombadil's* very speech is song.

Song is also part of the narrative action in key stories of the First Age.* In the tale of Beren and Lúthien, the elf-maiden,‡ the elven-king Finrod Felagund battles with Sauron* in song, and the singing of Lúthien* destroys Sauron's tower at Tol Sirion.* In Doriath,* her singing had enchanted Beren,* as her mother's singing had enchanted her father, Thingol,* in earlier days. In the tale of

Túrin Turambar,* after Túrin finds healing at the Pools of Ivrin, he is able to make a song for his lost friend, Beleg, and is thus able to act once more, in defiance of the enemy.

In the Third Age,* this direct power of song only seems to be retained by Galadriel.* Her lament in Lórien,* sung while the Company of the Ring* were there, mentions this power:

I sang of leaves, of leaves of gold, and leaves of gold there grew:
Of wind I sang, a wind there came and in the branches blew.

The power of song is the magical power lying behind creation, an idea C.S. Lewis‡ took up in the creation of Narnia in *The Magician's Nephew.*
See also The Road Goes Ever On.‡

Myth, mythology

Myths are normally attempts to explain or understand the reality in which we find ourselves. In Tolkien's fiction the myths belong to his secondary world of Middle-earth.* It is an invented mythology rather than one which embodies a belief system (such as the Babylonian cosmology, or northern myths of creation). Yet Tolkien intended his invented mythology to illuminate the real, primary world. He hoped that it would bring to his reader recovery† of a true view of things, escape† from the prison of inaccurate and misleading presuppositions, and true consolation,† consolation which pointed to the historical gospel story. Paradoxically, Tolkien's invented mythology can claim to be believed myth, myth in the usual sense – pointing to an objective state of affairs.

Tolkien sharply distinguished myth from allegory,† though he did believe in the applicability, and need to apply, stories. C.S. Lewis,‡ who thought rather similarly (though was more 'allegorical' than Tolkien), expressed this distinction of myth and allegory. He did this when writing to Tolkien after reading the early, unfinished poetic version of the tale of Beren and Lúthien, the elf-maiden:‡

> The two things that come out clearly are the sense of reality in the background and the mythical value: the essence of the myth being that it should have no taint of allegory to the maker and yet should suggest incipient allegories to the reader.

In reviewing his friend's *The Lord of the Rings*,‡ C.S. Lewis describes just how Tolkien's invented mythology is applicable to the primary, real world. Lewis concentrates on the aspect of recovery:

> The value of the myth is that it takes all the things we know and restores to them the rich significance which has been hidden by the veil of familiarity. The child enjoys his cold meat, otherwise dull to him, by pretending it is buffalo, just killed with his own bow and arrow. And the child is wise. The real meat comes back to him more savoury for having been dipped in a story; you might say that only then is it real meat. If you are tired of the real landscape, look at it in a mirror. By putting bread, gold, horse, apple, or the very roads into a myth, we do not retreat from reality: we rediscover it. As long as the story lingers in our mind, the real things are more themselves. This book applies the treatment not only to bread or apple but to good and evil, to our endless perils, our anguish and our joys. By dipping them in myth we see them more clearly. I do not think he could have done it in any other way.

Tolkien's view of myth, which deeply influenced C.S. Lewis, is captured in a poem written to Lewis at the time his scepticism about Christian belief was shattered. The poem, 'Mythopoeia'‡ (the making of myths), is reproduced in the new (1988) edition of *Tree and Leaf*.‡

C.S. Lewis regarded the nineteenth-century writer George MacDonald‡ as one of the greatest masters of myth-making, especially in *Phantastes* (which, Lewis says, 'baptized' his imagination long before he became a Christian believer) and *Lilith*. Tolkien did not hold MacDonald in such high regard as Lewis, although his work shows an indebtedness to him.

Tolkien persuaded Lewis that, at the heart of Christianity, is a myth that is also a fact – making the claims of Christianity unique. But by becoming fact it did not cease to be myth, or lose the quality of myth. Tolkien sets out his ideas in his seminal essay, 'On Fairy Stories'.‡

Tolkien spoke of the 'seamless web of story'. Human stories were interrelated and, by God's† grace, carried insights into the true nature of things. It is the gospel, however, that has broken into this web of story from the real world (*see* Joy†).

It is important to realize the way that Tolkien saw story (*see* Story, Tolkien's theology of†). The temptation is to source hunt Tolkien's invented mythology, for instance examining Old Norse mythology or biblical imagery. David Harvey, in *The Song of Middle-earth*, warns against this danger. Tolkien was concerned with universal mythological themes.

Tolkien's belief that God in his grace had prefigured the gospel *evangelium* in human stories, a view shared by C.S. Lewis, was a kind of natural theology.†

Natural theology, Tolkien and

Tolkien, by confession, was a Roman Catholic. Roman Catholicism always has given a high value to natural theology. The *New Dictionary of Theology* defines natural theology as 'Truths about God that can be learned from created things (nature, man, world) by reason alone'. The Reformation emphasized a return to Scripture alone as the source of knowledge of God,† and thus all else. Nature† was interpreted through the spectacles of Scripture.

In practice, Protestant apologists have tended to presuppose a common ground of reason which suggests an implicit natural theology. Roman Catholics, on the other hand, are inclined to see a continuum between natural and revealed theology. The issue is one of autonomy or neutrality in knowledge. Is there true knowledge of God without the enlightenment of Scripture? The problem with an autonomous view of human reason is the radical biblical doctrine of the fall,† which affected every aspect of the human, including the mind.

Tolkien's natural theology is unusual in that his stress is with the imagination,† rather than with reason. It is by imagination, he suggests, that there can be genuine insight into God and reality independently of the specific revelation of Scripture. However, he seeks to avoid autonomy by emphasizing, in his essay, 'On Fairy Stories',‡ that any such insights are acts of grace from the Father of Lights. They are a kind of pre-revelation, opening the way to receiving the special revelation of the gospel. Furthermore, fundamental to his fiction is the theme of the fall of humankind.

Whereas traditional Roman Catholic thought emphasizes the rational and cognitive in natural theology, Tolkien links it with imaginative meaning. It is a complementary revelation to that of the propositional. The story,† like language, is evidence of the image of God still remaining in fallen humankind. 'The tongue and the tale', believed Tolkien, 'are coeval'. He also spoke of 'the seamless web of story', the interrelationship of all storytelling. Tolkien, like C.S. Lewis,‡ believed that, in a sense, it was natural to believe in Christ, our Saviour. Damnation is in fact a wilful choice, against our knowledge of what is good.

For Tolkien, monotheism is 'natural religion', and is the faith of the Three Ages of Middle-earth* (the pre-Christian era, highlighting the best of such a situation).

David Harvey, in his *The Song of Middle-earth*, argues that Tolkien employs universal motifs from mythology rather than specific sources like Old Norse mythology or the Bible. Specific borrowing from the northern imagination, and the like, is always transformed (as in the story of Kullervo in the Kalavala and the Túrin* story). This universal emphasis, however, is not humanism (which Harvey seems to imply) but Tolkien's natural theology - which he felt pointed to the unique Christ, the sole Saviour who came in the history of the primary world.

Tolkien's natural theology is a great imaginative achievement. Natural theology is related, philosophically, to intuitionism. Tolkien's is an imaginative rather than intellectual intuitionism, perhaps like that of George MacDonald.‡

One important problem with intuitionism is illustrated in the famous ontological argument, which argues from a human idea of perfection to God's existence. That idea of perfection is not pure intuition, however, but formed in a classical and Christian tradition, so has presuppositional, language-based, archetypal elements. The same is true of Tolkien's natural theology of the imagination – he is in fact restating and restoring an imaginative tradition, rather than inventing or 'discovering' symbols and stories that, by natural intuition, the reader knows to be in some sense true. That tradition itself, however, is making truth-claims with great power, and Tolkien allows it to be heard once again.

Nature

Like his close friend C.S. Lewis,‡ Tolkien believed that worlds of the imagination† are properly based upon the humble and common things of life – what Lewis called 'the quiet fullness of ordinary nature'. Both Tolkien and Lewis defended fantasy on this basis against the charge of escapism (*see* Fairy stories†). What Lewis said about *The Wind in the Willows* (the popular children's story by Kenneth Grahame) could have been Tolkien's words: 'The happiness which it presents to us is in fact full of the simplest and most attainable things – food, sleep, exercise, friendship, the face of nature, even (in a sense) religion.' Such fantasy is the opposite of escapism. It deepens the reality of the real world for us – the terror as well as the beauty.

Again like Lewis, Tolkien believed that nature is better understood as God's† creation. When the storyteller is building up a convincing 'secondary world', he or she in fact is engaged in what Tolkien called 'sub-creation';† creating, as it were, in the image or as a miniaturization of the 'primary world'. Such story-making surveys the depth of space and time. It is the imaginative equivalent of the reason's attempt to capture reality in a single, unified theory.

For Tolkien, the natural world of God's creating imposes a fundamental limit to the human imagination. We cannot, like God, create *ex nihilo*, out of nothing. We can only rearrange elements that God has already made, and which are already brimful with his meanings. Sub-creation, the storytelling at least of humankind (that of elves* is different), reflects the brokenness of God's original creation. The fall† theme is intrinsic. Tolkien clarified this theme in the light of the claims of Christian revelation (*see* Christianity, Tolkien and†). To give just one example of the effect of the fall, evil† always results in the disruption or even the destruction of nature. Tolkien's work is full of symbolic landscapes of a spoiled world: the devastation of Ard-galen,* the ruin of Beleriand,* the drowning of Númenor,* the desolation of Smaug* – to name just a few. He even takes the basis of life – light† – and employs it symbolically to show the mischief that wickedness causes, particularly the malice of Morgoth.*

Tolkien uses his own sub-creation of Middle-earth* as a mirror of nature. There are considerable complexities in the structure of his world. Genetically, for example, there are differences between elves and humans, even though the two races can intermarry fruitfully. As a result of these differences one race is immortal and the other must face the mystery of death.† Elves are tied to the natural order in a way that humankind is not. Nevertheless (and, in Tolkien, because of this), elves represent the higher aspect of human nature (*see* Elven quality†). Another example of complexity in Tolkien's portrayal of his world is its geography.* At the drowning of Númenor the very shape of the world is changed, becoming the sphere that is familiar to us. Though an invented world, Tolkien supposes that it is our primary world in its pre-Christian history, especially as regards northern Europe.

This sense of familiar location is intensified by Tolkien in his creation of the Shire,* and of Tol Eressëa* in early versions of *The Silmarillion*.‡ The Shire, and the original Tol Eressëa, are homely places associated with Tolkien's experience of the West Midlands at the turn of the last century. This identity of the West Midlands was strengthened for Tolkien by his study of medieval English literature. Favourite works such as *Pearl* were written in a rich West Midlands English.

As well as this large-scale 'homeliness', Tolkien was fond of creating homely places such as the Cottage of Lost Play, Bag End, Crickhollow, the House of Tom Bombadil,* the Prancing Pony* pub, and Rivendell.*

By a powerful transposition, Tolkien portrayed a homeliness in his idea of the hero,† an idea which he took from the Bible. His real heroes, such as Bilbo Baggins* and Sam Gamgee,* are taken from ordinary life. Even more 'heroic' heroes like Beren* are in the opinion of the wise weak and frail. The great king Aragorn* must be disguised as a humble Ranger* for much of his life to be prepared for the great tasks required of him.

Tolkien had a great love for nature as a garden. His brother Hilary‡ was a market gardener, and Tolkien was an amateur gardener. His knowledge of flora is an important element in his fiction. He of course created Elanor,* Athelas* and Evermind. His love for the tree† became a central theme in his work. In Middle-earth, the tree is the crown of the flora of creation.

Nature and grace

Tolkien's imaginative creations work out the theme of nature and grace (*see* Story, Tolkien's theology of†; Elven quality†). The framework of nature and grace was originally largely an attempt to Christianize a Greek antithesis of form and matter in medieval times. Etienne Gilson points out that by the beginning of the thirteenth century an Aristotelian concept of the soul had gained a widespread acceptance among certain Christian philosophers and theologians. Before this a concept of the soul that had come from Plato, largely through Augustine's influence, had been popular. Aristotle's concept of the soul illustrates the dynamic pattern of form and matter. Etienne Gilson comments that 'the soul, according to Aristotle, is the act or form of an organized body having life potentially. Thus the relation of soul and body is a particular case of the general relationship between form and matter.'

Aquinas drew heavily on Aristotle's concept. The human being actualizes the potentiality of nature; for example, it makes nature knowable by the exercise of human reason. From this arose the idea of natural theology. Truths about God and the world could be known by the unaided human intellect. Only a fuller knowledge of God, the heavenly realm, and the spiritual, depended on grace. In relation to God, humankind is only potential, a potential actualized by the divine. Humanity is in a middle world, between form and matter, God and nature. After Aquinas the intellect became more and more independent of divine revelation and grace in relation to knowledge, helping to give rise to the modern sciences.

The framework of nature and grace was the pattern not only for theology and philosophy but throughout western culture, influencing artists and writers everywhere. In his essay, 'Nature and Grace in "The Faerie Queen"', A.S.P. Woodhouse points out that the model was still in existence in the seventeenth century, guiding the great poets. He observes:

In Spenser's day, as still in Milton's, the two orders of nature and of grace were universally accepted as a frame of reference, whether they were specifically named or not. Within this frame of reference there was room for every degree of difference in attitude and emphasis: it was a frame of reference, not a body of doctrine.

Integral to the framework is a hierarchy to the created world, ranging from the inanimate, through vegetable and sensible life, to the rational. Humankind straddled the hierarchy present on earth; they were a 'little world' or *microcosmos*. In a sense, persons in themselves are alternative worlds, potentially the creators of other worlds (*see* Sub-creation†). Such a view of humanity was immensely liberating to the imagination.† To the contrary, increasingly mechanistic views of reality reduced humans to a spatial segment of matter in motion, or to a dualism of mind and body. Expressing the view of humanity the microcosm, Gregory the Great wrote: 'Because man has existence in common with stones, life with trees, and understanding with angels, he is rightly called by the name of the world.' Such a view was also a feature of John Calvin's thinking, expressed in his commentary on the book of Genesis.

See also Natural Theology, Tolkien and.†

Numinous

This is a term created by the German Lutheran theologian, Rudolf Otto (1869–1937). He was concerned to isolate the universal element in human experience that is religious. He rejected the attempts to explain away such experience by materialistic theories. The experience could be called the Holy, but he was afraid that this term might only suggest a moral category. So, as an alternative, he tried to define the numinous. He did not give a simple, rational, definition, believing that the religious is ultimately inexpressible. Instead, he tried to invoke its reality. The numinous experience involves a sense of dependence upon what stands wholly other to humanity. This otherness (or other-worldliness) is unapproachable and awesome. At the same time it has a fascination and attraction. Rudolf Otto believed that Christianity has the clearest concept of the numinous.

Whatever the rights and wrongs of Otto's analysis, the implication is that the experience of the numinous is captured better by suggestion and allusion than by a theoretical analysis. It is also true that many realities captured in imaginative fiction could be described as having a quality of the numinous. C.S. Lewis‡ realized this, incorporating the idea into his apologetic for the Christian view of suffering, *The Problem of Pain*, and cited an event from Kenneth Grahame's fantasy for children, *The Wind in the Willows*, to illustrate it. Many elements in his fantasies, and in the fiction of Tolkien, convey a quality of the numinous.

Much of the numinous in Tolkien is the effect of his linguistic creativity (*see* Philology, Tolkien and†). His use of Elvish* names, words and phrases, which are beautiful and yet foreign, often invokes a numinous quality, similarly his employment of Runes.* The uncomprehended can have great imaginative power, as in dreams, or in George MacDonald's‡ *Phantastes*. Parts of *The Silmarillion*,‡ using an archaic yet powerfully attractive style, also convey the numinous – the 'Ainulindalë'‡ is the most successful.

Tolkien has great ability in capturing the numinous through the symbolic (*see* Symbolism†), whether in landscape (as in Doriath* or Lórien*) or the natural elements. He uses the element of light† with great power. The twilight which the elves* awoke to in Middle-earth,* before the creation of sun and moon, has a strong significance for the imagination.† Twilight is a traditional motif favoured by the Romantics (as in the link between darkness and moonlight and the sublime in Gothic literature), but Tolkien uses it with great delicacy in the world before the sun, where only the far west is lit by the light of the Two Trees.*

The numinous is embodied most of all, in Tolkien's work, in his idea of faerie (*see* Sub-creation†) – an other world in which it is possible for beings such as elves to live and move and have a history. The world of the elves is the focus of *The Silmarillion*,‡ and had a powerful attraction for his imagination. Some of his elves (like Lúthien* or Galadriel*) are incarnations of the numinous.

Where the numinous is captured, its appeal is firstly to the imagination, which also senses it most accurately. It belongs to the area of meaning rather than concept. C.S. Lewis found this when he read MacDonald's *Phantastes*, describing the effect as baptizing his imagination. It was years later that he was able to reconcile this experience with his thinking. Tolkien similarly seems to have taken years of reflection (reflection often captured in his letters) to come to terms with his imaginative discoveries (*see* Christianity, Tolkien and†).

Old West, Tolkien and the

Tolkien was by profession a philologist (*see* Philology, Tolkien and†), teaching Old English and Middle English, very much in connection with the literature of the period. His work was intimately related to his construction of the languages, peoples and history of Middle-earth.* From the burgeoning creation of Elvish* languages he reconstructed a forgotten world. Actually, he invented a world as if it were a forgotten world, patterned on the philologist's construction of forgotten contexts and earlier forms from vestiges of old languages. Tolkien particularly explored the possibility of a forgotten, old Western world in his unfinished tales of time travel, 'The Lost Road' and 'The Notion Club Papers'.‡ The same theme is implicit in the theme he returned to again and again, that of Aelfwine's* voyage to the Uttermost West by the lost road,* where he hears the forgotten tales of Middle-earth – or rather the tales of the cosmos to which Middle-earth belongs.

The instincts of a philologist are captured in the figure of the Cambridge philologist Elwin Ransom, in C.S. Lewis'‡ science-fiction story, *Out of the Silent Planet*. Ransom had been kidnapped to Malacandra (Mars), and in terror escaped his captors. He feared the alien life-forms on the planet until a startling event took place, which dramatically overturns his perceptions. He encounters an animal that speaks:

The creature, which was still steaming and shaking itself on the bank and had obviously not seen him, opened its mouth and began to make noises. This in itself was not remarkable; but a lifetime of linguistic study assured Ransom almost at once that these were articulate noises. The creature was talking . . . In the fraction of a second which it took Ransom to decide that the creature was really talking, and while he still knew that he might be facing instant death, his imagination had leaped over every fear and hope and probability of his situation to follow the dazzling project of making a Malacandrian grammar. *An Introduction to the Malacandrian language – The Lunar verb – A Concise Martian–English Dictionary* . . . the titles flitted through his mind. And what might one not discover from the speech of a non-human race? The very form of language itself, the principle behind all possible languages, might fall into his hands. (from Chapter 9)

Ransom's thought, 'what might one not discover from the speech of a non-human race?' is the kind of notion that would naturally arise in Tolkien's mind. Indeed, the creation of Elvish languages – non-human languages of a kind – were for him an explanation of the dazzling possibilities of language for illuminating our knowledge of reality, both natural and supernatural, seen and unseen.

The character of Elwin Ransom, in Lewis' story (and in its sequel, *Perelandra*), is actually based upon Tolkien, his close friend. Elwin means 'Elf-friend', like the name Aelfwine. Tolkien was aware of this resemblance. Ransom is both Lewis' voice in the story and representative of Tolkien.

The affinity between Lewis and Tolkien that allowed Lewis to fictionalize his friend, and allowed his friend modestly to recognize this fictional treatment, is not simply a linguistic one. Philology is undoubtedly an important element in *Out of the Silent Planet*, as it is in the foundation of all Tolkien's fiction. Equally important however, and present in both theory and fiction, is a commitment to the Old West, and a related antipathy to modernism. What the friends would have viewed as Old Western values are embodied in Elwin Ransom, values they each endorsed.

These Old Western values are embedded in the portrayal of Ransom, both positively and negatively. Positively they are displayed in Ransom's perception, which is pre-modernist and essentially medieval. Lewis, like Tolkien, loved the Renaissance and medieval cosmos, its imaginative model of reality, and it is this world-picture that is smuggled into the minds of modern readers as they enjoy Lewis' story. Negatively, Ransom's pre-modernist values are expressed in contrast to the attitudes of Professor Edward Weston, a scientist who represents all that Lewis dislikes about the modernist world. Weston is the person responsible for kidnapping Ransom, an act he considers completely justifiable. He has a disdain for all values of the Old West. His guiding value is the survival of humanity at any cost.

Lewis famously defended what he called the Old West in his inaugural lecture taking on the Chair of Medieval and Renaissance Literature at the University of Cambridge in 1954, a seat Tolkien helped him gain. Tolkien was an Elector of the newly established chair, along with F.P. Wilson and Basil Willey. Tolkien described Lewis as 'the precise man for the job'. Lewis claimed, in the lecture:

It is my settled conviction that in order to read Old Western literature aright you must suspend most of the responses and unlearn most of the habits you have acquired in reading modern literature. And because this is the judgement of a native, I claim that, even if the defence of my conviction is weak, the fact of my conviction is a historical *datum* to which you should give full weight. That way where I fail as a critic, I may yet be useful as a specimen. I would even dare to go further. Speaking not only for myself but for all other Old Western men whom you may meet, I would say, use your specimens while you can. There are not going to be many more dinosaurs. (from *De Descriptione Temporum*, 1955)

Tolkien, along with their mutual friend Owen Barfield,‡ was responsible for helping along the process which led Lewis to become aware of a dramatic shift from the Old to the Modernist West, a shift which made the change from medieval to Renaissance culture insignificant by comparison. Tolkien pointed out to Lewis that the values of pre-Christian paganism were not merely of aesthetic interest, but were life and death matters reflecting an objective state of affairs.

As a result of Tolkien's arguments, C.S. Lewis came to the conclusion that similarities between Christian teaching and ancient myths can argue for the truth of Christianity as well as against it. At the heart of Christianity, C.S. Lewis came to believe, is a myth that is also a fact – making the claims of Christianity unique. But by becoming fact, it did not cease to be myth, or lose the quality of myth (*see* Myth,† mythology).

Tolkien's fiction, significantly, largely has a pre-Christian setting. Of Lewis' corpus, only his novel, *Till We Have Faces*, has such a setting. It is such a significant work however, that it underlines the deep affinity between the two men. Tolkien embodies his love of and commitment to the Old West in his mythology.

Most obvious of all is the geographical – Valinor and Númenor symbolically embody the values of the Old West. Quests† for the Undying Lands figure often in the tales of Tolkien's sub-created world. Eärendil,* for instance, seeks the blessed realm of Valinor in order to intercede for the threatened peoples of Beleriand.* The tapestry of tales essentially begins and ends with quests for the West. After their awakening, the elves* journey towards the Uttermost West. Then, at the end of the Third Age* of Middle-earth, the Ring-bearers pass west over the Great Sea to seek the Undying Lands beyond the world. In our own history, Tolkien imagines Aelfwine's journey west to Tol Eressëa,* where he hears the elven tales. In the unfinished 'The Lost Road' and 'The Notion Club Papers', the lost western island of Númenor figures prominently in the setting of our world.

Tolkien's tales in their own manner embody anti-modernist themes as powerfully as any stories written by Lewis, disclosing his Old Western values. Anti-modernism can be seen clearly, for instance, in Tolkien's treatment of the related themes of possession† and power, themes central to his work.

In our time, modernism increasingly seems to be collapsing in on itself like a stellar black hole. The anti-modernism of Tolkien and Lewis is now acceptable to an extent that would have astonished them. It is not really surprising that the popularity of their writings is greater than ever – as the recent Waterstone's poll revealed. The current phase of post-modernism is difficult to characterize but, like pre-modernism, is identified in relation to what Lewis called the hideous strength of modernism. It is interesting that even back in 1954, Lewis defined the Old West by placing it in contrast to modernism. The Great Divide lay, he believed, somewhere in the nineteenth century. It was as much a sociological and cultural divide as a shift in ideas. However, with the recent rise of a new paganism, I think Lewis and Tolkien would caution against assuming that this is the same as the pre-Christian paganism they loved and explored, much as they might have welcomed features of it. The new paganism we are experiencing today is on our side of the Great Divide, not on the other side, the side of the Old West. Both Lewis and Tolkien, as we saw, found values in pre-Christian paganism that prefigured the Christian values that they championed. Lewis warned, in his inaugural Cambridge lecture:

> Christians and Pagans had much more in common with each other than either has with a post-Christian. The gap between those who worship different gods is not so wide as that between those who worship and those who do not ... A post-Christian man is not a Pagan; you might as well think that a married woman recovers her virginity by divorce. The post-Christian is cut off from the Christian past and therefore doubly from the Pagan past.

The continuing popularity of Lewis' and Tolkien's pre-modernism – their sustained rejection of modernism in favour of Old Western values – suggests the existence of a continuity between the Old West and now, despite the Great Divide. It indicates a strong though small stream that has never been eradicated, despite Tolkien's and Lewis' fears.

Philology, Tolkien and

According to Professor Shippey, in his book, *The Road to Middle-earth*, Tolkien's fiction results from the interaction between his imagination† and his professional work as a philologist. C.S. Lewis‡ put something of his friend into the fictional character of the philologist, Elwin Ransom, in his science fiction story, *Out of the Silent Planet*. In 1944, Tolkien wrote to his son Christopher: 'As a philologist I may have some part in him, and recognize some of my opinions Lewisified in him.' (*See* Old West.†)

The name, Elwin, means 'Elf friend', and is a version of the name of the central character in Tolkien's unfinished story, 'The Lost Road'. In that story he is named Alboin. From when he was a child he has invented, or rather discovered, strange and beautiful words, leading him to the theory that they are fragments from an ancient world. This slightly autobiographical story tells us much about the love which motivated Tolkien's work in philology, and how it was intimately tied up with his invented mythology† of Middle-earth.* Owen Barfield‡ said of C.S. Lewis that he was in love with the imagination. It could be said of Tolkien that he was in love with language.

The academic discipline of philology, once strong, has now been absorbed into the subject area of linguistics. It combined linguistic, literary and cultural study. *Everyman's Encyclopedia* attempts a definition: 'Philology is used either (and particularly in Europe) to include both literary scholarship and the linguistic study of literary languages, both text-oriented; or purely to mean linguistics, particularly historical or diachronic linguistics (terms to which it is losing ground).' For a taste of Tolkien's professional work, see his *The Monsters and the Critics and other Essays*,‡ where he remarks, 'Philology is the foundation of humane letters.'

At Oxford, Tolkien taught mostly Early English, Middle English and the history of the English language. This professional work was intimately related to his construction of the languages, peoples and history of the three Ages of Middle-earth.* He commented in a letter that he sought to create a mythology for England, but it might be argued that he also tried to create a mythology for the English language. The earliest expression of the mythology embodied in *The Silmarillion*,‡ a poem written in 1914 about the voyage of Eärendil,* was inspired by a line from Cynewulf's Old English poem *Christ, 'Eala Earendel engla beorhtost'* ('Behold Earendel brightest of angels').

In his essay, 'The Oxford English School' (1930), Tolkien makes clear that he regarded both literary and linguistic approaches as too narrow to gain a full response to works of art. He felt that this was particularly true of early literary works, very distant from contemporary culture. Philology was a necessary dimension of both approaches. It could give a proper depth of response. Professor Shippey points out that Tolkien saw works of literary art philologically, and his own fiction came out of a philological vision.

The philological instinct is demonstrated in the quest† for an Indo-European language in the deep past. As the old philologists sought for Indo-European, many Tolkien readers try to unravel a proto-Elvish language, the ancestor of the two distinct branches of Tolkien's invented Elvish* – Quenya* and Sindarin.* It is interesting that, while Tolkien constructs a plausible family relationship between the two branches of Elvish, the two languages that inspired them – Finnish and Welsh – are not related in this way, according to linguists.

It is also interesting, as Professor Shippey points out, that the philologist Jakob Grimm produced collections of fairy tales as well as learned scholarship, just as Tolkien's imaginative work sprang out of his philological study.

Further reading

James Allan (ed.), *An Introduction to Elvish* (1978).
Ruth S. Noel, *The Languages of Tolkien's Middle-earth* (1980).
T.A. Shippey, *The Road to Middle-earth* (1982).

Possession and power

In his mythology† and tales of Middle-earth,* Tolkien explores power in relation to possession. Possession is a unifying theme, from the desire of Morgoth* (Melkor) to have God's† power of creation to the temptation of wielding the One Ring.* In a letter (Letter 131) Tolkien commented, '"Power" is an ominous and sinister word in all these tales, except as applied to the gods.'

The wrong use of power is often expressed in Tolkien in magic, the mechanical and the technological. Morgoth, Sauron* and Saruman* experiment with genetic engineering, and use or encourage the use of machines. Sauron, in fact, is the supreme technocrat; the Ring itself is a product of his technological skill. Tolkien contrasts art with magic, typified in the elves* (*see* Elven quality†), who have no desire for domination. Tolkien, like C.S. Lewis‡ and Jacques Ellul, saw a machine attitude, or technocracy, as the modern form of magic, seeking to dominate and possess nature,† rather than husband it. Though Tolkien tried to recreate a rural past in the Shire,* he was not anti-cultural. He was rather opposed to a machine mentality. The Shire he portrayed could only exist because of the sacrifice† and effort of its secret guardians such as Aragorn* and Gandalf.*

The magical power – the instinct to possess at any cost – of modern technocracy is recognized not only by Tolkien and Lewis (as in his science-fiction novel, *That Hideous Strength*). Lord Zuckerman commented about the nuclear arms race: 'It is he, the technician, not the commander in the field, who is at the heart of the arms race, who starts the process of formulating a so-called military nuclear need . . . They have become the alchemists of our times, working in secret ways which cannot be divulged, casting spells which embrace us all' (*Apocalypse Now?*, page 25).

Domination does not necessarily imply possession in Tolkien; it is not wholly bad. Possession however is a perversion of stewardship. Denethor* and Gandalf can be contrasted as bad and good stewards, as they exercise responsibility over others. Tom Bombadil* is also a good model of stewardship; the guardian of the Old Forest* who has no desire to possess, and who is thereby invulnerable to the desire of the Ring. The earlier Ages of Middle-earth* are dominated by elves, who avoided possession. The dominance of humankind in the Fourth Age* is intended to be modelled on elven values, not to be a destructive territorial rivalry. Tolkien condemns the process in Númenor* from a stewardly civilization to one which lusted for possession and sought to enslave others.

The two central motifs of the stories of Middle-earth, the Silmarils* and the Ring, focus the theme of possession. The Silmarils are wholly good, and the Ring is wholly evil, yet each test those who come into contact with them. Thingol* tragically falls morally in desiring a Silmaril; Beren* has no desire to possess it. Rather he loves the greater treasure, Lúthien,* who is better than any possession. Boromir* succumbs to the desire of the Ring; Bilbo* resists it, as does Galadriel*; it has little power over the humble Sam.*

Another powerful symbol relating to the theme of possession is the dragon† with its hoard. Though the hoard cannot be of any use to the dragon, he is jealous over the smallest item that may be stolen, as Smaug* is in *The Hobbit*.‡

Power

See Possession and power.†

Providence

According to Ruth S. Noel, in *The Mythology of Middle-earth*, the concept of predestined fate is common in myth.† In Tolkien's invented mythology, he grapples with the relationship between fate and free will.

His solution is a Christian one which sees the hand of God,† or providence, behind human history and the natural world. Working out this solution imaginatively must mean grappling with the complexity of reality. Even an invented reality is complex, for Tolkien sees it as sub-creation,† having an 'inner consistency of reality'.

In the northern imagination† to which Tolkien was so deeply indebted, fate was a fundamental principle. There is fated to be a twilight of the gods. In Greek mythology, and philosophical thought, the gods are ultimately ruled by principles greater than themselves. The personal creator-god of Plato's *Timaeus* is a demiurge. It is only in the biblical narratives of Judeo-Christianity that there is a personal creator who is not conditioned, who is infinite, making an order of being out of nothing, a reality distinct from his own.

Fundamental to Tolkien's invented mythology is the fact that the demiurges or powers involved in the creation of the world are themselves creatures of Ilúvatar,* the one God. The divine providence thus overrules all principles and powers found in created reality, including the shadow-evil. From the perspective of created beings such as elves, humans and hobbits,* it can often seem that evil† is winning, that an indifferent or negative fate rather than providence is in command. Tolkien believed that a work of imagination like his own, an attempt at proper sub-creation, should reveal providence rather than evil or fate as the master principle. By its nature, providence (unlike evil or fate) does not do away with free will, but respects it (*see* Natural theology, Tolkien and†). Rather like John Milton, writing *Paradise Lost*, Tolkien was concerned to justify the ways of God to humanity in a world spoiled by suffering and evil.

Tolkien picked up on themes of providence found in fairy stories.† Frequently, bans and prohibitions are placed by the Valar* on elves and humans. Fëanor* refused to stay in Valinor* after Morgoth's* theft of the Silmarils,* provoking judgment on himself and his family. The Númenoreans were forbidden to set foot on the shores of Valinor. As well as bans and prohibitions, Tolkien employed the theme of prophecy. One key prophecy in *The Lord of the Rings*‡ was that the king, returning to Gondor,* would be recognized by his healing† hands. Aragorn* also carried a sword that had been broken, fulfilling another prophecy.

The complex pattern of free will and providence is captured in the incident where Sam,* Frodo* and others look in the mirror of Galadriel.* It showed not only what would happen, but also what might happen. Events in Middle-earth* were not 'closed' but 'open'; free will had a bearing in the outcome of events. Sam and Frodo chose to go to Mordor.* The audacious strategy of seeking to destroy the Ring* under Sauron's* nose depended upon freely chosen sacrifice† and a deliberate act of foolishness.

Tolkien tried to retain a mood or tone from the northern imagination, one of courage and dignity before fate or doom. Though the way forward seemed impossible of success, as with the quest† of Frodo and Sam, or the march of the western allies to the Black Gate of Mordor, it had to be taken with full heart. Here Tolkien was emulating the Christian author of the poem, *Beowulf* (*see* 'Beowulf: The Monsters and the Critics'‡). A characteristic symbol† and presence of providence in Middle-earth are eagles.† They can mean judgment, as in the eagle-shaped clouds before the destruction of Númenor,* or, more usually, divine assistance.

There are numerous examples of the providential assistance of eagles in Tolkien's narratives of Middle-earth. Maedhros* is rescued by the eagle Thorondir.* Beren* and Lúthien* escape with the help of eagles after coming out of Angband* with the Silmaril cut from the Iron Crown of Morgoth. Bilbo* and the party of dwarves* are taken to the eyries of the eagles in *The Hobbit*.‡ Gandalf* is plucked from captivity in Isengard* by an eagle in *The Lord of the Rings*. In the same story, the otherwise desperate Frodo and Sam are lifted from Mount Doom after the Ring's destruction by the great eagle. In *The Silmarillion*,‡ eagles have their eyries in the Crissaegrim, peaks south of Gondolin,* strategically placed to view events within a wide radius. There they act as the messengers and servants of Manwë* the Vala.* Manwë ordained that eagles nest in mountains not high trees† so that they can hear and report to him the voices of humans and elves that called to him.

All means of light† are signs of providence, placed by the Valar. Stars have a particular significance, associated with Elbereth.* When Eärendil* the mariner was set to sail the heavens his star was a powerful symbol of hope to the faithful peoples of Middle-earth.

Another indication of providence was the arrival of the wizards† in Middle-earth in the Third Age.* Their work of guardianship was echoed to a lesser but vital extent by the Rangers* who, for example, protected the boundaries of the Shire.* One of the wizards, Gandalf, functions as a key interpreter of events (and thus of providence) in the story of *The Lord of the Rings*. Gandalf's sacrifice itself is providential. A sub-theme of providence is the place of oaths and curses, a traditional element in fairy stories.† Mandos* puts a doom or curse on Fëanor and his family after the kinslaying* at Alqualondë.* Most notable is the curse of Morgoth on the children of Húrin,* described as one of his greatest evils. This curse is a chief element in the tale of Túrin Turambar.* Artistically, this narrative is a great challenge to Tolkien in weaving the interrelationship between free will and the consequences of the curse. His greater task is to demonstrate that the great evil of this curse does not frustrate the larger purposes of providence.

The creation song† – the 'Ainulindalë'‡ – reveals that the discord of Morgoth is subsumed into the musical harmony of Ilúvatar.* The Túrin story is the great test of this claim. At the end of the story, despite the depths of its tragedy,† Túrin is a dragon-slayer, a great hero† in the battle of good against evil, light† against dark.

In another tale, Fingon attempts to end a feud between elves, the feud being a result of the curse or Doom of Mandos.* He traces his friend Maedhros.* Maedhros begs him to kill him to end the misery of his captivity. Fingon cries to Manwë to guide his arrow. Instead, the Vala, in answer to Fingon's prayer, sends one of his watching eagles, King Thorondir, to carry Fingon to rescue Maedhros.

Gandalf must be allowed to have the last word about providence, as he is so often its spokesman. At the end of *The Hobbit* he says to Bilbo:

'Surely you don't disbelieve the prophecies, because you had a hand in bringing them about yourself? You don't really suppose, do you, that all your adventures and escapes were managed by mere luck, just for your sole benefit? You are a very fine fellow, Mr Baggins, and I am very fond of you; but you are only quite a little fellow in a wide world after all!'

'Thank goodness!' said Bilbo laughing, and handed him the tobacco jar.

Quest

The quest often takes the form of a journey in symbolic literature (*see* Symbolism†), in fiction such as Tolkien's. Life and experience has the character of a journey, and this character can be intensified by art. The Christian possibilities of the quest have been explored by Thomas Malory (in *Morte d'Arthur*), by John Bunyan (in *The Pilgrim's Progress*) and by Tolkien – to name a few writers.

The greatest quests in Tolkien's fiction are Beren's* for the Silmaril* (but really for the hand of his beloved, Lúthien*), and

Frodo* and Sam's* for the destruction of the one Ring.* In Tolkien's profound little tale, *Leaf by Niggle*,‡ there is both a quest (to complete the painting of the tree) and a journey – from Niggle's call by the Inspector to his arrival at the beginning of the mountains.

The tales of Middle-earth* abound with quest heroes: Beren, Lúthien, Tuor,* Eärendil,* Bilbo,* Frodo, Sam, Aragorn,* to instance a few. For Tolkien, the ultimate model of the quest hero is Christ, with his mission to die, and then to turn the cosmic table by rising again (*see* Hero†).

The main quest heroes of Middle-earth follow the traditional theme. Each has a specific task or tasks to undertake, sometimes taking up much of his or her life. Some of them marry into the Elvish* race, like Beren and Eärendil, creating a pattern of relationships. Beren marries the elven Lúthien. Their child, Dior,* is father of Elwing,* who becomes the wife of Eärendil. The children of Eärendil are Elros and Elrond.* Aragorn is a descendent of Elros, who became the first king of Númenor.* Aragorn's wife, Arwen,* is the daughter of Elrond.

Each of the quests is different. Beren seeks marriage with Lúthien, his motivation is romantic love, and the quest of the Silmarils arises out of this. Eärendil seeks the blessed realm of Valinor* in order to intercede for the threatened people of Beleriand.* Aragorn seeks the return of kingship in the Númenorean tradition, to uphold civilization in a reunited Middle-earth. As these quests are conducted, all aspects of Christ (love, resurrection, mediation, sacrifice,† kingship, conquering of death,† healing†) are illuminated (*see* Christianity, Tolkien and†).

The fiction of Middle-earth essentially begins and ends with a quest. After the awakening of the elves† at Cuiviénen* they are called on a Great Journey to the Uttermost West, Aman,* by the Valar,* their guardians. At the end of the Third Age,* after the War of the Ring,* the Ring-bearers Bilbo and Frodo, and many of the elves, pass from Grey Havens* over the great sea by the straight road* to seek the Undying Lands beyond the world.

Recovery

In the fiction of Tolkien, recovery is related to escape† and conso-lation† (*see* Fairy stories†). Tolkien, like C.S. Lewis,‡ believed that, through story, the real world becomes a more magical place, full of meaning. We see its pattern and colour in a fresh way. The recovery of a true view of things applies both to individual things like hills and stones, and to the cosmic – the depths of space and time itself. For in sub-creation,† Tolkien believed, there is a survey of space and time. Reality is captured in miniature. Through sub-creative stories – the type to which *The Lord of the Rings*‡ and 'The tale of Beren and Lúthien, the elf-maiden'‡ belong – a renewed view of reality in all its dimensions is given – the homely, the spiritual, the physical, the moral.

Tolkien, like Lewis, rejected what he saw as the restless quest of the modern world to be original. Meaning was to be discovered in God's† created world, not somehow to be created by humanity (*see* Imagination†). G.K. Chesterton in *Orthodoxy* speaks of the way that children normally are not tired of familiar experience. In this sense they share in God's energy and vitality; he never tires of telling the sun to rise each morning. The child's attitude is a true view of things, and dipping into the world of story can restore such a sense of freshness.

For Tolkien, fairy stories help us to make such a recovery – they bring healing† – and 'in that sense only a taste for them may make us, or keep us, childish'.

Ring, One Ring

See Rings of Power.†

Rings of Power

Also called the Rings or the Great Rings, these were fashioned by Noldorin* elves* in Eregion* and by Sauron* in the Second Age* of Middle-earth.* They made Three Rings* for the elves, Seven Rings* for the dwarves,* and Nine Rings* for humanity. In characteristic treachery, Sauron later created the One Ring* to rule the others.

Just as the tales of the First Age* of Middle-earth are dominated by the motif of the Silmarils,* the events of the Third Age,* particularly as it reached its climax with the War of the Rings,* are dominated by the motif of the Rings.

The significance of the Rings is interpreted vividly by Gandalf* at the last debate in Gondor.† The wizard warns the leaders of the triumphant armies of the west that they have not won the final victory over Sauron; such a victory could not be won by military might. He tells them:

> I still hope for victory, but not by arms. For into the midst of all these policies comes the Ring of Power, the foundation of Barad-dur, and the hope of Sauron ... If he regains it, your valour is vain, and his victory will be swift and complete: so complete that none can foresee the end of it while this world lasts. If it is destroyed, then he will fall; and his fall will be so low that none can foresee his arising ever again. For he will lose the best part of the strength that was native to him in his beginning, and all that was made or begun with that power will crumble, and he will be maimed for ever, becoming a mere spirit of malice that gnaws itself in the shadows, but cannot again grow or take shape. And so a great evil of this world will be removed. (*The Return of the King*, Book Five, Chapter 9)

The Road

The Road, which 'goes ever on', is a potent and central image in Tolkien, particularly in *The Hobbit*‡ and *The Lord of the Rings*.‡ As in John Bunyan's *The Pilgrim's Progress*, there is the path to be taken by choice, leading to perils and adventures. As Frodo* and Sam* set off with the Ring,* at first 'the road wound away before them like a piece of string'. This road, which leads across rivers,

through the underworld, over the dreadful bridge in Khazad-dûm,*
and finally into Mordor* itself through Shelob's* Lair, is charted in
Barbara Strachey's *Journeys of Frodo*.

The link between the Road and the theme of quest† is brought
out by Elrond,* at his Council in Rivendell,* speaking of the need
to go into Mordor* to destroy the Ring:

> Now at this last we must take a hard road, a road unforeseen.
> There lies our hope, if hope it be. To walk into peril – to
> Mordor . . . The road must be trod, but it will be very hard. And
> neither strength nor wisdom will carry us far upon it. This
> quest may be attempted by the weak with as much hope as the
> strong. Yet such is oft the course of deeds that move the wheels
> of the world: small hands do them because they must, while the
> eyes of the great are elsewhere. (*The Fellowship of the Ring*, Book
> Two, Chapter 2)

Sacrifice

In the tales of Middle-earth,* there are many examples of sacrifice,
a constant theme. In *The Silmarillion*,‡ we read of Lúthien* aban-
doning her immortality for love of Beren,* and of first Eärendil*
and then Amandil* sailing to the undying lands of the West to
intercede on behalf of humanity before the Valar,* knowing they
could not return. In *The Lord of the Rings*‡ we learn of the sacrifice
of Frodo* and Sam* in their quest† to destroy the Ring.* The
burden of the sacrifice falls most on Frodo, revealed in his words
to Sam as he prepares to leave Middle-earth:

> 'But,' said Sam, and tears started in his eyes, 'I thought you were
> going to enjoy the Shire, too, for years and years, after all you
> have done.'
> 'So I thought too, once. But I have been too deeply hurt, Sam.
> I tried to save the Shire, and it has been saved, but not for me.
> It must often be so, Sam, when things are in danger: some one

has to give them up, lose them, so that others may keep them . . .'

One supreme example of sacrifice in the story of *The Lord of the Rings* is that of Gandalf,* on the dreadful bridge of Khazad-dûm,* fighting a Balrog.* In Middle-earth, Tolkien points out (*Letters*,‡ letter 156) 'angelic'† powers such as wizards† are capable of error, or worse, especially as they are incarnate. Of the wizards, writes Tolkien,

> Gandalf alone fully passes the tests, on a moral plane anyway (he makes mistakes of judgement). For in his condition it was for him a sacrifice to perish on the Bridge in defence of his companions, less perhaps than for a mortal Man or Hobbit, since he had a far greater inner power than they; but also more, since it was a humbling and abnegation of himself in conformity to 'the rules': for all he could know at that moment he was the only person who could direct the resistance to Sauron success-fully, and all his mission was vain. He was handing over to the Authority that ordained the Rules, and giving up personal hope of success.

See also Providence;† Christianity, Tolkien and;† Hero(ism).†

Song
See Music.†

Story, Tolkien's theology of
Tolkien's frame of reference is not a modern one, but rather has deep affinities with the medieval and pre-Enlightenment period. This is the framework of nature† and grace. He therefore presents an alternative to modernism at a time when there is somewhat of an intellectual and imaginative vacuum. In presenting this alternative he has struck a chord with millions of his readers throughout the

world, from California to Canberra, and from Cape Town to Kyoto.

It is helpful and probably necessary to apply the frame of nature and grace, and a theology of story, in order to appreciate the richness and depths of Tolkien's ideas. Like C.S. Lewis,‡ Tolkien is not readily classifiable theologically though both men were orthodox Christians. To understand Tolkien simply as a traditional Roman Catholic is as likely to be as misleading, perhaps, as describing Lewis as an Ulster Protestant! Both are deceptive descriptions (*see* Christianity, Tolkien and†).

Sub-creation, natural theology and nature in Tolkien

Tolkien believed that the art of authentic fantasy or fairy story† writing is sub-creation†: creating another or secondary world with such skill that it has a compelling 'inner consistency of reality'. It is tied up with a profound human desire to end the separation between humanity and nature, and between nature and grace. This accounts for the universal appeal of deeply imaginative writing.

Tolkien's natural theology† is unusual in that he stresses imagination,† rather than reason. However, he emphasizes that any such insights are acts of grace from the Father of Lights. They open the way to receiving the special revelation of the gospel (*see* Fairy story†). Story in particular, like language, is evidence of the image of God† still remaining in fallen humankind. For Tolkien, monotheism is 'natural religion', and is the faith of the Three Ages of Middle-earth* (the pre-Christian era, highlighting the best of such a situation). Like his close friend C.S. Lewis, Tolkien believed that worlds of the imagination are properly based upon nature, the humble and common things of life. Such fantasy is the opposite of escapism.

Sub-creation, the storytelling at least of humans (that of elves† is different), reflects the brokenness of God's original creation. The theme of fall† is intrinsic. Tolkien clarified this theme in the light of the claims of Christian revelation. Tolkien uses his own sub-creation of Middle-earth* as a mirror of nature.

Sub-creation, nature and grace in Tolkien

Looked at in connection with the frame of nature and grace, Tolkien's conception of sub-creation has important consequences for our understanding of how we know reality (epistemology). Tolkien seems to say that, in sub-creation, stories take on an inevitable structure, which anticipates or refers to the Christian gospel. Grace thus intervenes in the activity of sub-creation (the epitome of human storytelling), leading to insight into, and contact with, reality.

Here the medieval concept of humankind as a microcosm throws light on Tolkien's basic idea. Secondary worlds of the imagination – the fruit of sub-creation – are for him miniature worlds, focusing primary reality on their limited scale. They provide an imaginative survey of space and time. The great social thinker Giambattista Vico (1668–1744) taught that people can best know what they make themselves, namely history. Similarly, Leonardo earlier had a concept of operational knowledge, where human beings redesign and reorder the world in creating, and thus uncover its hidden structures. The early scientists (perhaps like some modern cosmologists) believed that they were thinking God's thoughts after him. For Tolkien, in perhaps a similar way, his imaginative making, or sub-creation, unlocks the meaning of God's primary creation, even discovering hints of his plan to redeem mankind and set a spoiled world right (*see* Providence†). This is why Tolkien disliked allegory† to be predominant in storytelling. Allegory as invention is too conscious, with not enough imaginative making. At its most successful, sub-creation makes myth.† Pre-eminently the gospel story has the quality of myth while, uniquely, being true in the actual, primary world rather than only in a secondary world. One such quality of myth is to bring together in a satisfactory way elements which are paradoxes, imponderables, or even contradictions to abstract thought – such as responsible, free human agency and divine providence.

Story, grace and the centrality of elves

Tolkien saw a fundamental quality of good fantasy or fairy story as consolation.† Here grace – the presence, will and mind of God – enters the story. The story of the incarnation, death and resurrection of Christ has all the features of the best stories, as the result of a divine shaping of real, historical events. The gospel story reveals the mark of God, the greatest storyteller. His intervention in history rends the 'seamless web' of human storytelling, enriching and fulfilling it.

The fairy story is at the heart of human storytelling, whether of northern Europe or of the classical world, or elsewhere. The concept of faerie had been mutilated, and Tolkien sought to rehabilitate it, both in his scholarship and in his own storytelling. In his works his name for fairies is, of course, elves. In the equation of story and grace, elves have a significant place. In his invented mythology of Middle-earth, Tolkien intended that his elves were an extended metaphor of a key aspect of human nature. This elven quality† in human life was an abiding preoccupation of Tolkien's. Elves, like dwarves,* hobbits,* and the like, 'partially represent' human beings. They are an extended metaphor of human life and culture.

In Tolkien's tales the elves are dominant in the early Ages of Middle-earth. In the period in which *The Lord of the Rings*‡ is set, the elves are in decline and will soon fade. However, key tales (such as that of Beren and Lúthien the elf-maiden,‡ and Aragorn* and Arwen*) record intermarriages between elves and humans which introduce the elven quality dramatically into human history, or vivify it. By the time of the Fourth Age* and those beyond, including our own, the elven quality mainly persists in human form. The three Ages recorded in Tolkien's Middle-earth stories and annals are pre-Christian. After them the elven quality will be pre-eminently a spiritual one, associated with Christianity, the grace of the gospel (or *evangelium*), and the presence of the Holy Spirit.

The embodiment of this 'elven quality' in human figures is a central feature of Tolkien's conception. This embodiment is more complex because, in his fiction, humans are subject to the 'gift of Ilúvatar', death,† whereas elves are immortal. The Númenorean humans, though, represented by Aragorn* in *The Lord of the Rings*, were granted a lifespan three times the normal. They were however to view death positively (the association of punishment for rebellion against God had been removed, unlike in actual history). Death was meant to highlight the eternal quality within themselves, which carried the promise of continuing life in the future within the plan of Ilúvatar.* The good Númenoreans were in fact enriched by their acceptance of providence. In culture, laws and the arts, theirs was a great civilization, a standard for all human society. In these enlightened people, the negativity of death was overcome with grace.

In his *Letters* (Letter 181) Tolkien describes the 'mythology' of Middle-earth as being 'Elf-centred'. The mythology is embodied in *The Silmarillion*.‡ The Elvish* framework of *The Silmarillion* particularly shows up where it is compared with *The Hobbit*,‡ and *The Lord of the Rings*, both of which could be said to be hobbit-centred, the narrative being composed by hobbits. This striking shift of perspective reflects the process whereby the elven quality is increasingly embodied in human beings. Hobbits belong to humanity, even though they are diminutive.

The embodiment or indeed incarnation of an elven quality in human lives is part of Tolkien's solution to the reconciliation of nature and grace. Elves in themselves are ideal beings, with a few exceptions a cut above the concerns of ordinary mortals. King Thingol,* typically, is dismissive of Beren* and his wish to marry Lúthien, even though Beren is a hero† spoken of even by the elves. We do not normally enter the lives of elves sympathetically, as we do with the lives of hobbits and humans in Middle-earth. Their qualities of grace and spirituality are not generally humanized. Elves are superior to nature and the ordinary. It is true that, according to Tolkien, they are for ever tied to the existing order of nature. Their destiny however is not home for humans. Eärendil* does not have his humanity deepened in the Uttermost West. Rather, he becomes more spiritual and idealized. By contrast, the Ring-bearers only go into the far west temporarily for healing† – their destiny and true home is elsewhere, and they remain human. In contrast, Lúthien's choice of Beren (and later Arwen's of Aragorn) reconcile nature and grace. Lúthien retains her grace and spirituality even though becoming fully human – an image of Christ's incarnation, or rather, in Tolkien's timescale, a foretaste of it.

Paganism

In exploring the pattern of nature and grace in Tolkien a consideration of paganism is inevitable. It seems that for Tolkien, paganism was a central case study for the intervention and integration of grace in nature. Tolkien's tales of Middle-earth are thoroughly set in a pagan context. It is a pagan world, like the setting of his great model, *Beowulf* (*see* 'Beowulf: The Monsters and the Critics'‡). In the poem Beowulf 'moves in a northern heroic age imagined by a Christian, and therefore has a noble and gentle quality, though conceived to be a pagan'. The *Beowulf* poet indicates for Tolkien the good that may be found in the pagan imagination, a theme also powerfully explored by C.S. Lewis. Tolkien's world in general is replete with Christian heroes and yet it is a pagan world. Ultimately, grace successfully spiritualizes nature. The fading of the elves is sad for the elves. Aragorn however stands at the end of the Third Age with Arwen at his side, a reminder of Lúthien in her grace and beauty. The future Ages are full of the promise of the *evangelium*. The White Tree had at last flowered, a sign of permanent and ultimate victory over evil.

Tolkien's treatment of paganism has the same potency that he found in *Beowulf*. The potency is there also in C.S. Lewis' own great exploration of pre-Christian paganism, *Till We Have Faces*. This novel strikingly reveals the imaginative and theological affinity between the two men. In Lewis' novel, Princess Psyche is prepared to die for the sake of the people of Glome, a country somewhere to the north of the Greeklands. She represents a Christ-likeness, though she is not intended as an allegory of Christ. Lewis wrote in explanation to Clyde S. Kilby:

> Psyche is an instance of the *anima naturaliter Christiana* making the best of the pagan religion she is brought up in and thus being guided (but always 'under the cloud,' always in terms of her own imagination or that of her people) towards the true God. She is in some ways like Christ not because she is a symbol of Him but because every good man or woman is like Christ.

Tolkien as a Christian artist

Tolkien is a pre-modern rather than post-modern author who has outstanding contemporary appeal. This appeal transcends the universal attraction of a good story. The qualities of what he considered authentic sub-creation are there in his work – consolation, joy†, recovery† and myth – what Tolkien might describe as the presence of grace derived from the *evangelium*, God's story or the Godspell. Tolkien has an important place as a Christian artist because his fiction successfully embodies Christian meaning in artistic form, suitable for a contemporary readership that generally doesn't share his Christian beliefs. In this sense, Tolkien is a twentieth-century apologist or defender of the Christian faith. We are perhaps used to thinking of C.S. Lewis' fiction and popular theology as of a piece as apologetics. Tolkien's fiction is in the same apologetic framework, recovering and restoring a Christian way of seeing reality. The appeal of Tolkien's thinking was pivotal in persuading Lewis of the truth of the Christian claims (*see* Christianity, Tolkien and‡).

Tolkien's distinctive contribution as a Christian artist resulted from his concept of sub-creation. Though he saw it in terms of fantasy, the applicability might well prove to be much wider. Secondary worlds can take many forms. In his book, *Art in Action*, the philosopher Nicholas Woltersdorff sees 'world-projection' as one of the universal and most important features of art, particularly fiction. It has large-scale metaphorical power. Nicholas Woltersdorff claims: '*by way of* fictionally projecting his distinct world the fictioneer may make a claim, true or false as the case may be, about our actual world.' Its metaphorical quality deepens or indeed modifies our perception of the meaning of reality (*see* Symbolism†). The power of metaphor underlies the thinking of both Tolkien and Lewis, each deeply influenced by Owen Barfield's‡ reflections on metaphor, truth and language. Tolkien has also contributed to a Christian understanding of imagination, in association with Lewis and Barfield.

Though Tolkien and Lewis are within a tradition of Romanticism, they are distinctive in not identifying imagination and truth. In the terms of C.S. Lewis, imagination is the organ of meaning, not truth. Imagination perceives reality. In a sense, reality *is* meaning, in being a dependent creation of God's, referring to him as its source, and not having meaning in itself. These are familiar Christian ideas of meaning, found for example in such diverse thinkers as Michael Polanyi and Herman Dooyeweerd, yet dramatically applicable to the imagination.

Conclusion

Tolkien's Christian theology emerges through a pattern of nature and grace. He attempts to reconcile and integrate the two realities in various ways. Particularly, his view of sub-creation expresses a kind of natural theology, while his notion of the 'seamless web of story' has story alive with God's presence, through the intervention of the gospel narrative. Central to Tolkien's fiction is the creation of elves. These are representative of human spirituality and culture, and human spirituality itself has an elven quality. This explains his portrayal of a pre-Christian, pagan world, with *Beowulf* as his model. If nature and grace can be integrated, as Tolkien desired, the position of the pre-Christian world is highly significant. Indeed, most of Tolkien's fiction is set in such a world. Ultimately, Tolkien is successful in integrating nature and grace in *The Lord of the Rings* as a Christian artist.

Sub-creation

J.R.R. Tolkien believed that the art of true fantasy or fairy story† writing is sub-creation: creating another or secondary world with such skill that it has an 'inner consistency of reality'. This inner consistency is so potent that it compels secondary belief or primary belief (the belief we give to the primary or real world) on the part of the reader. Tolkien calls the skills to compel these two degrees of belief 'fantasy' and 'enchantment' respectively. A clue to the concept of sub-creation lies in the fact that the word 'fairy', or more properly 'faerie', etymologically means 'the realm or state where faeries have their being'. A faerie story is not thus a story which simply concerns faery beings. They are in some sense other-worldly, having a geography and history surrounding them.

Tolkien's key idea is that Faerie, the realm or state where faeries have their being, contains a whole cosmos. It contains the moon, the sun, the sky, trees† and mountains, rivers, water and stones, as well as dragons,† trolls,* elves,† dwarves,* goblins,* talking animals, and even a moral person when he or she is enchanted (through giving primary belief to that other world). Faerie is sub-creation rather than either representation or allegorical interpretation of the 'beauties and terrors of the world'. Sub-creation comes, says Tolkien, as a result of a twofold urge in human beings: (1) the wish to survey the depths of space and time; and (2) the urge to communicate with living beasts other than humans, to escape†

from hunger, poverty, death,† and to end the separation between humanity and nature.† Just as the reason wishes for a unified theory to cover all phenomena in the universe, the imagination† also constantly seeks a unity of meaning appropriate to itself.
See Fairy Stories.†

Symbolism

Tolkien belongs to the tradition of Romanticism, but with important differences, one being that the imagination† is not the organ of truth. As with the Romantics, symbols play an integrating part in his fiction. His symbolism helps to make his work a lamp as well as a mirror; depicting reality, but also illuminating it. In this book is included a number of his characteristic symbols or symbolic themes, such as death,† angels,† dragons,† eagles,† an elven quality,† healing,† light,† music,† the numinous,† the quest,† the Ring,† the Road,† the tree† and underground places and journeys.†

On a greater scale, the geography* and history of Middle-earth* are symbolic, enriching the stories that come from the various Ages. Further enrichment is obtained from invented beings such as the Valar,* the Maiar,* Balrogs,* elves,† dwarves* and hobbits.*

The process of invention that Tolkien calls sub-creation† allows the imagination to employ both unconscious and conscious resources of the mind. This is particularly so with regard to language, which is intimately connected to the whole self, and not just theoretical thought. Sub-creation allows powerful archetypes to became an effective part of an art-work. This accounts for the universal appeal of deeply imaginative writing like Tolkien's. Archetypes are recurrent symbols, plot structures, and character types that make up much of the material of literature. In symbolic literature like Tolkien's, the archetypes are focused and definite, but so-called realistic fiction is also replete with hidden archetypes. Tolkien takes many archetypes from the Bible (see Christianity, Tolkien and†), which Northrope Frye called 'a grammar of literary archetypes', and Leland Ryken described as 'the great repository of archetypes in Western literature'.

Tragedy

Traditionally, in tragedy, the tragic person or hero† has within him or herself a fatal weakness. Tragedy however also involves a moral fall,† a before and after. In tragedy, therefore, there is a complex mixture of subjective and objective evil.† For a Christian writer like Tolkien, there is the additional question: Has tragedy a place in Christian art, or only 'comedy' and triumph? Tolkien shows it has (as does the Bible, with its continual emphasis on the necessity of suffering in a distorted world). Tragedy in the Bible however is subsidiary to what Tolkien calls eucatastrophe (*see* Consolation†), the denial of ultimate defeat. In *The Silmarillion*‡ tragedy is a major element, in the characters of such as Melkor (Morgoth*), Fëanor,* and particularly Túrin Turambar.* Tolkien (*Letters*,‡ Letter 131) remarks that Túrin is 'a figure that might be said (by people who like that sort of thing, though it is not very useful) to be derived from elements in Sigurd the Volsung, Oedipus and the Finnish Kullervo'.

Túrin is flawed in being swift to anger, proud and unteachable. Yet, as Paul Kocher points out, Túrin has free will, even though cursed by the oath of Morgoth against his father, Húrin* (whose innocent suffering is Job-like). His mistaken wrath and pride make him an outlaw and cut him off from Thingol* of Doriath* (with terrible consequences for Nienor* and his mother). His arrogance at Nargothrond* means that he rejects the wisdom of both Ulmo* and King Orodreth,* bringing ruin, death,† and the dragon,† Glaurung, to the realm.

The fall of Númenor* is a tragedy, as seems to be suggested by Tolkien (*Letters*, Letter 131): 'The Downfall is partly the result of an inner weakness in man . . . Its central theme is (inevitably, I think, in a story of Men) a Ban, or Prohibition.' *The Lord of the*

Rings‡ records a number of tragic characters: Gollum,* Boromir,* Denethor,* and Saruman,* to name a few of the most significant.

David Harvey, in his *The Song of Middle-earth*, believes that Frodo* is a tragic figure. He believes that Frodo's tragedy lies in his choice, in weakness, not to destroy the One Ring* at the decisive moment. Providence† has to intervene in the form of Gollum (who, significantly, is only there because of Frodo's earlier pity – as well as the pity of Sam* and Bilbo*).

Tree

This is a seminal symbol in Tolkien's life and writings. It is characteristic that his illustration of a tree appears on the cover of *Tree and Leaf*,‡ a fact that gave Tolkien pleasure. It is a symbol too that has a key integrating role in the biblical message (*see* Christianity, Tolkien and†). Clyde Kilby pointed out that the image of the tree, in both Tolkien's writings and the Bible, is persistent 'particularly as symbol of beginnings and endings, of significant people and of highly historical events'.

The Bible opens with a garden that includes the tree of life and closes with the same tree in the New Jerusalem, the heavenly city. In Middle-earth,* there are in its early history Two Trees,* one white and one golden, Telperion* and Laurelin,* that illuminated Valinor.* At the end of the Third Age* a seedling modelled on Telperion flowered. This marked the restoration of the realm of King Elessar (Aragorn*).

Isildur* had brought the seed from Númenor,* from a tree which went back to Tol Eressëa,* and before that, to Valinor. Minas Tirith* presages the New Jerusalem. Significantly, Gondor's* emblem is the White Tree and seven stars on a black field. The seven stars are an apocalyptic† symbol in the biblical book of Revelation. The flowering of the White Tree was a reassurance to Aragorn, a sign of permanent and ultimate victory over evil.† Kilby points out that the sapling of a tree on a barren mountainside is parallel to Isaiah's prophecy of the coming Christ (Isaiah 53:2). In Aragorn's case, the shooting tree looks forward to the Fourth Age* and the arrival of the Christian centuries. Aragorn himself is identified with the sapling, a parallel with a forerunner of Christ in the Old Testament, King David (2 Samuel 11).

Tolkien had a deep sense in his invented mythology† of a Final Ending, where the earth would be remade, the trees rekindled into life, and the lands under the sea restored.

Underground places and journeys

In the descent into the underworld, Ruth Noel points out in her book, *The Mythology of Middle-earth*, extraordinary events take place. Sometimes they have the character of the darker side of the numinous† – a dreadful encounter with the supernatural. It is common for underground places to be protected by magic. Examples of such protection are the magic doors in Thranduil's* halls, and Melian's* spell around Menegroth.*

Heroism† is involved in subterranean descent. There is the courage of Bilbo* before Smaug,* and of Frodo* in the Barrow, when he calls to Tom Bombadil* for help. There is the courage and sacrifice of Gandalf* against the balrog.* Lúthien* displays extra-ordinary resolve in facing Mandos* on behalf of Beren.* The courage of Sam* against Shelob* in her dark lair is notable. For Tolkien, monstrous spiders and dragons† symbolize the enemy of humankind, greater than death;† Sam faced no ordinary danger. Examples of underground places and paths abound in Tolkien's world. They include the Gate of the Noldor* (found by Tuor*), the Halls of Mandos,* Nargothrond,* Menegroth, Angband* (into which Beren and Lúthien ventured), orc* tunnels, Thranduil's realm, Smaug's lair, the Barrow-wight's Chamber, Khazad-dûm,* Shelob's lair, the Paths of the Dead, and the Glittering Caves.

Further reading

Ruth S. Noel, *The Mythology of Middle-earth* (1977).

Underworld

See Underground places and journeys.†

West

See Old West, Tolkien and the.†

Wizards

The most well-known of the wizards are Gandalf* and Saruman.* The origin of the five or so wizards was known only by a small number, such as Elrond* and Galadriel.* They appeared in Middle-earth* about the year 1000 of the Third Age.* This was the time when the shadow and menace of Sauron* began to reappear. They were sent as emissaries from the Valar* to encourage the native powers of the enemies of Sauron. They were capable of error and failure, and power of the One Ring* affected them. The wizards were Maiar* in human form.

The three of the wizards who are agents in the tales are Saruman the White, Gandalf the Grey, and Radagast* the Brown. Another two wizards are called the Ithryn Luin, the Blue Wizards, in *Unfinished Tales*.‡ Their names were Alatar and Pallando. The Blue Wizards had the role of 'missionaries to enemy occupied lands' away from the familiar lands that are the setting of *The Lord of the Rings*.‡ Typically, in a letter, Tolkien writes of his suspicion that the Blue Wizards failed, as Saruman did. He suspected that they were founders or beginners of secret cults and 'magic'† traditions that persisted into the Fourth Age.* Though Tolkien could find no modern word to say what Istari or wizards were, they could be described as incarnate angels† or, more strictly, messengers (of the Valar). In another place, he characterizes them as guardian angels. By 'incarnate', Tolkien meant that

they were embodied in physical bodies capable of pain, and weariness, and of afflicting the spirit with physical fear, and of being 'killed', though supported by the angelic spirit they might endure long, and only show slowly the wearing of care and labour (Letter 156).

In another letter to a publisher he explains:

> Their powers are directed primarily to the encouragement of the enemies of evil, to cause them to use their own wits and valour, to unite and endure. They appear always as old men and sages, and though (sent by the powers of the True West) in the world they suffer themselves, their age and grey hairs increase only slowly.

Gandalf's function is particularly to watch over human affairs. By 'human', Tolkien explicitly means 'Men and Hobbits' (Letter 131). *See also* Providence.†

EIGHT

PEOPLE AND PLACES
IN HIS LIFE

Auden, W.H. (1907–73)

A major figure in Anglo-American poetry, and a literary critic, W.H. Auden was born in Britain and later became a US citizen. Like Tolkien, his family took him to Birmingham‡ as an infant. He went up to Oxford‡ in 1925, the year Tolkien moved there from Leeds to become Professor of Anglo-Saxon. His tutor was Nevill Coghill.‡ As an undergraduate, Auden developed a particular liking for Old English literature. Like Tolkien, he had a deep interest in Northern mythology.† Like C.S. Lewis,‡ he was a late convert to Christianity.

Auden referred to the effect that Tolkien had on him during his inaugural lecture delivered as Professor of Poetry before the University of Oxford on 11 June 1956:

> I remember [a lecture] I attended, delivered by Professor Tolkien. I do not remember a single word he said but at a certain point he recited, and magnificently, a long passage of Beowulf. I was spellbound. This poetry, I knew was going to be my dish. I became willing, therefore, to work at Anglo-Saxon because, unless I did, I should never be able to read this poetry. I learned enough to read it, however sloppily, and Anglo-Saxon and Middle English poetry have been one of my strongest, most lasting influences.

Tolkien was greatly encouraged by Auden's enthusiasm for *The*

Lord of the Rings.‡ He wrote on the quest† hero† in Tolkien's work, and corresponded and discussed with him about the meaning of his work (*see The Letters of J.R.R. Tolkien*‡).

His reviews counteracted some of the negative criticism of the trilogy. In Humphrey Carpenter's biography of Auden there is reproduced a photograph of him absorbed in reading *The Hobbit*,‡ taken in the 1940s. In 1965 Auden intended to collaborate with the writer Peter Salus on a short book on Tolkien in the Christian Perspectives series. He failed however to gain Tolkien's approval for such a project and, so, unfortunately, it was dropped.

Further reading

W.H. Auden, *Secondary Worlds* (1968).
Humphrey Carpenter, *W.H. Auden: A Biography* (1981).
Neil D. Isaacs and Rose A. Zimbardo (eds), *Tolkien and the Critics* (1968).

Barfield, Owen (1898–1997)

A core member of the Inklings,‡ Owen Barfield was a child of 'free-thinking' parents, one a London solicitor. After serving in World War I, he studied at Wadham College, Oxford,‡ reading English. At Oxford he formed a lifelong friendship with C.S. Lewis,‡ and also became an anthroposophist, an advocate of the religious school of thought developed by Rudolf Steiner. For several years he was a freelance writer, before joining his father's legal firm. His first book deeply influenced C.S. Lewis and Tolkien. The influence on Tolkien has been cogently argued by Verlyn Flieger in her study, *Splintered Light*.

Birmingham

A major city in England that, along with the West Midlands, Tolkien regarded as home. When his father, Arthur Tolkien,‡ died in 1896, the family settled at Sarehole Mill,‡ at that time outside of the city boundary. Tolkien attended King Edward's School, then located near the city centre. The TCBS,‡ which started life as a schoolboy club, would meet at the tea room in Barrow's Stores in Corporation Street.

Birmingham had gained city status in 1889. It is the largest manufacturing city in England, and the chief hardware city in the world. The Industrial Revolution began in nearby Ironbridge. Birmingham's metal industries have been important since the last half of the seventeenth century.

Birmingham was an Anglo-Saxon settlement, mentioned in the Domesday Book. After the Norman Conquest it became the property of the Bermingham family. By the end of the thirteenth century a market town had grown up at the Bull Ring where several routes intersected. The Bull Ring remains the name of the modern city centre, rebuilt after wartime bombing.

Coghill, Nevill (1899–1980)

Professor of English Literature at Oxford‡ from 1957 to 1966, and a member of the Inklings.‡ After serving in World War I, he read English at Exeter College, Oxford, and in 1924 was elected a Fellow there. As an undergraduate attending the Essay Club at Exeter College, he heard Tolkien read aloud 'The Fall of Gondolin',* from *The Silmarillion*.‡ He was also a member of the Kolbitar‡ club. Coghill was admired for his theatrical productions, and for his translation of Chaucer's *Canterbury Tales* into modern English couplets.

d'Ardenne, Simonne

A philologist who was a student of Tolkien's in the 1930s, studying for an Oxford‡ B.Litt. She was a Belgian graduate who eventually taught at the University of Liège. She and Tolkien collaborated on several projects, including her edition of *The Life and Passion of St Juliene*. The advent of the Second World War interrupted their association, and they did little work together after the war though their friendship continued.

See also Philology, Tolkien and.†

Dyson, H.V.D. 'Hugo' (1896–1975)

A member of the Inklings,‡ Dyson was seriously wounded at Passchendaele before reading English at Exeter College, Oxford.‡ As an undergraduate, he heard Tolkien read 'The Fall of Gondolin'* (part of *The Silmarillion*‡) to the Essay Club at Exeter College. On a momentous night in 1931, he helped Tolkien to persuade C.S. Lewis‡ of the truth of Christianity. After lecturing in English at Reading University he was, in 1945, elected Fellow and Tutor in English Literature at Merton College. He retired in 1963.

Gilson, R.Q. 'Rob'

A close friend of Tolkien's youth, and member of the TCBS.‡ Like another member, G.B. Smith,‡ he was killed on active service in the First World War. Gilson was the son of the headmaster at King Edward's School, Birmingham,‡ which Tolkien and the others attended. He was artistic and intelligent, and attended Cambridge before being swallowed up by war.

Gordon, E.V.

A Canadian, who had been a Rhodes Scholar at Oxford,‡ was appointed to teach in the English department at Leeds University soon after Tolkien. The two men became firm friends, and were soon collaborating on a major piece of scholarship. It was a new edition of a favourite Middle English poem of Tolkien's, *Sir Gawain and the Green Knight*. Further projects came to nothing, with Tolkien moving to Oxford, and Gordon eventually moving to Manchester University. In 1938, he died suddenly, at the age of 42, and Tolkien lost a friend and much-needed collaborator.

Havard, R.E 'Humphrey' (1901–85)

Affectionately known as the 'Useless Quack', he was the doctor of Tolkien and C.S. Lewis,‡ and member of the Inklings.‡ The son of an Anglican clergyman, 'Humphrey' Havard was received into the Roman Catholic Church aged 30. He studied medicine after reading chemistry and became a doctor. In 1934 he took over a medical practice in Oxford‡ with surgeries in Headington and St Giles (near the Eagle and Child public house, haunt of the Inklings).

The Inklings

J.R.R. Tolkien was a central figure in the Inklings, a literary group of friends held together by the zest and enthusiasm of C.S. Lewis.‡ Tolkien described it in a letter as an 'undetermined and unelected circle of friends who gathered around C.S.L[ewis]., and met in his rooms in Magdalen . . . Our habit was to read aloud compositions of various kinds (and lengths!)'.

As Tolkien's description suggests, there is a problem of definition. The group called the Inklings was so informal and casual, such a wide variety of writers passed through it, that very little common entity remains. However, along with Tolkien and Lewis, Charles Williams‡ was a focal person. These three men were united in the defence of reason, Romanticism and Christianity. Owen Barfield‡ was also a defining influence, though he rarely attended after moving to London to work as a solicitor in his father's firm.

Tolkien points out that 'The Inklings had no recorder and C.S. Lewis no Boswell'. However, glimpses of meetings can be seen in the letters of Tolkien and Lewis, and in the diaries of Lewis' brother, Major Warren Hamilton Lewis. The preface of *Essays Presented to Charles Williams* is also informative.

According to John Wain, after Charles Williams' death in 1945, the two most active members of the group became Tolkien and Lewis. In his autobiography, *Sprightly Running*, Wain describes the Inklings as 'a circle of instigators' encouraging each other 'in the task of redirecting the whole current of contemporary art and life'. He writes:

> While Lewis attacked on a wide front, with broadcasts, popular-theological books, children's stories, romances, and controversial literary criticism, Tolkien concentrated on the writing of his

colossal 'Lord of the Rings' trilogy. His readings of each successive installment were eagerly received, for 'romance' was a pillar of this whole structure.

C.S. Lewis provides a rare window into the Inklings in his preface to *Essays Presented to Charles Williams*, to which Tolkien contributed. Lewis points out that three of the essays in the collection are on literature, and, specifically, one aspect of literature, the 'narrative art'. That, Lewis says, is natural enough. Charles Williams'

> *All Hallow's Eve* and my own *Perelandra* (as well as Professor Tolkien's unfinished sequel to *The Hobbit*) had all been read aloud, each chapter as it was written. They owe a good deal to the hard-hitting criticism of the circle. The problems of narrative as such – seldom heard of in modern critical writings – were constantly before our minds.

The Inklings embodied the ideals of life and pleasure of Tolkien and Lewis, especially Lewis, who spoke of good evenings full of 'the cut and parry of prolonged, fierce, masculine argument'. Both Tolkien and Lewis were 'clubbable' – Tolkien had been in the TCBS‡ group of school friends and in the Kolbitar* (along with Lewis) in previous years. The Inklings' most important years were the 1930s and 1940s, especially the war years when Charles Williams was resident in Oxford.‡

Tolkien occasionally refers to the group in his letters. Writing approvingly to his publisher about Lewis' science-fiction story, *Out of the Silent Planet*, he speaks of it 'being read aloud to our local club (which goes in for reading things short and long aloud). It proved an exciting serial, and was highly approved. But of course we are all rather like-minded.' It is clear from his letters that the Inklings provided valuable and much-needed encouragement as he struggled to compose *The Lord of the Rings*.‡

A letter to his son Christopher,‡ away with the RAF in South Africa, is typical, written in 1944:

Monday 22 May... It was a wretched cold day yesterday (Sunday). I worked very hard at my chapter – it is most exhausting work; especially as the climax approaches and one has to keep the pitch up: no easy level will do; and there are all sorts of minor problems of plot and mechanism. I wrote and tore up and rewrote most of it a good many times; but I was rewarded this morning, as both C.S.L[ewis]. and C[harles]. W[illiams]. thought it an admirable performance, and the latest chapters the best so far. Gollum continues to develop into a most intriguing character...

One of the favourite haunts of the Inklings was 'The Eagle and Child' public house in St Giles (known more familiarly as 'The Bird and Baby'). Many a discussion or friendly argument was washed down with beer.

Further reading

Humphrey Carpenter, *The Inklings: C.S. Lewis, J.R.R. Tolkien, Charles Williams and Their Friends* (1978).

Colin Duriez and David Porter, *The Inklings Handbook* (2001).

John Wain, *Sprightly Running: Part of an Autobiography* (1962).

The Kolbitar

An informal reading club initiated by Tolkien soon after he became a professor at Oxford‡ to explore Icelandic literature such as the Poetic Edda. The name meant those who crowd so close to the fire in winter that they seem to 'bite the coal'. C.S. Lewis‡ attended meetings, as did Nevill Coghill.‡ It predated the Inklings.‡

Lewis, C.S. (1898–1963)

Tolkien's deep friendship with C.S. Lewis was of great significance to both men. Tolkien found in Lewis an appreciative audience for his burgeoning stories and poems of Middle-earth,* a good deal of which was not published until after his death. Without Lewis' encouragement over many years, *The Lord of the Rings*‡ would probably have never appeared in print. Lewis equally had cause to appreciate Tolkien. His views on myth† and imagination,† and the relation of both to reality, helped to convince Lewis (who had not long before been a convinced atheist) of the truth of Christianity. Seeing mind to mind on both imagination and the truth of Christianity was the foundation of their remarkable friendship. The Inklings,‡ the group of literary friends around Lewis, grew out of this rapport between Lewis and Tolkien. A.N. Wilson, in his biography *C.S. Lewis*, remarks that, at the very beginning of the association between Lewis and Tolkien: 'It must have seemed clear to him at once that Tolkien was a man of literary genius.' On Tolkien's side, thinking with sadness in 1929 of his marriage, he wrote: 'Friendship with Lewis compensates for much.'

Known to his friends as 'Jack' (he didn't like 'Clive Staples'), C.S. Lewis was born in the outskirts of Belfast on 29 November 1898, and died in his Oxford‡ home, the Kilns, almost 65 years later. Like Tolkien, he was equally a scholar and a storyteller. The story of his early life, his conversion from atheism to Christianity, and his awareness of joy† and longing for a fulfilment outside of his own self, is told in his autobiography *Surprised by Joy* and his allegory *The Pilgrim's Regress*.

Jack Lewis was devoted to his brother W.H. 'Warnie' Lewis. The two brothers were brought together by their common interest in creating imaginary worlds as boys, and also by the death of their mother of cancer. Mrs Flora Lewis died when Jack was nine. Their father never got over the loss and relations between father and sons became more and more strained as time went on. C.S. Lewis portrays his father, Albert Lewis, as having little talent for happiness, and withdrawing into the safe monotony of routine.

When the Great War broke out Warnie was already on active duty. Lewis himself was not old enough to enlist until 1917. He spent his nineteenth birthday on the front-line. In spring 1918 Lewis was wounded in action and was eventually discharged after a spell in hospital. During all this time he, like Tolkien, had been writing poetry. By 1923 Lewis had confirmed his brilliance by gaining a Triple First at Oxford University. He won a temporary lectureship in philosophy at University College. Then Magdalen College appointed him as a Fellow, lecturing and tutoring in English. He was an Oxford don until 1954, when Cambridge University invited him to the new Chair of Medieval and Renaissance Literature, where he described himself as an 'Old Western Man' in his inaugural lecture (*see* Old West†).

In the early Oxford days Tolkien became one of C.S. Lewis' lifelong friends. They would criticize one another's poetry, drift into theology and philosophy, pun or talk university English School politics. Tolkien helped to force Lewis to reconsider the claims of Christianity. He was first 'cornered' by theism and then biblical Christianity.

In 1953 Lewis met an American woman, Helen Joy Davidman, with whom he had corresponded for some time. (The film *Shadowlands* is based upon their friendship.) She was a poet and novelist who had been converted from atheism and Marxism to Christianity. Lewis' love for Joy Davidman, and earlier friendship with Charles Williams, weakened the intimacy between him and Tolkien, much to the latter's grief. When she was free to remarry, and was dying of cancer, Lewis married her. She came home to die in the summer of 1957, but had a miraculous stay of execution. In fact she lived until 1960. The happiness that had come to him so late in life, and subsequent bitter bereavement, is recorded in his *A Grief Observed*.

As well as *The Chronicles of Narnia* for children, C.S. Lewis wrote a classic science-fiction trilogy, a novel (*Till We Have Faces*), other fiction, literary criticism, cultural criticism, ethics, theology and poetry.

Further reading

Humphrey Carpenter, *The Inklings: C.S. Lewis, J.R.R. Tolkien, Charles Williams and Their Friends*. George Allen and Unwin: London, 1978; Houghton Mifflin: Boston, 1979.

Colin Duriez, *The C.S. Lewis Encyclopedia.* Crossway Books: Wheaton, 2000.

Roger Lancelyn Green and Walter Hooper, *C.S. Lewis: A Biography.* Collins: London, 1974.

Clyde S. Kilby and Marjorie L. Meade (eds), *Brothers and Friends: The Diaries of Major Warren Hamilton Lewis.* Harper and Row: New York, 1982.

Letters of C.S. Lewis. Geoffrey Bles: London, 1966; revised edition, edited by Walter Hooper, 1988.

C.S. Lewis, *The Pilgrim's Regress.* J.M. Dent: London, 1933, 1943.

C.S. Lewis, *Surprised by Joy: The Shape of My Early Life.* Geoffrey Bles: London, 1955.

George Sayer, *Jack: C.S. Lewis and His Times.* Macmillan: London, 1988.

A.N. Wilson, *C.S. Lewis: A Biography.* Collins: London, 1990.

MacDonald, George (1824–1905)

The Scottish writer George MacDonald was born in Huntly in rural Aberdeenshire, the son of a weaver. C.S. Lewis‡ regarded his own debt to him as inestimable. Tolkien's attitude to the fantasist was more ambivalent, and often critical. Yet there were many affinities. The theme of death† is central to the fiction of both Tolkien and MacDonald. The Scot's thinking about the imagination† has a number of striking similarities with Tolkien's. The goblins in Tolkien's children's story, *The Hobbit*,‡ are reminiscent of the goblins in MacDonald's Curdie stories for children, not as terrifying and malicious as the orcs* of *The Lord of the Rings*‡ and *The Silmarillion*.‡ There are hints of rudimentary 'sub-creation'† in MacDonald. His distinctive Great-Great-Grandmother figures have an elven quality† that could belong to Tolkien's world. He has powerful feminine images of spirituality and providence† that are akin to Tolkien's Galadriel* and Varda.*

Like Tolkien and C.S. Lewis, MacDonald lost his mother in boyhood, a fact that touched his thought and writings. His views on the imagination anticipated those of Lewis as well as Tolkien, and inspired G.K. Chesterton. He was a close friend of Charles Dodgson (Lewis Carroll) and John Ruskin, the art critic. His insights into the unconscious mind predated the rise of modern psychology. Like Lewis and Tolkien he was a scholar as well as a storyteller. Lewis regarded him as his 'master'.

MacDonald's sense that all imaginative meaning originates with the Christian creator became the foundation of C.S. Lewis' thinking and imagining. Such a view is also central to Tolkien. Two key essays, 'The Imagination: Its Functions and Its Culture' (1867) and 'The Fantastic Imagination' (1882), remarkably foreshadow Tolkien's famous essay 'On Fairy Stories'.‡ Tolkien's views on imagination persuaded C.S. Lewis of the truth of Christianity on a significant night in 1931. Many years before Lewis had stumbled across a copy of MacDonald's *Phantastes* (1858), resulting in what he famously described as a baptism of his imagination.

George MacDonald wrote nearly 30 novels, several books of sermons, a number of abiding fantasies for adults and children, short stories and poetry. His childhood is captured in his semi-autobiographical *Ranald Bannerman's Boyhood* (1871). George MacDonald entered Aberdeen University in 1840, and had a scientific training. For a few years he worked as a tutor in London. Then he entered Highbury Theological College and married. The rapidly growing family were always on the brink of poverty. Fortunately, the poet Byron's widow, recognizing MacDonald's literary gifts, started to provide financial help. The family moved down to London, living in a house then called 'The Retreat', near the Thames at Hammersmith, later owned by William Morris.

For a time George MacDonald was Professor of Literature at Bedford College, London. Because of continued ill-health the family eventually moved to Italy, where MacDonald and his wife were to remain for the rest of their lives. There were, however, frequent stays in Britain during the warmer months, and a long and successful visit to the United States on a lecture tour. One of his last books, *Lilith* (1895) is among his greatest, a fantasy with the same power to move and to change a person's imaginative life as *Phantastes*.

Further reading

C.S. Lewis, *George MacDonald: An Anthology*. Geoffrey Bles: London, 1946.

Greville MacDonald, *George MacDonald and His Wife*. George Allen and Unwin: London, 1924.

Michael Phillips, *George MacDonald: Scotland's Beloved Storyteller*. Bethany House: Minnesota, 1987.

William Raeper, *George MacDonald*. Lion: Oxford, 1987.

Morgan, Father Francis

The guardian of Tolkien and his brother Hilary,‡ appointed by their mother, Mabel Tolkien.‡ Father Morgan was a Roman Catholic parish priest, attached to the Birmingham‡ Oratory, founded by John Henry Newman. He provided friendship and counsel for the fatherless family. Half-Welsh and half-Spanish, he was an extrovert, whose enthusiasm helped to better the lot of the Tolkien family. With the boys often ill, and the mother developing diabetes, Father Morgan hit on the plan of moving them to Rednal, in the countryside, for the summer of 1904. It was like being back at their beloved Sarehole.‡ Mabel Tolkien died there later that year, and Father Morgan was left with the responsibility of the boys. He helped them financially, found them lodgings in Birmingham, and took them on holiday. When Tolkien later married Edith Bratt,‡ and their first son was born, Father Francis travelled from Birmingham to baptize him. Sometimes he joined the growing family on their seaside holidays at Lyme Regis.

Oxford

City and county town of Oxfordshire, England. It was J.R.R. Tolkien's home from 1925, when he was elected Rawlinson and Bosworth Professor of Anglo-Saxon, to his death in 1973, except for a few retirement years in Poole.

Oxford is located at the meeting of the rivers Thames and

Cherwell, about 50 miles north-west of London. Its importance as early as the tenth century is evident from its mention in the Anglo-Saxon Chronicle for 912.

Before World War I Oxford was known as a university city and market town. Then printing was its only major industry. Between the wars, however, the Oxford motor industry grew rapidly, much to Tolkien's sorrow.

University teaching has been carried on at Oxford since the early days of the twelfth century, perhaps as a result of students migrating from Paris. The university's fame quickly grew, until by the fourteenth century it rivalled any in Europe. Tolkien was associated with three Oxford colleges: Exeter, Pembroke and Merton. Between 1911 and 1915 he was an undergraduate at Exeter College, studying first classics then English language and literature. In 1925 he returned from Leeds University to became Professor of Anglo-Saxon, with Pembroke as his college. After he changed chairs to become Professor of English Language and Literature in 1945, he became a Fellow of Merton College. A professor's first responsibility was to the whole Oxford faculty.

The Tolkien family lived in a succession of houses in suburban Oxford. In 1925, Tolkien bought a house at 20 Northmoor Road, in the north of the city, and then, in 1930, moved to a larger house next door, number 22. It was the mutilation of a favourite poplar tree in the street which inspired Tolkien's story, *Leaf by Niggle*.‡ In 1947 the family moved to a smaller house in 3 Manor Road, as John and Michael Tolkien had now left home, but this proved too small. The house the Tolkiens moved to in 1950, in Holywell Street, had much more character, but they soon found that the Oxford traffic made living there unbearable. Tolkien wrote that 'This charming house has become uninhabitable: unsleepable-in, unworkable-in, rocked, racked with noise, and drenched with fumes. Such is modern life. Mordor in our midst.' Three years later they found a house in Headington, a quiet suburb to the east of the city, near to C.S. Lewis'‡ home, the Kilns. This was 76, Sandfield

Road, where the Tolkiens lived until 1968, when they moved to Poole in Dorset. After Edith's death in 1971, Tolkien was able to move back to Oxford, living in college rooms in 21 Merton Street. He lived there from March 1972 until his death the following year.

Sarehole Mill

In 1896, Mabel Tolkien‡ took her two young sons to live in a rented house in Sarehole, Warwickshire, then in the countryside outside Birmingham‡ city limits. Here an old brick mill stood, with a tall chimney. A stream ran under its great wheel. The mill, with its frightening miller's son, made a permanent impression on the young Tolkien's imagination. In Hobbiton,* located on the Water, stood a mill which was torn down and replaced by a brick building which polluted both the air and water.

Sisam, Kenneth

Tolkien's tutor in the English school at Exeter College, Oxford,‡ when he was an undergraduate. Sisam was a young New Zealander who greatly inspired Tolkien in the area of medieval literature. Later the two men collaborated on a book of extracts from Middle English, Tolkien painstakingly supplying the glossary. Sisam eventually joined the Clarendon Press (Oxford University Press).

Smith, G.B.

A close friend of Tolkien's from schooldays and member of the society, the TCBS.‡ He commented on a number of Tolkien's early poems, including his original verses about Eärendil* (then written 'Earendel'). Smith was killed on active service in the winter of 1916. He wrote to Tolkien shortly before his death, speaking of how the TCBS – the 'immortal four' – would live on, even if he died that night. He concluded: 'May God bless you, my dear John Ronald, and may you say the things I have tried to say long after I am not there to say them, if such be my lot.'

The TCBS

A club of four friends formed while Tolkien was a schoolboy in King Edward VI Grammar School. The other members included G.B. Smith,‡ R.Q. 'Rob' Gilson,‡ and Christopher Wiseman.‡ Only Wiseman and Tolkien survived the First World War. At first the original group was called the Tea Club (TC), and then later the Barrovian Society (BS), as the tea room in Barrow's Stores in Corporation Street, Birmingham,‡ became a favourite place to meet. TCBS members combined the two groups. Constant members were Tolkien, Gilson and Wiseman, and later Smith. Tolkien's friends enjoyed his interest in Norse sagas and medieval English literature. After leaving school, the four core members of the TCBS continued to meet up occasionally, and to write to each other, until the war destroyed their association. The TCBS left a permanent mark on Tolkien's character, which he captured in the idea of 'fellowship', as in the Fellowship of the Ring. Friendship with C.S. Lewis‡ helped to satisfy this important side of his nature.

Tolkien, Arthur (1857–96)

The father of J.R.R. Tolkien, and a manager for Lloyds Bank. He moved to South Africa to improve his prospects, and Mabel Suffield (*see* Mabel Tolkien‡) left Birmingham‡ to marry him there. They married in April 1891. Arthur died quickly from rheumatic fever. He contracted the illness while the rest of the young family were visiting England, to improve the young J.R.R. Tolkien's health. The child was just four.

Tolkien, Christopher

The third son of J.R.R. Tolkien, born in 1924. He was called Christopher in honour of Christopher Wiseman,‡ one of the TCBS.‡ The father was especially fond of Christopher, finding a great affinity with him (perhaps captured in the unfinished story, 'The Lost Road'). During the war years, when Christopher was posted to South Africa with the RAF, Tolkien sent him instalments of his work in progress, *The Lord of the Rings*.‡ In a sense, he was the original audience for the work. In earlier years, he had listened intently as his father read to him from the material making up *The Silmarillion*.‡ Christopher also prepared maps for the publication of that work. After his father's death he devoted himself to editing his unfinished work, such as the published *The Silmarillion* (1977), as was Tolkien's wish.

Christopher Tolkien was a member of the informal literary group, the Inklings.‡ He studied at Trinity College, Oxford‡ and became a Fellow at New College. He eventually resigned his academic duties to devote himself to editing his father's work.

Tolkien, Edith (1889–1971)

Née Bratt, the wife of J.R.R. Tolkien. No mean illustrator, Tolkien affectionately sketched his young wife from behind in the early days of their marriage, attending to her hair, washing herself from a large bowl, and playing the piano. He met Edith in 1908 when he and his brother Hilary‡ were lodged in a house behind the Birmingham‡ Oratory by Father Francis.‡ Like the boys, Edith was an orphan, three years older than Tolkien. She was born on 21 January 1889, in Gloucestershire. A cousin helped her mother bring her up. Edith's formal education was poor but she was very gifted musically. After her mother's death she wanted to become a music teacher.

After her move to Birmingham she and Tolkien fell in love, which necessitated Father Francis moving the boys out of her lodgings. Tolkien continued to write to and meet Edith. They married in 1916. Later that year Tolkien sailed for France and the Battle of the Somme. Their first child, John, was born the following year. She regularly played the piano at home throughout her life until arthritis made this too painful. After the war she settled into the life of an academic's wife and a mother of young children, pursuing her more homely interests. Much of Tolkien's life was separate from Edith's world, in his study, and in the male dominated world of Oxford University, which included regular meetings with C.S. Lewis,‡ the Kolbitars‡ and later the Inklings.‡ Their golden wedding celebrations in 1966 included a performance at Merton College of Donald Swann's song cycle, *The Road Goes Ever On*.‡ As Edith's health deteriorated the couple spent more and more time on holidays and visits to Bournemouth, where they eventually bought a bungalow.

Tolkien, Hilary

The younger brother of J.R.R. Tolkien, born in South Africa, February 1894. After leaving school, he helped run a farm with an aunt before enlisting as a bugler in 1914. After the war he bought a small orchard and market garden near Evesham, in Worcestershire, the ancestral home of his mother's family. Worcestershire was one of the inspirations for the Shire* in his brother's fiction.

Tolkien, J.R.R. (1892–1973)

See Chapter 1: The Life and Work of J.R.R. Tolkien.

Tolkien, Mabel (1870–1904)

The mother of J.R.R. Tolkien. Her family, the Suffields, were associated with Evesham, Worcestershire, and Tolkien identified himself with these West Midland roots of his mother. When she was 21, Mabel sailed to South Africa to marry Arthur Tolkien,* who had sought to better himself by being posted there for Lloyd's Bank. Mabel had to adjust to life in Bloemfontein. Arthur Tolkien died in 1896, while Mabel and her two young sons were visiting England. Soon the family moved to Sarehole,‡ in the countryside south of Birmingham.‡ Mabel, a highly talented woman, educated the boys until they entered formal education.

Mabel's religious background was mixed, and she eventually moved from a high church position to Roman Catholicism. Both the Tolkien and Suffield families were non-conformist or Anglican, so her conversion created great tension, especially as the boys were now exposed to Roman Catholicism. Tolkien came to believe that the effect on her health of this opposition eventually proved fatal. She succumbed to diabetes in 1904. She had arranged for the boys to have the guardianship of Father Francis Morgan.‡

Warwick

A market town and county town of Warwickshire, and part of Tolkien's early mythology† as Kortirion. (Tirion in Elvish* means 'a mighty tower, a city on a hill'). Kortirion was the chief town in a region of elms in Tol Eressëa.* Warwick is 33 kilometres southeast of Birmingham.‡ Its history is linked to its great castle, which still stands on a hilly site fortified from Saxon times. The river Avon runs alongside the castle. From 1913 until her marriage to Tolkien in 1916 Edith Bratt‡ lived in Warwick and Tolkien visited her from Oxford.‡ Tolkien wrote his poem, 'Kortirion Among the Trees' in 1915, dedicated to Warwick. Warwickshire was part of the inspiration for Tolkien's Shire.*

Welsh

A language much loved by Tolkien, ever since as a child he saw Welsh place-names on railway coal trucks near his home. He learnt the language, and based one of his main variants of Elvish* – Sindarin* – upon its structure. He writes of Welsh in the collection of essays, *The Monsters and the Critics and Other Essays*.‡

Williams, Charles (1886–1945)

Enigmatic both as an author and in his person, Charles Williams was introduced to the literary circle of Lewis,‡ Tolkien, and the Inklings,‡ in the 1930s. He exerted a deep and lasting influence on Lewis, but not on Tolkien. Tolkien did respect Williams, however, and appreciated his comments on chapters of the unfinished *The Lord of the Rings*‡ as they were read. He contributed his essay, 'On Fairy Stories'‡ to a posthumous tribute, *Essays Presented to Charles Williams*. At one stage, Tolkien wrote an affectionate poem to

Williams, complaining about difficulty in understanding his writings, but valuing his person nonetheless:

> When your fag is wagging and spectacles are twinkling,
> when tea is brewing or the glasses tinkling,
> then of your meaning often I've an inkling,
> your virtues and your wisdom glimpse . . .

Charles Williams' writings encompassed fiction, poetry, drama, theology, church history, biography and literary criticism. Anne Ridler perhaps captured the essence of Charles Williams when she wrote: 'In Williams' universe there is a clear logic, a sense of terrible justice which is not our justice and yet is not divorced from love.' For Anne Ridler 'the whole man . . . was greater even than the sum of his works'. Similarly T.S. Eliot – who greatly admired Charles Williams – said, in a broadcast talk:

> It is the whole work, not any one or several masterpieces, that we have to take into account in estimating the importance of the man. I think he was a man of unusual genius, and I regard his work as important. But it has an importance of a kind not easy to explain.

Charles Williams was in his early forties when his first novel, *War in Heaven*, was published in 1930. Prior to this he had brought out five minor books, four of which were verse, and one of which was a play. His important work begins with the novels; it is after 1930 that his noteworthy works appear, packed into the last 15 years of his life. During these final years 28 books were published (an average of almost two a year) as well as numerous articles and reviews. The last third of these years of maturity as a thinker and writer were spent in Oxford.‡ They involved Williams' normal editorial duties with Oxford University Press, lecturing and tutorials for the university, constant meetings with the Inklings, and frequent weekends in his London home. His wife stayed behind to look after the flat when Williams was evacuated to Oxford with OUP.

When Williams was evacuated with the OUP to Oxford he made a vivid impact there, captured in John Wain's autobiography, *Sprightly Running*. He comments: 'He gave himself as unreservedly to Oxford as Oxford gave itself to him.' Williams' arrival in Oxford, and Lewis' friendship with him, was not perhaps entirely welcome to Tolkien, as it meant he had less of Lewis' attention. In his letters he often mentions seeing Lewis 'and Williams' rather than Lewis alone. When Williams died suddenly in 1945 however Tolkien felt deep sorrow over the loss of his friend, writing a letter to his widow, Michal.

Further reading

Humphrey Carpenter, *The Inklings: C.S. Lewis, J.R.R. Tolkien, Charles Williams and Their Friends*. George Allen and Unwin: London, 1978; Houghton Mifflin: Boston, 1979.

Colin Duriez and David Porter, *The Inklings Handbook*. SPCK Azure: London, 2001.

Alice Hadfield, *Charles Williams: An Exploration of His Life and Work*. Oxford University Press: Oxford, 1983.

John Wain, *Sprightly Running: Part of an Autobiography*. Macmillan: London, 1962, 1965.

Wiseman, Christopher

A close friend of Tolkien's youth, and member of the TCBS.‡ Though he was from a Methodist family, he found a great affinity with the Roman Catholic Tolkien. According to Tolkien's biographer, Humphrey Carpenter, they shared an interest in Latin and Greek, Rugby football, and a zest for discussing anything under the sun. Wiseman was also sympathetic with Tolkien's experiments in invented language, as he was studying the hieroglyphics and language of ancient Egypt. Tolkien and Wiseman continued to meet after the latter went up to Cambridge University. He served in the Royal Navy during the First World War and was the only one of

Tolkien's close friends to survive it; other TCBS members, G.B. Smith‡ and R.Q. Gilson,‡ perished.

After the war, Wiseman eventually became head of Queen's College, a public school in Taunton, and the two men didn't meet very frequently. When they did meet, they found they had less and less in common. The gap in Tolkien's friendship was then filled by C.S. Lewis,‡ whom he met in Oxford‡ in 1926. The friendship with Wiseman was never entirely forgotten, however. There is a note of Tolkien visiting him in his retirement. Tolkien's last published letter mentions him.

Wright, Joseph (1855–1930)

As a schoolboy Tolkien was delighted to acquire a second-hand copy of Joseph Wright's *Primer of the Gothic Language*. As a student at Oxford‡ Tolkien chose comparative philology as his special subject (*see* Philology, Tolkien and†), so he had the same Joseph Wright as a lecturer and tutor. This Yorkshireman of humble origins (he started as a woollen-mill worker from the age of six) had, by a long struggle, become Professor of Comparative Philology. The struggle included teaching himself to read at the age of 15. Among the many languages he later studied were Sanskrit, Gothic, Russian, Old Norse, and Old and Middle High German. One of his achievements was the six large volumes of his *English Dialect Dictionary*. Joseph Wright communicated to Tolkien his love for philology, and was a demanding teacher.

NINE

TOLKIEN'S WRITINGS

The Adventures of Tom Bombadil (1961)

A collection of light verses from the Red Book of Westmarch,* supposedly written by Bilbo Baggins,* Sam Gamgee,* and other hobbits,* and rendered into English from Westron* by J.R.R. Tolkien, who adds an explanatory note. They are mainly concerned with legends and jests of the Shire* at the end of the Third Age.* Tolkien's talent for songs, ballads and witty riddles fits well into a hobbitish setting. The collection is named after a major piece in it. The contents include two poems about Tom Bombadil.* Both are regarded by the hobbits, says Tolkien, as 'benevolent persons, mysterious maybe and unpredictable but nonetheless comic'. The first poem beautifully reveals Bombadil's affinity with nature.†

'Ainulindalë'

In *The Silmarillion*,‡ this is 'The music of the Ainur' (the Ainur* are the angelic† beings, Valar* and Maiar*). It is also called 'The Great Music' or 'The Great Song'. It is the name of the narrative of creation attributed to Rúmil* of Tirion* in the First Age.* The music† expressed the blueprint of creation, the providence† and design of Ilúvatar.* The music parallels the personification of Wisdom in one of the most beautiful passages of the Bible, Proverbs 8. There Wisdom represents the standard by which God† works as he envisages the creation he is to make.

The music develops three themes of Ilúvatar, the creator. The first theme, in which the Ainur, the angelic powers, were allowed to participate, presented the form of the yet-to-be-created world. Into this theme Morgoth* (then called Melkor) introduced discord as a result of his rebellion. The second theme, in which the development of the world was revealed, overcame the discord, using it to enhance the music. This theme is prophetic of divine providence in creation. The third theme, in which the Ainur or powers played no part, had as its subject the creation of 'The Children of Ilúvatar',* that is, the elves† and humankind.

The Great Music was thus synonymous with the conception and creation of the world out of nothing, as well as its subsequent development. The rebellion of Morgoth works out throughout the invented history of Middle-earth,* a central theme in Tolkien's work.

The Valar first take on the role of preparing the world for the arrival of elves and, later, humankind. They steward the world, and provide its light,† first the Two Lamps,* then the Two Trees,* and finally the sun and moon. The stars also play an important function in revealing the care and design of Ilúvatar. In the Third Age,* several lesser Valar, or Maiar, take on human form in order to serve as guardians against the reviving power of Sauron,* originally Morgoth's lieutenant. One of these is Gandalf.*

C.S. Lewis‡ may have been inspired by the 'Ainulindalë' in the creation of Narnia by the song of Aslan in his *The Magician's Nephew*, and in the Great Dance at the climax of his science-fiction story, *Perelandra*. Music is an important theme throughout Tolkien's fiction, for instance in the tale of Beren and Lúthien, the elf-maiden.‡ Several of his poems were set to music by Donald Swann and Stephen Oliver for the BBC Radio production of *The Lord of the Rings*‡ in 1981.

Further reading

J.R.R. Tolkien:
'Ainulindalë' in *The Lost Road* (1987).
'The Ambarkanta' or 'The Shape of the World' in *The Shaping of Middle-earth* (1986).
'The Music of the Ainur' in *The Book of Lost Tales*, I (1983).
The Silmarillion (1977).

Beleriand, The Lays of
See *The Lays of Beleriand.*‡

'Beowulf: The Monsters and the Critics' (1936)

Like J.R.R. Tolkien's essay, 'On Fairy Stories',‡ this lecture provides on important key to his work both as a scholar and a writer of fiction. *Beowulf* is one of the greatest works of English literature, from the early English period. He is concerned to understand the poem as a unified work of art. In particular, he saw the two monsters which dominant it – Grendel, and the dragon† – as the centre and focus of the poem. Tolkien argued that what he called the 'structure and conduct' of the poem arose from this central theme of monsters. He may have been influenced by *Beowulf* in placing Gollum* and Smaug* the dragon at the centre of the plot of *The Hobbit*,‡ each of which give a particular kind of danger to be faced, and evoke a special kind of heroism† in response.

It was clear to Tolkien that the *Beowulf* poet created, by art, an illusion of historical truth and perspective. (C.S. Lewis‡ called such illusion, 'realism of presentation'.) The poet had an instinctive historical sense which he used for artistic, poetic ends. Tolkien observed:

> So far from being a poem so poor that only its accidental historical interest can still recommend it, Beowulf is in fact so interesting as poetry, in places poetry so powerful, that this quite overshadows the historical content, and is largely independent even of the most important facts . . . that research has discovered.

In considering the monsters, which are so pivotal to *Beowulf*, Tolkien points out what he believes is the rarity and esteem of dragons in northern literature. Only two he finds significant, one of which is Beowulf's 'bane', and the other Fafnir, the dragon of the Volsungs, is alluded to in the poem.

The author of *Beowulf*, for all his greatness and nobility of mind, was sure-footed in his artistic choice of theme. This choice actually accounts for the greatness of the poem, argues Tolkien. The poem's power comes from 'the mythical mode of imagination'. Tolkien was to take this idea further in his lecture, 'On Fairy Stories', delivered several years later. The significance of created myth in *Beowulf* cannot be dissected analytically. It is best presented, as it is in this poem, by a 'poet who feels rather than makes explicit what his theme portends; who presents it incarnate in the world of history and geography, as our [Beowulf] poet has done'. This comment is strikingly true of Tolkien's own creations.

Beowulf was a dragon slayer, as was Túrin in *The Silmarillion*.‡ Tolkien sees the dragon as a potent symbol.

> Something more significant than the standard hero, a man faced with a foe more evil than any human enemy of house or realm, is before us, and yet incarnate in time, walking in heroic history, and treading the named lands of the North.

The *Beowulf* author not only uses the old legends in a fresh and original fashion, but provides 'a measure and interpretation of them all'. In the poem we see 'man at war with the hostile world, and his inevitable overthrow in time'. The question of the power of evil,† the question of Job, is central. Beowulf 'moves in a northern heroic age imagined by a Christian, and therefore has a noble and gentle quality, though conceived to be a pagan'. In *Beowulf* there is a fusion of the Christian and the ancient north, the old and the new. The imagination of the *Beowulf* author was not allegorical. Allegory† was a later development in English literature. His dragon, as a symbol of evil, retains the ancient force of the pagan northern imagination; it is not an allegory of evil in reference to the individual soul's redemption or damnation. He is concerned with 'man on earth' rather than the journey to the Celestial City. 'Each man and all men, and all their works shall die . . . The shadow of its despair, if only as a mood, as an intense emotion of regret, is still there. The worth of defeated valour in this world is deeply felt.' The poet feels this theme imaginatively or poetically rather than literally, yet with a sense of the ultimate defeat of darkness.

Tolkien concludes that the poem explores the insights into goodness that may be found within the limits of the pagan imagination.

In Beowulf we have, then, an historical poem about the pagan past, or an attempt at one ... It is a poem by a learned man writing of old times, who looking back on the heroism and sorrow feels in them something permanent and something symbolical. So far from being a confused semi-pagan – historically unlikely for a man of this sort in the period – he brought probably first to his task a knowledge of Christian poetry ...

Tolkien undoubtedly found a great affinity between his own vision as a writer and this ancient poem. Like the *Beowulf* poet Tolkien is a Christian scholar looking back to an imagined northern European past. The *Beowulf* author was a Christian looking to the imaginative resources of a pagan past. Both made use of dragons and other potent symbols, symbols that unified their work. Both are concerned more with symbolism† than allegory. Like the ancient author, also, Tolkien took care to create an illusion of history and a sense of depths of the past. Behind *The Lord of the Rings*‡ stands the vast history and geography of *The Silmarillion*.‡

Beren and Lúthien the elf-maiden, The tale of

This is one of the chief stories of *The Silmarillion*,‡ alluded to, and briefly retold in song by Aragorn,* in *The Lord of the Rings*.‡ Like that book it is a heroic romance, though on a smaller scale. There are both poetic and prose versions, though none of the poetic versions is complete (*see* The Lays of Beleriand‡).

The tale of Beren* and Lúthien* is set in Beleriand,* during the First Age* of Middle-earth.* Lúthien was the daughter of the elven

King Thingol,* ruler of Doriath,* and Queen Melian,* and thus immortal. Beren was a mortal man. (For a fuller account of the story see Chapter 5: How *The Lord of the Rings* Relates to *The Silmarillion.*)

Many of Tolkien's characteristic themes emerge in this story, including healing† and sacrifice,† evil,† death† and immortality, and romantic love. Through the eventual marriage of Beren and Lúthien, an elvish quality† was preserved in humankind in future generations – even into the Fourth Age* when humanity became ascendant, and the elves† waned. This theme is repeated in *The Lord of the Rings* with the marriage of Arwen* and Aragorn. In future Ages the story of Beren and Lúthien brought hope and consolation† both to elves and to those of humanity who were faithful against the darkness. This hope is often picked up in *The Lord of the Rings*, by Aragorn and others.

The Book of Lost Tales
See under *The History of Middle-earth.*‡

Farmer Giles of Ham (1949)
This light-hearted short story is subtitled, 'The Rise and Wonderful Adventures of Farmer Giles, Lord of Tame, Count of Worminghall and King of the Little Kingdom.' It begins with a mock-scholarly Foreword about its supposed authorship, translation from Latin, and the extent of the 'Little Kingdom' in 'a dark period of the history of Britain'. Tolkien concludes that the setting is before the days of King Arthur, in the valley of the Thames.

Farmer Giles, of the village of Ham, had a dog named Garm. One night a rather deaf and short-sighted giant wandered by mistake near Farmer Giles' farm, trampling his fields and animals. The nervous farmer let fly with an anachronistic blunderbuss, stuffed with wire, stones, and other bits. The giant, not hearing the bang, supposed himself stung, and quickly left that place with its apparently unpleasant horseflies. Farmer Giles was now the village hero.† Even the King of the Little Kingdom heard of his deed and sent him the gift of a long sword.

The Farmer enjoyed his reputation until a dragon† heard of the rich kingdom from the giant, and times were hard. The name of the dragon was Chrysophylax Dives, and he came to investigate the land. The fiery dragon made a nuisance of himself, but the King's knights were unwilling to take him on.

Meanwhile, the scaly beast got closer and closer to Ham. It turned out that the sword given to Giles was called Tailbiter, and had belonged to a renowned dragon-slayer. The pressure was on for the reluctant hero to go dragon-hunting. With Garm, his dog, and his old grey mare, the Farmer set off.

Much to Giles' surprise, the wily dragon greeted him with a 'Good morning', thinking of his next meal. (He had earlier eaten a stringy Parson, whereas Giles was large and fat.) The sword, Tailbiter, however, nonplussed the dragon – with good reason, for, after challenging the dragon, Farmer Giles wounded his wing, making him unable to fly.

Instead he ran, pursued by the fat Farmer on his grey mare. The folk of Ham cheered at the pursuit. Eventually the exhausted dragon bargained to save his skin. If Farmer Giles would let him go home, the dragon would return with treasure. The Farmer agreed, and the dragon left for home in the far-off mountains, with no intention of returning.

The King, hearing of the events, decided that the dragon's wealth should be his. He encamped with his entourage in Farmer Giles' field, draining the local economy. The day soon came when the dragon had agreed to return, but of course he didn't. The furious King ordered Giles to come to his court and lead his knights to punish the dragon.

After four tiring days Farmer Giles on his grey mare, and the King's knights on their horses, reached the far-away mountains. The mare became lame, so she and Giles found themselves behind the party as it reached Chrysophylax's territory. Suddenly the dragon leapt out of his cave. Farmer Giles rushed to give battle, holding the eager sword, Tailbiter. The knights were either killed or fled, but the old mare stood her ground. The dragon became nervous at the sight of his old enemy with the fearful sword. As Giles insisted to the dragon on having treasure the old grey mare began to worry about how it was going to be carried. However, Farmer Giles forced the dragon to carry a great load of it on his back.

Instead of returning to the King's court, the odd procession made its way to Ham. The King was outraged, and made his way to the village, not realizing that the dragon was still there. He was unable to insist that Giles gave him the treasure, and from that time the Farmer was Lord of the region around the village, backed up by his tamed dragon – or, Tame Worm – who was housed in a 'hall', a barn. Giles was called Lord of the Tame Worm, and eventually Lord of Tame. This title led to the name, Thame, as Ham and Tame became conflated. The humbled dragon was eventually allowed by Giles to return home to the mountains.

This humorous story, though on the surface very different from the tales of Middle-earth,* is characteristic of Tolkien in its themes. The story's inspiration is linguistic: it provides a spoof explanation for the name of an actual village east of Oxford‡ called Worminghall, near Thame. An uneaten Parson in the story is a grammarian (the equivalent of a philologist), making him shrewd and wise (*see* Philology, Tolkien and†). The Little Kingdom has similarities with the Shire,* particularly the sheltered and homely life of Ham. Farmer Giles is like a complacent hobbit,* with unexpected qualities. The humour – with its mock scholarship – is similar to that in the collection of hobbit verses, *The Adventures of Tom Bombadil.*‡

The Father Christmas Letters (1976)

This is a collection of letters, edited by Baillie Tolkien (wife of Christopher Tolkien‡), to his children in the 1920s and 30s. He writes them as from Father Christmas, illustrates them vividly (*see Pictures*‡).

The Fellowship of the Ring (1954)

The first volume of *The Lord of the Rings*,‡ comprising Books One and Two (*see* Chapter 3: Introducing *The Lord of the Rings*).

The History of Middle-earth

The title of a series of volumes of unfinished or preliminary material edited and published after Tolkien's death by his son, Christopher,‡ who also provides a detailed commentary. The volumes are *The Book of Lost Tales, The Lays of Beleriand, The Shaping of Middle-earth, The Lost Road,* and the four books of *The History of the Lord of the Rings.*

The Book of Lost Tales, 1 and 2 (1983, 1984)

These make up the first two volumes of *The History of Middle-earth.* Explanatory commentaries are added. *The Book of Lost Tales* represents Tolkien's first major imaginative work. He began it during the First World War, and abandoned it several years afterwards.

The first volume contains narratives relating to Valinor,* the Undying Lands to the Uttermost West of Middle-earth.* The second is made up of stories set in Beleriand* in the First Age.* *The Book of Lost Tales* is the first form of the 'Quenta Silmarillion',‡ 'The Silmarillion' proper which only constitutes part of the published book, *The Silmarillion.*‡

A striking feature of *The Book of Lost Tales* is Tolkien's attempt to put *The Silmarillion* into an accessible narrative framework. It concerns Aelfwine* (or Eriol) who, by chance, sails to Tol Eressëa,* an elvish island close by the coast of Valinor.* There, in a Warwick-shire-like setting, he discovers The Cottage of Lost Play. Here is narrated to him the tales of the creation of the world, Morgoth's* destruction of the light of the Two Trees* of Valinor, and other stories of *The Silmarillion.* There are significant differences of detail from the final form of the stories, but they are clearly recognizable. In *The Book of Lost Tales* are the only full narratives of the Necklace of the Dwarves (Nauglamir*) and the Fall of Gondolin.* The second volume contains the history of Aelfwine, a narrative picked up in *The Lost Road*.

The Lays of Beleriand

This is the third volume of *The History of Middle-earth*. It mainly consists of substantial unfinished narrative poems, one telling the story of Túrin Turambar,* and the other, the tale of Beren and Lúthien.‡ These are two of what Tolkien regarded as the four narratives that stood independently of the complex annals of the First Age* of Middle-earth. (The others were the tale of Tuor* and the Fall of Gondolin, and the story of Eärendil the Mariner.*

The Túrin poem, entitled 'The Lay of the Children of Húrin', consists of two versions, both unfinished. It was a bold experiment in alliterative verse, which Tolkien confessed he wrote 'with pleasure'. Unlike the summary tale published in *The Silmarillion* it has vividness and what C.S. Lewis‡ elsewhere called 'realism of presentation'. The poem is early, begun around 1918, so some names differ from the final *Silmarillion*. Gwindor for instance is called Flinding go-Fuilin.

It is valuable to read this poem in conjunction with the long prose version (alas, also incomplete) in *Unfinished Tales*.‡ These, along with the summary in *The Silmarillion*, will help the reader to have a fuller enjoyment of one of Tolkien's greatest stories.

The Beren* and Lúthien* poem, entitled 'The Lay of Leithian' (meaning, 'release from bondage'), is also in two versions, the first much longer than 'The Lay of the Children of Húrin', and the other quite brief. It is written in octosyllabic couplets, a form Tolkien uses with great power and effectiveness. Tolkien abandoned the first version in 1931, returning to it in 1949 or 1950 and beginning the second version. At this time he still hoped that *The Silmarillion* might be published. As with the Túrin poem, this beautiful poem, telling the love story of Beren and Lúthien and the quest† for the Silmaril,* adds reality to the summary version in the published *Silmarillion*. C.S. Lewis, in the early days of his friendship with Tolkien, provided diplomatic and ingenious criticism of the unfinished poem. Lewis' commentary is reproduced as an appendix to *The Lays of Beleriand*. It was Lewis' encouragement that kept Tolkien writing *The Lord of the Rings*‡ which otherwise might too have remained unfinished. A.N. Wilson vividly describes the development of friendship between Lewis and Tolkien in his biography of C.S. Lewis, and speaks highly of 'The Lay of Leithian': 'Though at times the verse is technically imperfect, it is full of passages of quite stunning beauty; and the overall conception must make it, though unfinished, one of the most remarkable poems written in English in the twentieth century.'

The Shaping of Middle-earth (1986)
This is the fourth volume of the series. The book is sub-titled, 'The Quenta, the Ambarkanta and the Annals'. Christopher Tolkien provides an exhaustive commentary on the development of his father's invention.

'The Quenta' is sometimes given the fuller name, 'The Quenta Silmarillion', another name for 'The Silmarillion' (meaning, 'The history of the Silmarils'). The book includes the original 'Silmarillion', written by Tolkien in 1926, and also the 'Quenta Noldorinwa' of 1930 (the largest section of the book). The latter was the only form of the mythology† of the First Age* that Tolkien ever completed. To it is appended a fragment translated into Old English, supposedly by Aelfwine.* 'The Ambarkanta' (or 'The Shape of the World'), is the only account found of the nature of Tolkien's imagined universe. Though a short work, it throws valuable light on his cosmology, and the effect of the change of the world at the time of the destruction of Númenor.*

'The Annals' are in effect annotated chronologies, reflecting Tolkien's preoccupation with chronology. This book gives the earliest 'Annals of Valinor' (there were three versions in all), and also the earliest version of the 'Annals of Beleriand' (other versions followed).

The Shaping of Middle-earth shows the development of Tolkien's mythology up to some time in the 1930s. He continued to work on and modify 'The Silmarillion' up to his death in 1973.

The Lost Road and Other Writings (1987)

This is the fifth volume in the series. Under pressure to produce a sequel to the popular The Hobbit, Tolkien at the end of 1937 reluctantly set aside his mythology and tales of the First and Second Ages of Middle-earth. This fifth volume completes the presentation and commentary on his invention up to that time.

At this point, Tolkien had composed later versions of 'The Annals of Valinor' and 'The Annals of Beleriand', and a greatly amplified version of 'The Silmarillion' was nearly complete. He had also started work on the history of the Downfall of Númenor and the change in the world which resulted from this. All this material is included. There is also an account of the development of the Elvish* languages, 'The Lhammas' ('Account of Tongues'), supposedly written by Rúmil.*

Tolkien was also wrestling with the problem of the narrative framework of 'The Silmarillion'. One of the most interesting sections of this book is his unfinished tale of time-travel, 'The Lost Road', which, if it had been successful, would have provided such a framework. Tolkien tried to absorb his earlier framework, whereby the traveller Aelfwine was told the tales of the First Age, into the story of 'The Lost Road'. As it happened, the telling of The Lord of the Rings provided some kind of resolution to the problem of the narrative framework for 'The Silmarillion'.

Tolkien never prepared a sustained Elvish vocabulary, but did construct an etymological dictionary of word relationships. This is included in the book under the title, 'The Etymologies'.

See also Philology, Tolkien and.†

The History of the Lord of the Rings

A series of four books, parts 6 to 9 of *The History of Middle-earth*, which collect early drafts of *The Lord of the Rings*. The books are *The Return of the Shadow*, *The Treason of Isengard*, *The War of the Ring* and *Sauron Defeated*.

The Return of the Shadow (1988) is made up of Tolkien's early drafts of what was to become the first volume of *The Lord of the Rings*, *The Fellowship of the Ring*.‡ Frodo Baggins* is here called Bingo, and Strider (Aragorn*) has the name of Trotter. The collection provides fascinating insights into Tolkien's manner of composition.

The Treason of Isengard is Volume 7 of *The History of Middle-earth*, and Part 2 of *The History of the Lord of the Rings*. It helps to show the development of *The Lord of the Rings* by publishing earlier drafts.

The War of the Ring (1990) is also made up of early drafts of what was the become part of *The Lord of the Rings*. The book concerns the battle of Helm's Deep, the destruction of Isengard* by the Ents,* the journey of Frodo,* Sam* and Gollum* to the Pass of Cirith Ungol,* the war in Gondor,* and the parley between Gandalf* and the ambassadors of Sauron* in front of the Black Gate of Mordor.* Developments unforeseen by Tolkien include the emergence of the Palantir* at Isengard and the appearance in the story of Faramir.* The book contains illustrations and plans, including Orthanc,* Dunharrow,* Minas Tirith* and the tunnels of Shelob's* lair. Faramir speaks of ancient history, and the languages of Gondor and the Common Speech (*see* Westron*), material not retained in *The Two Towers*.‡

Sauron Defeated (1992) shows Tolkien's developing conception of the final part of the story of *The Lord of the Rings*. It also includes 'The Notion Club Papers'‡ and 'The Drowning of Anadune'. Anadune is the Adûnaic* form of Númenor.

Morgoth's Ring

Volume 10 of *The History of Middle-earth*, tracing the evolution of

The Silmarillion from the completion of *The Lord of the Rings* in 1949 until Tolkien's death. It draws upon unpublished papers to show this development. Volume 10 follows the narrative up to Morgoth's theft of the precious Silmarils.*

War of the Jewels (1994)

This takes the narrative up to the conflict between the elves* and the evil Morgoth, containing many of the legends of Beleriand.

The Peoples of Middle-earth

The twelfth and last volume of *The History of Middle-earth*. This volume reveals the genesis of the Appendices to *The Lord of the Rings*, as well as issuing two stories that Tolkien soon abandoned, including 'The New Shadow'.

The Hobbit (1937)

A children's story that belongs to the Third Age* of Middle-earth,* and chronologically precedes *The Lord of the Rings*.‡ It provides the conditions for the plot of the later work (*see* Chapter 3: Introducing *The Lord of the Rings*).

The Lays of Beleriand

See under *The History of Middle-earth*.‡

Leaf by Niggle (1945)

First published in January 1945 in *The Dublin Review*, this short allegory† was republished in *Tree and Leaf*.‡ The allegory, an unusual form for Tolkien, is also untypical in having autobiographical elements.

Niggle, a little man and an artist, knew that he would one day have to make a Journey.† Many matters got in the way of his painting, such as the demands of his neighbour, Mr Parish, who had a lame leg. Niggle was soft-hearted, and rather lazy.

Niggle was concerned to finish one painting in particular. This had started as an illustration of a leaf caught in the wind, then became a tree.† Through gaps in the leaves and branches a Forest and a whole world opened up. As the painting grew (with other, smaller paintings tacked on) Niggle had had to move it into a specially built shed on his potato plot.

Eventually Niggle fell ill after getting soaked in a storm while running an errand for Mr Parish. Then the dreaded Inspector visited to tell him that the time had come for him to set out on the Journey.

Taking a train his first stop (which seemed to last for a century) was at the Workhouse, as Niggle had not brought any belongings. He worked very hard there on various chores. At last, one day, when he had been ordered to rest, he overheard two Voices discussing his case. One of them spoke up for him. It was time for gentler treatment, he said.

Niggle was allowed to resume his Journey in a small train which led him to the familiar world depicted on his painting of long ago, and to his tree, now complete. 'It's a gift!' he exclaimed. Niggle then walked towards the Forest (which had tall Mountains behind). He realized that there was unfinished work here, and that Parish could help him – his old neighbour knew a lot about plants, earth and trees. At this realization he came across Parish, and the two of them worked busily together. At last, Niggle felt that it was time to move on into the Mountains. Parish wished to remain behind to await his wife. It turned out that the region they had worked in together was called Niggle's Country, much to their surprise. A guide led Niggle into the Mountains.

Long before, back in the town near where Niggle and Parish had lived before the Journey, a fragment of Niggle's painting had survived and been hung in the Town Museum, entitled simply, 'Leaf by Niggle'. It depicted a spray of leaves with a glimpse of a mountain peak.

Niggle's Country became a popular place to send travellers as a holiday, for refreshment and convalescence, and as a splendid introduction to the Mountains.

Tolkien's little story suggests the link between art and reality. Even in heaven there will be place for the artist to add his or her own touch to the created world.

The allegorical element could be interpreted as follows, much as suggested by Tom Shippey in his *The Road to Middle-earth*:

The Journey† = death
Niggle the painter = Tolkien the writer
Painting leaves rather than trees = Tolkien's perfectionism, and ability to be easily distracted
Niggle's leaf = *The Hobbit*‡
Niggle's tree = *The Lord of the Rings*‡ (and *The Silmarillion*‡)
The country that opens up = Middle-earth*
Other pictures tacked on = poems and other works
The neglected garden = Tolkien's professorial responsibilities
Parish's excellent potatoes = 'proper' work
The Workhouse = Purgatory
Niggle = creative element in humans (*see* Elvish quality†)
Parish = practical element in humans
The Mountains = heaven, and the resolution of Niggle's two sides
Potatoes = scholarship
Trees = fantasy

This interpretation emphasizes the autobiographical aspect of the story. The tale has equal applicability to the artist in general, however. In particular, there is a poignancy to the unfinished nature of Niggle's work. There are very few artists (or, indeed, other people) who can say at the end of their lives, 'It is finished'.

The Letters of J.R.R. Tolkien (1981)

This substantial 463-page book is a selection of Tolkien's letters from the mid-1930s (when he was in his mid-forties), as *The Hobbit*‡ was being prepared for the press, to just before his death in 1973 at the age of 81. Only eight letters come from the period before that. The collection was edited by Humphrey Carpenter, Tolkien's biographer, with the assistance of Christopher Tolkien,‡ Tolkien's son, to whom a number of the letters are addressed. The letters greatly concern Tolkien's fictional works, including their development and interrelationship. Much is also revealed of the life and personality of this remarkable and complex man. Far from mentally inhabiting an 'unreal' world of imagination,† the letters unveil Tolkien's sharp observation and critique of the foibles of the modern age.

Much like his close friend C.S. Lewis,‡ Tolkien probably would have been happy to be seen as a specimen or even relic of the almost lost age of 'Old Western Man' (*see* Old West†). Like Lewis, he was able successfully to look at, and write for, our modern age with command and pertinence. The letters constantly give clues to Tolkien's thought and world-view, unlike Lewis almost totally expressed in his fiction (*but see* Fairy stories†). His deep Christian faith is evident in the letters, where he in one place answers a child's letter (Letter 310) about 'the purpose of life' (*see* Christianity, Tolkien and†).

As deep as his Christian insight is his love for language. He was a philologist by profession (*see* Philology, Tolkien and). His genius with language is nowhere more evident than in his creation of names for people and places in Middle-earth.* Many of the letters concern his invented languages, including Elvish.*

Mainly since the cult popularity of Tolkien's fiction in the 1960s, numerous interpretations of his work have appeared in journals and books. These letters have embedded in them Tolkien's own interpretation of, and commentary on, his work. An author's own view of his or her work is not necessarily the final say, or the best, but because of the unique nature of Tolkien's invention, his comments provide a framework and standard for understanding his work. Without the letters interpretation would be much more difficult, especially as so much of Tolkien's work is unfinished. The letters reinforce the fact that Tolkien's work demands to be taken seriously, in the terms in which it was written, including its linguistic inspiration.

There are many memorable letters in the corpus, a few of which are as follows:

Letter 131 – A letter of around 10,000 words to Milton Waldman, of the publisher Collins, demonstrating the integral relationship between *The Silmarillion*,‡ and other matter from the first two Ages of Middle-earth,* and *The Hobbit*‡ and *The Lord of the Rings*,‡ set in the Third Age.* The letter reveals a great deal about the development of Tolkien's work. It was written around 1951, when Tolkien hoped that *The Silmarillion* and *The Lord of the Rings* might be published together.

Letter 144 – Addressed to the author Naomi Mitchison in 1954, this letter answers key questions about *The Lord of the Rings*.

Letter 153 – A bookseller challenged the metaphysics of *The Lord of the Rings*, and Tolkien wrote this careful and revealing letter, which he never finished. He thought he was taking himself too seriously, but it illustrates the theological seriousness of his fiction.

Letter 163 – This letter to W.H. Auden‡ in 1955 casts light on Tolkien's life in relation to the development of his fiction.

Letter 165 – A letter written to Tolkien's US publisher, Houghton Mifflin Co., to provide publicity material about what 'made him tick'. It was used as the basis for this information.

Letter 212 – This is a draft, never sent, continuing a previous letter to Rhona Beare. It speaks of the difference between Tolkien's invented mythology (*see* Myth†) and the biblical narrative, for instance, on the nature of the fall.†

Letter 257 – This letter, written in 1964, reveals much about Tolkien's development.

The Lord of the Rings (1954–55)

See Chapter 3: Introducing *The Lord of the Rings*; *The History of Middle-earth.*‡

The Lost Road and other writings

See under *The History of Middle-earth.*‡

The Monsters and the Critics and Other Essays (1983)

A collection of general essays on linguistic or literary topics. They are all lectures given over a long period of time, from the mid-1930s to Tolkien's retirement in 1959 as Merton Professor of English Language and Literature. The essays are as follows:

'Beowulf: The Monsters and the Critics'‡

The now famous essay defending the artistic unity and integrity of the great Old English poem.

'On Translating Beowulf'

Tolkien defends a prose translation of the poem as an aid to study. He points out that 'Old English (or Anglo-Saxon) is not a very difficult language . . . But the idiom and diction of Old English verse is not easy. Its manner and conventions, and its metre, are unlike those of modern English verse. Also it is preserved fragmentarily and by chance'. Tolkien later discusses alliterative verse, in which he was skilled.

'Sir Gawain and the Green Knight'

This presents Tolkien's main thinking about a medieval English poem that was a particular favourite of his, and which he translated. He devoted a great deal of study to it. He states that

It is indeed a poem that deserves close and detailed attention, and after that . . . careful consideration, and re-consideration. It is one of the masterpieces of fourteenth-century art in England, and of English Literature as a whole ... It belongs to that literary kind which has deep roots in the past, deeper even than its author was aware. It is made of tales often told before and elsewhere, and of elements that derive from remote times, beyond the vision or awareness of the poet: like Beowulf, or some of Shakespeare's major plays, as a King Lear or Hamlet.

'On Fairy Stories'

This was an Andrew Lang lecture delivered at the University of St Andrews on 8 March 1939. It presents the heart of Tolkien's thinking about fantasy, sub-creation,† and the nature of fiction. It provides a key into his work, and that of C.S. Lewis‡ and George MacDonald‡ (see Fairy stories†).

'English and Welsh'

In this lecture, given at Oxford‡ the day after the publication of *The Return of the King*, Tolkien speaks of the attraction that the Welsh language has for him (see Elvish*). He also mentions its preference for a hard 'c' over 'k'. Tolkien also speaks of the growth of his love of language, in which Welsh played an important part (see Philology, Tolkien and†).

'A Secret Vice'

This lecture is of particular interest because of its autobiographical elements. Tolkien speaks of the pleasure of inventing languages, and believes that this 'hobby' is natural in childhood. He gives examples of his own invention, including Elvish.

'Valedictory Address to the University of Oxford'

In this lecture, Tolkien reflects back over the more than 30 years in which he had held two chairs in the university. He is particularly interested in the relationship between the teaching of language and literature.

Mr Bliss (1982)

A children's story, illustrated in colour throughout by Tolkien. Mr Bliss is noted for his tall hats, and lives in a tall house. In 1932 Tolkien bought a car (he later abandoned car ownership on principle, because of the environmental effect of massive car ownership and production). The erratic consequences of this possession suggested the story of Mr Bliss' adventures after buying a bright yellow car for five shillings. Tolkien showed the story to his publishers in 1937, when the publication of *The Hobbit*‡ had created a demand for more from the pen of the professor. Colour printing costs at that time, however, were prohibitive. It was not until after Tolkien's death that the book was published.

See also Pictures.‡

'Mythopoeia'

A poem in rhyming couplets that Tolkien addressed to his friend, C.S. Lewis,‡ then pre-Christian, defending the imagination† and myth† as a means of truth, against Lewis' materialism. Similar ideas are set out in his essay 'On Fairy Stories' (*see* Fairy stories†). The poem is written as from Philomythus to Misomythus (from lover to distruster of myth). It is included in the second edition of *Tree and Leaf*‡ (1988).

'The New Shadow'

A story intended to be set in the Fourth Age,* abandoned by Tolkien. It was to tell of events about 100 years after the death of Aragorn,* where people had soon become bored with goodness. There were secret revolutionaries involved in Satanism (whether extolling Sauron* or Morgoth,* Tolkien does not say), and boys of Gondor* played at being orcs.*

'The Notion Club Papers'

An incomplete work published in *The History of the Lord of the Rings*.‡ In a letter to his publisher in July 1946, he mentioned having written three parts of this. He said that it took up material employed in the unfinished 'The Lost Road', but in an entirely different frame and setting. Like 'The Lost Road' it is a time-travel book, having the purpose of introducing the tales of Númenor.* The Inklings'‡ meetings at that time (which were much larger than in earlier days) provide the inspiration for the setting of an informal literary group. Members of the Notion Club resemble C.S. Lewis,‡ Hugo Dyson,‡ Dr Humphrey Havard,‡ and others. The text is made up of papers supposedly found early in the twenty-first century, and constitute the minutes of discussion of the Notion Club in Oxford‡ during 1986–87 – the years of the great storm.

Tolkien wrote the unfinished papers during 1945–46. Associated with the Notion Club Papers was a new version of the Númenorean legend – 'The Drowning of Anadune'. The Papers are a second attempt (the first being *The Lost Road*) at time-travel, in response to a challenge that Lewis and Tolkien set themselves to write a time or space travel story. Lewis' response was his *Out of the Silent Planet*, admired by Tolkien.

'The Notion Club Papers' idealizes the Inklings but contains neither direct biography nor autobiography. They concern the discovery of clues to the lost world of Númenor through strange words that contain clues for philologically aware people, people exceptionally sensitive to language. The work appreciates the value of a group or community of people in building up together an imaginative picture of the past. The insights into the past achieved imaginatively are in a curious way as objective as the seemingly hard facts of traditional history. This objectivity is demonstrated by the intrusion of a great storm in late twentieth-century Oxford that derives from the calamity which befell Númenor. The world of Númenor – specifically its terrible destruction – in fact intrudes into the future western world in the summer of 1987. (Interestingly, there was a great storm – a hurricane – in Britain that autumn which had a devastating impact!)

As well as language, the Inklings-like discussions of the Notion Club concern the status of dreams, and time and space travel via that medium. Behind it is an exciting exploration of the place imagination† has in putting us in contact with objective reality, resisting the view that imagination is purely subjective and individualistic.

'On Fairy Stories'

Reproduced in *Essays Presented to Charles Williams* (1947), *Tree and Leaf,*‡ and *The Monsters and the Critics and Other Essays,*‡ this lecture is the key source for J.R.R. Tolkien's thinking and theology behind his creation of Middle-earth* and its stories. *See* Fairy stories.†

Pictures by J.R.R. Tolkien (1979)

Collected, with notes, by Christopher Tolkien.‡ This large format book contains 48 sections of paintings, drawings and designs by J.R.R. Tolkien, mostly relating to *The Hobbit,*‡ *The Lord of the Rings,*‡ and *The Silmarillion.*‡ Tolkien had great skills as an illustrator. His visualization of settings from his fiction is of particular interest. Those from *The Silmarillion* (such as the illustrations of Nargothrond*) are especially valuable due to the unfinished nature of that work. Tolkien was unable to detail the stories of that period of Middle-earth* as vividly as in *The Lord of the Rings*. The illustrations emphasize the great care Tolkien took in visualizing and creating his geography* of Middle-earth. We glimpse Tol Sirion,* with the shadow of Thangorodrim* on the horizon. We see the beautiful city of Gondolin,* encircled by mountains. There is a powerful depiction of Taniquetil,* its peak in the stars.

From the Third Age* of Middle-earth is included Tolkien's crayon drawing of the Mallorn trees of Lórien* in spring, capturing the numinous† quality of the region. There are many other illustrations, including a picture of Hobbiton* that was the frontispiece to the original edition of *The Hobbit* in 1937. One of Tolkien's illustrations of Mirkwood* is based on an earlier painting of Taur-nu-Fuin,* illustrating Beleg's finding of Gwindor. The depiction of the elven-king's Gate from *The Hobbit* is somewhat reminiscent of Tolkien's portrayal of Nargothrond. One of Tolkien's beautiful, stylized drawings of trees† is used on the cover of *Tree and Leaf*.‡ A more naturalistic crayon drawing powerfully depicts Old Man Willow.

The Quenta Silmarillion

Literally, 'the history of the Silmarils'.
See Chapter 5: How *The Lord of the Rings* Relates to *The Silmarillion*.

The Return of the King (1955)

The third volume of *The Lord of the Rings*,‡ comprising Books Five and Six, and extensive appendices.
See Chapter 3: Introducing *The Lord of the Rings*.

The Road Goes Ever On: A Song Cycle (1968, 1978)

Poems by Tolkien on the theme of the Road,† set to music by Donald Swann. The musical scores are included, along with notes on, and translations of, the Elvish* poems by Tolkien. The first edition included 'The road goes ever on', 'Upon the hearth the fire is red', 'In the Willow-Meads of Tasarinan', 'In Western lands', 'Namarie (Farewell)', 'I sit beside the fire', and 'Errantry'. In the second edition, 'Bilbo's last song' was added. A recording of the poems, sung by William Elvin, and accompanied at the piano by the composer, is available. The recording, *Poems and Songs of Middle-earth*, also contains recordings of Tolkien reading the poems.

Roverandom

A story both written and illustrated by Tolkien and not published until 1998, over 70 years later. In 1925, while the family was on holiday at Filey in Yorkshire, four-year-old Michael Tolkien lost

his little lead dog on the beach. In sympathy, his father wrote
Roverandom, about a real dog Rover, turned into a toy by a wizard.†
When dropped on the beach by a small boy, the toy is transported
to the moon along the path of light the moon makes when it
shines over the sea. The Man in the Moon renames him
Roverandom and gives him wings. Roverandom and Moondog
set out on a series of adventures, encountering the Great White
Dragon† and other moon fauna like giant spiders and dragon-
moths. Finally, back on Earth, Roverandom travels under the sea
inside Uim, oldest of the whales, to ask the wizard who changed
him into a toy to undo the spell.

The Silmarillion (1977)

A book of tales and annals chronicling the early days that include
the First Age* of Middle-earth.* Its unifying motif is that of the
Silmarils* and their fate.
See Chapter 5: How *The Lord of the Rings* relates to *The
Silmarillion*.

Sir Gawain and the Green Knight (1925)

Edited by J.R.R. Tolkien and E.V. Gordon.‡ This presentation of
the text of the finest of all the English medieval romances helped
to stimulate study of this work, much loved by Tolkien. It contains
a major glossary. His own translation of it was published in 1975.
A new edition of Tolkien's and Gordon's book came out in 1967,
edited by Norman Davis.

Sir Gawain and the Green Knight, Pearl, and Sir Orfeo (1975)

Tolkien's own translations of three major medieval English poems
that he particularly loved. His verse translations skilfully represent
the poetic structures of the original poems. The Sir Gawain and Pearl
poems are by the same unknown author from the West Midlands,
an area of England with which Tolkien identified, basing the
Shire* upon it.

Smith of Wootton Major (1967)

A short story that complements the essay, 'On Fairy Stories' in tracing the relationship between the world of faery and the primary world (*see* Fairy stories†). Tolkien described it as 'an old man's book, already weighted with the presage of "bereavement".' It was as if, like Smith in the story with his elven star, Tolkien expected his imagination† to come to an end. Like *Farmer Giles of Ham*,‡ the story has an undefined medieval setting. The villages of Wootten Major and Minor could have come out of the Shire.* As in Middle-earth,* it is possible to walk in and out of the world of faerie (the realm of Elves*). The story contains an elven-king in disguise, Alf, apprentice to the bungling cake-maker Nokes. Nokes has no concept of the reality of faerie, but his sugary cake for the village children, with its crude Fairy Queen doll, can stir the imagination of the humble. A magic elven star in the cake is swallowed by Smith, giving him access to faerie. In the village it is the children who can be susceptible to the 'other', the numinous,† where their elders are only concerned with eating and drinking.

As in *Leaf by Niggle*‡ glimpses of other worlds transform art and craft in human life (*see* Elven quality†). The humble work of the village smith is transformed into the sacramental.

The Tolkien Reader (1966)

Published only in the United States, this collection contains an introduction by Peter S. Beagle, and the following pieces by Tolkien:

'The Homecoming of Beorhtnoth Beorhthelm's Son' (a short play);
'On Fairy Stories'‡ (an essay)
'Leaf by Niggle'‡ (an allegorical short story);
'Farmer Giles of Ham'‡ (a comic short story);
'The Adventures of Tom Bombadil'‡ (a collection of hobbit* verses).

The collection was important for introducing devotees of *The Lord of the Rings*‡ to the wider range of Tolkien's writings.

Tree and Leaf (1964, 1988)

This book by Tolkien includes his famous essay, 'On Fairy Stories' (*see* Fairy story†), explaining his view of fantasy and sub-creation,† and an allegory† with autobiographical elements, *Leaf by Niggle*.‡ The new edition of 1988 adds a poem written to C.S. Lewis,‡ 'Mythopoeia', ‡ incorporating ideas about the relationship between myth† and fact which were influential in Lewis' conversion to Christianity (*see* Christianity, Tolkien and†).

The Two Towers (1954)

The second volume of *The Lord of the Rings*,‡ comprising Books Three and Four. It tells the adventures of the members of the Company of the Ring* after the break-up of their fellowship, up to the beginning of a great darkness from Mordor* and the start of the War of the Ring.*
See Chapter 3: Introducing *The Lord of the Rings*.

Unfinished Tales of Númenor and Middle-earth (1980)

A collection of incomplete or unfinalized tales and narratives supplementing *The Silmarillion*,‡ *The Hobbit*‡ and *The Lord of the Rings*,‡ edited by Christopher Tolkien.‡

The book is divided into four parts, three of which are devoted to the First, Second and Third Ages of Middle-earth,* while the fourth concerns the strange Dúnedain,* wizards† and the Palantíri,* or Seeing Stones. There is a useful glossary. Part One begins with a beautiful, but sadly unfinished, tale of Tuor* and his coming to Gondolin,* most probably written in 1951. Had it been completed it would have been a major work, concerning as it does one of the four independent stories of the First Age* (*see* 'The Fall of Gondolin'*). Then follows a long, but also unfinished, account of the life of Túrin Turambar,* another of the four major stories of 'The Silmarillion'. This too is marked by great beauty, complemented by the unfinished poetic version in the *Lays of Beleriand*‡ (*see* Chapter 5: How *The Lord of the Rings* Relates to *The Silmarillion*).

Part Two, concerned with the Second Age* of Middle-earth,* opens with a description of the island of Númenor.* This helps to give flesh to the often annalistic accounts of Númenorean history. Then follows a reconstructed story, the only one in existence about Númenor, entitled 'Aldarion and Erendis'. It is also called 'The tale of the Mariner's Wife', and gives the first hints of the shadow which is to fall, not least in its tone of sadness. After this is a record of the Line of Elros in Númenor, then an account of the history of Galadriel* and Celeborn,* including a piece on the origin of the Elessar, the brooch eventually bequeathed to Aragorn* by Arwen.*

In Part Three, several events from the Third Age:* 'The Disaster of the Gladden Fields' and 'Cirion and Eorl and the Friendship of Gondor and Rohan' (both from the earlier history of Gondor* and Rohan*); 'The Quest of Erebor'(setting out more fully the links between *The Hobbit* and *The Lord of the Rings*); 'The Hunt for the Ring'; and 'The Battles of the Fords of Isen'.

BIBLIOGRAPHY OF
J.R.R. TOLKIEN

MAJOR WRITINGS OF J.R.R. TOLKIEN,
IN ORDER OF FIRST PUBLICATION

A Middle English Vocabulary. The Clarendon Press: Oxford, 1922. Prepared for use with Kenneth Sisam's *Fourteenth Century Verse and Prose* (The Clarendon Press: Oxford, 1921) and later published with it.

Sir Gawain and the Green Knight. Edited by J.R.R. Tolkien and E.V. Gordon. The Clarendon Press: Oxford, 1925 (new edition, revised by Norman Davis, 1967).

The Hobbit, or There and Back Again. George Allen and Unwin: London, 1937; revised edition.

Farmer Giles of Ham. George Allen and Unwin: London, 1950.

The Fellowship of the Ring: Being the First Part of the Lord of the Rings. George Allen and Unwin: London, 1954.

The Two Towers: Being the Second Part of the Lord of the Rings. George Allen and Unwin: London, 1954.

The Return of the King: Being the Third Part of the Lord of the Rings. George Allen and Unwin: London, 1955.

The Adventures of Tom Bombadil and Other Verses from the Red Book. George Allen and Unwin: London, 1962.

Ancrene Wisse: The English Text of the Ancrene Riwle. Edited by J.R.R. Tolkien. Oxford University Press: London, 1962.

Tree and Leaf. George Allen and Unwin: London, 1964.

The Tolkien Reader. Ballantine Books: New York, 1966.

The Road Goes Ever On: A Song Cycle. Poems by J.R.R. Tolkien, music by Donald Swann. Houghton Mifflin Company: Boston, 1967. (Enlarged edition, 1978.)

Smith of Wootton Major. George Allen and Unwin: London, 1967.

287

POSTHUMOUS WRITINGS

Sir Gawain and the Green Knight, Pearl and Sir Orfeo. Translated by J.R.R. Tolkien; edited by Christopher Tolkien. George Allen and Unwin: London, 1975.

The Father Christmas Letters. Edited by Baillie Tolkien. George Allen and Unwin: London, 1976.

The Silmarillion. Edited by Christopher Tolkien. George Allen and Unwin: London, 1977.

Pictures by J.R.R. Tolkien. Edited by Christopher Tolkien. George Allen and Unwin: London, 1979.

Unfinished Tales of Númenor and Middle-earth. Edited by Christopher Tolkien. George Allen and Unwin: London, 1980.

The Letters of J.R.R. Tolkien. Edited by Humphrey Carpenter, with the assistance of Christopher Tolkien. George Allen and Unwin: London, 1981; Houghton Mifflin Company: Boston, 1981.

Old English Exodus. Text, translation and commentary by J.R.R. Tolkien; edited by Joan Turville-Petre. The Clarendon Press: Oxford, 1981.

Finn and Hengest: The Fragment and the Episode. Edited by Alan Bliss. George Allen and Unwin: London, 1982.

Mr Bliss. George Allen and Unwin: London, 1982; Houghton Mifflin Company: Boston, 1983.

The Monsters and the Critics and Other Essays. Edited by Christopher Tolkien. George Allen and Unwin: London, 1983.

The History of Middle-earth. Edited by Christopher Tolkien. Published in 12 volumes between 1983 and 1996, by George Allen and Unwin, Unwin Hyman and HarperCollins.

Roverandom. Edited by Christina Scull and Wayne G. Hammond. HarperCollins: London, 1998.

SELECTED WRITINGS ABOUT J.R.R. TOLKIEN

Allan, James (ed.). *An Introduction to Elvish and to Other Tongues and Proper Names and Writing Systems of the Third Age of the Western Lands of Middle-earth as Set Forth in the Published Writings of Professor John Ronald Reuel Tolkien.* Bran's Head Books: Hayes, Middlesex, 1978.

Andrews, Bart with Bernie Zuber. *The Tolkien Quiz Book: 1001 Questions About Tolkien's Tales of Middle-earth and Other Fantasies.* Signet Books: New York, 1979.

Armstrong, Helen. *Digging Potatoes, Growing Trees: 25 Years of Speeches at the Tolkien Society's Annual Dinners*, vols 1 and 2, the Tolkien Society, 1997–98.

Battarbee, K.J. (ed.). *Scholarship and Fantasy: Proceedings of the Tolkien Phenomenon, May 1992, Turku, Finland.* University of Turku: Turku, Finland, 1993.

Becker, Alida (ed.). *The Tolkien Scrapbook.* Grosset and Dunlap: New York, 1978.

Becker, Alida (ed.). *A Tolkien Treasury.* Courage Books: Philadelphia, Pennsylvania, 1989.

Blackwelder, Richard E. *Tolkien Phraseology: A Companion to a Tolkien Thesaurus.* Tolkien Archives Fund: Marquette University, Milwaukee, Wisconsin, 1990.

Blount, Margaret. *Animal Land: The Creatures of Children's Fiction.* Hutchinson: London, 1974; William Morrow: New York 1975.

Carpenter, Humphrey. *The Inklings: C.S. Lewis, J.R.R. Tolkien, Charles Williams and Their Friends.* George Allen and Unwin: London, 1978; Houghton Mifflin: Boston, 1979.

Carpenter, Humphrey. *J.R.R. Tolkien: A Biography.* George Allen and Unwin: London, 1977; Houghton Mifflin: Boston, 1977.

Carter, Lin. *Tolkien: A Look Behind the Lord of the Rings.* Ballantine: New York, 1979.

Clute, John and John Grant. *The Encyclopedia of Fantasy.* Orbit: London, 1997.

Collins, David R. *J.R.R. Tolkien: Master of Fantasy.* Lerner: Minneapolis, 1992.

Curry, Patrick. *Defending Middle-earth.* HarperCollins: London, 1997.

Day, David. *A Tolkien Bestiary.* Mitchell Beazley: London, 1979; Ballantine: New York, 1979.

Duriez, Colin. "'Art Has Been Verified . . .': The Friendship of C.S. Lewis and J.R.R. Tolkien' in Armstrong, Helen. *Digging Potatoes, Growing Trees: 25 Years of Speeches at the Tolkien Society's Annual Dinners*, vol. 2, the Tolkien Society, 1998.

Duriez, Colin. 'J.R.R. Tolkien' in *British Children's Authors 1914–1960*, a volume of the *Dictionary of Literary Biography*. Bruccoli Clark Layman: Columbia, South Carolina, 1996.

Duriez, Colin. *The J.R.R. Tolkien Handbook*. Baker Book House: Grand Rapids, Michigan, 1992.

Duriez, Colin. 'Sub-creation and Tolkien's Theology of Story' in K.J. Batterbee (ed.), *Scholarship and Fantasy*. University of Turku: Turku, Finland, 1993.

Duriez, Colin. 'The Theology of Fantasy in C.S. Lewis and J.R.R. Tolkien' in *Themelios*, vol. 23, no. 2, February 1998.

Duriez, Colin. *The Tolkien and Middle-earth Handbook*. Monarch: Eastbourne, 1992; Angus and Robertson: Pymble, NSW, 1992.

Duriez, Colin. 'Tolkien and the Old West' in Armstrong, Helen. *Digging Potatoes, Growing Trees: 25 Years of Speeches at the Tolkien Society's Annual Dinners*, vol. 2, the Tolkien Society, 1998.

Duriez, Colin. 'Tolkien and the Other Inklings' in Reynolds, Patricia and Glen H. GoodKnight. *Proceedings of the J.R.R. Tolkien Centenary Conference: Keble College, Oxford, 1992*. The Tolkien Society: Milton Keynes and The Mythopoeic Press: Altadena, California, 1995.

Elgin, Don D. *The Comedy of the Fantastic: Ecological Perspectives on the Fantasy Novel*. Greenwood, London, 1985.

Ellwood, Gracia Fay. *Good News from Tolkien's Middle-earth: Two Essays on the 'Applicability' of the Lord of the Rings*. W.B. Eerdmans: Grand Rapids, Michigan, 1970.

Etkin, Anne (ed.). *Eglerio! In Praise of Tolkien*. Quest Communications: Greencastle, Pennsylvania, 1978.

Evans, Robley. *J.R.R. Tolkien*. Crowell: New York, 1976.

Flieger, Verlyn. *Splintered Light: Logos and Language in Tolkien's World*. W.B. Eerdmans: Grand Rapids, Michigan, 1983.

Fonstad, Karen Wynn. *The Atlas of Middle-earth*. Houghton Mifflin: Boston, 1981.

Foster, Robert. *The Complete Guide to Middle-earth: From the Hobbit to the Silmarillion*. George Allen and Unwin: London, 1978; Ballantine Books: New York, 1978.

Fuller, Edmund. *Books with Men Behind Them*. Random House: New York, 1962.

Garbowski, Christopher. *Recovery and Transcendence for the Contemporary*

Mythmaker: The Spiritual Dimension in the Works of J.R.R. Tolkien. Lublin: Maria Curie-Skłodowska University Press, 2000.

Giddings, Robert (ed.). *J.R.R. Tolkien: This Far Land.* Vision: London; Barnes and Noble: Totowas, New Jersey, 1983.

Giddings, Robert and Elizabeth Holland. *J.R.R. Tolkien: The Shores of Middle-earth.* Eletheia Books: Maryland, 1981.

Grotta, Daniel. *The Biography of J.R.R. Tolkien: Architect of Middle-earth.* Running Press: Philadelphia, 1978.

Hammond, Wayne G. with the assistance of Douglas A. Anderson. *J.R.R. Tolkien: A Descriptive Bibliography.* St Paul's Bibliographies: Winchester and Oak Knoll Books: New Castle, Delaware, 1993.

Hammond, Wayne G. and Christina Scull. *J.R.R. Tolkien, Artist and Illustrator.* London: HarperCollins, 1995.

Harvey, David. *The Song of Middle-earth: J.R.R. Tolkien's Themes, Symbols and Myths.* Allen and Unwin: London, 1985.

Helms, Randel. *Tolkien and the Silmarils.* Houghton Mifflin: Boston, 1981.

Helms, Randel. *Tolkien's World.* Houghton Mifflin: Boston, 1974.

Hillegas, Mark R. (ed.). *Shadows of Imagination: The Fantasies of C.S. Lewis, J.R.R. Tolkien and Charles Williams.* Southern Illinois University Press: Carbondale, 1969, new edition 1979.

Huttar, Charles A. (ed.). *Imagination and the Spirit: Essays in Literature and the Christian Faith.* W.B. Eerdmans: Grand Rapids, Michigan, 1971.

Isaacs, Neil D. and Rose A. Zimbardo (eds). *Tolkien: New Critical Perspectives.* The University Press of Kentucky: Kentucky, 1981.

Kilby, Clyde S. *Tolkien and the Silmarillion.* Harold Shaw: Wheaton, Illinois, 1976; Lion: Tring, 1977.

Knight, Gareth. *The Magical World of the Inklings.* Elements Books: Longmead, Dorset, 1990.

Kocher, Paul H. *Master of Middle-earth: The Fiction of J.R.R. Tolkien.* Houghton Mifflin: Boston, 1972. British edition: *Master of Middle-earth: The Achievement of J.R.R. Tolkien.* Thames and Hudson: London, 1972.

Kocher, Paul H. *A Reader's Guide to the Silmarillion.* Thames and Hudson: London, 1980.

Lichański, Jakub (ed.). *J.R.R. Tolkien: Recepcja Polska.* Wydawnictwa

Uniwersytetu Warszawskieso: Warsaw, 1996. (Includes Abstracts in English.)

Lobdell, Jared. *England and Always: Tolkien's World of the Rings*. W.B. Eerdmans: Grand Rapids, Michigan, 1981.

Lobdell, Jared. *A Tolkien Compass*. Open Court Publishing: La Salle, Illinois, 1975; Ballantine: New York, 1980.

Lochhead, Marion. *Renaissance of Wonder: The Fantasy Worlds of C.S. Lewis, J.R.R. Tolkien, George MacDonald, E. Nesbit and Others*. Canongate: Edinburgh, 1973; Harper and Row: San Francisco, 1977.

Manlove, C.N. *Modern Fantasy*. Cambridge University Press: Cambridge, 1975.

Matthews, Richard. *Lightning from a Clear Sky: Tolkien, the Trilogy and the Silmarillion*. Borgo: San Bernardino, 1978.

Melmed, Susan Barbara. *John Ronald Reuel Tolkien: A Bibliography*. University of Witwatersrand Department of Bibliography, Librarianship and Typography: Johannesburg, 1972.

Miesel, Sandra. *Myth, Symbol and Religion in the Lord of the Rings*. TK Graphics: Baltimore, 1973.

Miller, Stephen O. *Middle-earth: A World in Conflict*. TK Graphics: Baltimore, 1975.

Montgomery, John Warwick (ed.). *Myth, Allegory and Gospel: An Interpretation of J.R.R. Tolkien, C.S. Lewis, G.K. Chesterton and Charles Williams*. Bethany Fellowship: Minneapolis, 1974.

Moorman, Charles. *The Precincts of Felicity: The Augustinian City of the Oxford Christians*. University of Florida Press: Gainesville, 1966.

Morrison, Louise D. *J.R.R. Tolkien's the Fellowship of the Ring: A Critical Commentary*. Monarch: New York, 1976.

Morse, Robert E. *Evocation of Virgil in Tolkien's Art*. Bolchazy Carducci Publishers: Oak Park, Illinois, 1987.

Moseley, Charles. *J.R.R. Tolkien*. Northcote House: Plymouth, 1997.

Nitzsche, Jane Chance. *Tolkien's Art: A 'Mythology for England'*. St Martin's Press: New York, 1979.

Noel, Ruth S. *The Languages of Tolkien's Middle-earth*. Houghton Mifflin: Boston, 1980.

Noel, Ruth S. *The Mythology of Middle-earth*. Houghton Mifflin: Boston, 1977; Thames and Hudson: London, 1977.

O'Neill, Timothy R. *The Individuated Hobbit: Jung, Tolkien and the Archetypes of Middle-earth*. Houghton Mifflin: Boston, 1979.

Palmer, Bruce. *Of Orc-rags, Phials and a Far Shore: Visions of Paradise in the Lord of the Rings*. TK Graphics: Baltimore, 1976.

Pearce, Joseph (ed.). *Tolkien: A Celebration, Collected Writings on a Literary Legacy*. Fount: London, 1999.

Petty, Anne Cotton. *One Ring to Rule Them All: Tolkien's Mythology*. University of Alabama Press, Tuscaloosa, Alabama, 1979.

Purtill, Richard. *C.S. Lewis's Case for the Christian Faith*. Harper and Row: San Francisco, 1982.

Purtill, Richard L. *J.R.R. Tolkien: Myth, Morality and Religion*. Harper and Row: San Francisco, 1985.

Purtill, Richard L. *Lord of the Elves and Eldils: Fantasy and Philosophy in C.S. Lewis and J.R.R. Tolkien*. Zondervan: Grand Rapids, Michigan, 1974.

Ready, William. *The Tolkien Relation*. Regnery: Chicago, 1968.

Reilly, Robert J. *Romantic Religion: A Study of Barfield, Lewis, Williams and Tolkien*. University of Georgia Press: Athens, 1971.

Reynolds, Patricia and Glen H. GoodKnight. *Proceedings of the J.R.R. Tolkien Centenary Conference: Keble College, Oxford, 1992*. The Tolkien Society: Milton Keynes and The Mythopoeic Press: Altadena, California, 1995.

Rogers, Deborah Webster and Ivor A. Rogers. *J.R.R. Tolkien*. Twayne Publishers: Boston, 1980.

Rossi, Lee D. *The Politics of Fantasy*. UMI Research: Epping, 1984.

Sale, Roger. *Modern Heroism: Essays on D.H. Lawrence, William Empson and J.R.R. Tolkien*. University of California Press: Berkeley and Los Angeles, 1973.

Salu, Mary and Robert T. Farrell (eds). *J.R.R. Tolkien, Scholar and Storyteller: Essays in Memoriam*. Cornell University Press: Ithaca, 1979.

Shippey, T.A. *The Road to Middle-earth*. George Allen and Unwin: London, 1982; Houghton Mifflin: New York, 1983.

Shippey, Tom. *J.R.R. Tolkien: Author of the Century*. HarperCollins: London, 2000.

Shorto, Russell. *J.R.R. Tolkien: Man of Fantasy*. (Foreword by G.B. Tennyson.) The Kipling Press: New York, 1988.

Strachey, Barbara. *Journeys of Frodo*. Unwin Paperbacks: London, 1981.

The Filmbook of J.R.R. Tolkien's 'The Lord of the Rings'. Ballantine Books: New York, 1978.

Tolkien, Christopher. *The Silmarillion by J.R.R. Tolkien: A Brief Account of the Book and Its Making*. Houghton Mifflin: Boston, 1977.

Tolkien, John and Priscilla. *The Tolkien Family Album*. Unwin/Hyman: London, 1992.

Tyler, J.E.A. *The New Tolkien Companion*. St Martin's Press: New York, 1979.

Tyler, J.E.A. *The Tolkien Companion*. Macmillan: London, 1976.

Urang, Gunnar. *Shadows of Heaven: Religion and Fantasy in the Writing of C.S. Lewis, Charles Williams and J.R.R. Tolkien*. SCM Press: London, 1970; United Church Press: Philadelphia, 1971.

West, Richard C. *Tolkien Criticism: An Annotated Checklist*. Kent State University Press: Kent, Ohio, 1970.

Wilson, Colin. *Tree by Tolkien*. Covent Garden Press: London, 1973; Capra Press: Santa Barbara, 1974.

Zipes, Jack. *Breaking the Magic Spell: Radical Theories of Folk and Fairy Tales*. University of Texas Press: Austin, 1979.

THE TOLKIEN SOCIETY

In a hole in the ground there lived a hobbit . . .

Published in 1937, these words introduced a new world, Middle-earth, to the reading public; they were written by J.R.R. Tolkien. Seventeen years later his epic work *The Lord of the Rings* was published to critical acclaim. The years that followed saw many people become fans of his work, many of whom wanted to know more about Middle-earth and its peoples.

In 1969 the Tolkien Society was founded, its aim being to further interest in the life and works of J.R.R. Tolkien, CBE, the author of *The Hobbit*, *The Lord of the Rings* and other works of fiction and philological study. Based in the United Kingdom and registered as an independent, non-profit making charity, the Society boasts an international membership.

The Society helps to bring together those with like minds, both formally and informally, with gatherings throughout the year. There are three such events at a national level: an Annual General Meeting and Dinner, the Seminar and Oxonmoot.

The AGM is held in the spring in a different town or city in the UK each year, at the AGM committee members are elected and the running of the Society is discussed while after the formal dinner there is always a guest speaker, often someone who knew J.R.R. Tolkien, or a scholar and author on Tolkien's works such as Rayner Unwin, Prof. Tom Shippey and the author of this book.

The second event, the seminar, takes place in the summer at which a programme of talks are given on a Tolkien-related subject. These range from the serious to the light in tone and there is always something for everyone. Past topics have included 'Tolkien: A Mythology for England?' and 'The Change of Ages'.

The special event of the Tolkien Society year is the Oxonmoot, held over a weekend in September in an Oxford college. There are a range of events such as talks, discussions, slide-shows and a costume party. It is a great time for learning more, having fun and making new friends.

The society produces two publications; the bulletin, *Amon Hen*, appears six times a year with Tolkien-related reviews, news, letters, artwork and articles, both humorous and serious. The annual journal, *Mallorn*, is more serious in nature with longer critical articles, reviews and essays.

Within the Society there are local groups spread throughout Britain and the world called 'Smials' (after hobbit homes). Here both members and non-members can gather to discuss Tolkien's works, as well as other writers and topics. The formality and seriousness of meetings vary depending on the inclinations of members. There are also postal smials for those who live far from a local group, with regular newsletters and occasional meetings. In addition to these there are also Special Interest Groups, covering topics such as collecting, biography and Tolkien's languages.

For Young Members there is an active group, 'Entings', which has its own section in the Society bulletin. We also maintain an extensive Lending Library and Archive, both of which are accessible to members.

The Society has a web-site which provides members and non-members with general information about itself and the world of Tolkien:

http://www.tolkiensociety.org/

For further details please write to:

> The Secretary (CD),
> 210 Prestbury Road,
> Cheltenham,
> GL52 3ER
> United Kingdom

The Tolkien Society
Registered Charity No. 273809